Contents

List of Tables   vii

Preface   xi

Chapter 1: Background to Study   1

1. Services for children in care   2
2. Previous research on substitute child care and related fields   16
3. Subject of research and method of approach   31

Chapter 2: Characteristics of Research Settings, Children and Caretakers   41

1. The research settings   41
2. The children   45
3. The caretakers   57

Chapter 3: Four Dimensions of Care   69

1. The management of recurrent - mainly daily - social events   69
2. Children's community contacts   79
3. The physical environment   84
4. Controls and sanctions   88

Chapter 4: Caretakers' Roles, and Behaviour and Attitudes
            Towards Children   102

1.   The roles of foster parents and residential staff   102
2.   Caretaker behaviour toward children observed   116
3.   Caretaker attitudes toward children   121

Chapter 5: Children's Perceptions and Behaviours   133

1.   Children's behaviour towards caretakers observed   133
2.   Children's perceptions of their social environments   139
3.   Children's progress during their placements   148

Chapter 6: Summary and Discussion   162

1.   Summary of major findings   162
2.   Factors which help to define care practice   170
3.   Implications of the study   183

Appendices   190

Appendix (a) Internal Organisation of Settings Interview
                 Questionnaire (IOSIQ)   190
Appendix (b) Children's Characteristics Questionnaire (CCQ)   193
Appendix (c) Index of Child-Management (ICM)   204
Appendix (d) Revised Index of Community Involvement (RICI)   226
Appendix (e) Revised Index of Physical Environment (RIPE)   233
Appendix (f) Index of Controls and Sanctions (ICS)   238
Appendix (g) Staff/Foster Parent Interview Questionnaire (ST/FPIQ)   245
Appendix (h) Staff/Foster Parent Attitude Scale (ST/FPAS)   253
Appendix (i) Narrative Recording Schedule (NRS)   258
Appendix (j) Revised Social Climate Scale (RSCS)   268

Bibliography   272

DIMENSIONS OF SUBSTITUTE CHILD CARE

Dimensions of Substitute Child Care

A Comparative Study of Foster and Residential Care Practice

M. J. COLTON
Department of Social and Administrative Studies
University of Oxford

Avebury

Aldershot · Brookfield USA · Hong Kong · Singapore · Sydney

© M.J. Colton, 1988

Published by

Avebury   ⌐13388459

Gower Publishing Company Limited,
Gower House, Croft Road, Aldershot,
Hants. GU11 3HR, England

Gower Publishing Company,
Old Post Road, Brookfield, Vermont 05036
USA

Reprinted 1996

British Library Cataloguing in Publication Data
Colton, M.J., 1955-
  Dimensions of substitute child care : a
  comparative study of foster and residential
  care practice
  1. Great Britain. Children. Residential
  care compared with foster care 2. Great
  Britain. Children. Foster care compared
  with residential care
  I. Title
  362.7'32'0941

Library of Congress Cataloging-In-Publication Data
Colton, M.J., 1955-
  Dimensions of substitute child care : a comparative study of
  foster and residential care practice / M.J. Colton.
  p.   cm.
  Bibliography: p.
  1. Children–Institutional care–England 2. Foster home care-
  -England.   I. Title
  HV866.G72E543 1988
  362.7'3'0942–dc19

ISBN 0 566 05612 7

Printed and bound in Great Britain by
Cedric Chivers Ltd, Bristol

Tables

1.1   Gross revenue expenditure on personal social services for children   3

1.2   Children in care of local authorities (1977-1981) by age group   6

1.3   Manner in which children in care are accommodated   8

2.1   Total numbers of foster parents and children living at foster homes where data on care practice collected   42

2.2   Total numbers of staff and children at Children's Homes   42

2.3   Composition of staff groups   44

2.4   Ratio of foster parents to children living at foster homes where data on care practice collected   44

2.5   Ratio of residential child care staff to children   44

2.6   Numbers of foster children and natural children of foster parents living at foster homes where data on care practice collected   45

2.7   Ages of foster and residential children on which CCQ data collected   47

2.8   Sex of foster and residential children studied   47

2.9   Legislation in force with respect to foster and residential children   48

2.10   Reasons associated with children's latest admissions to care   49

2.11   Duration of sample children's placements   51

2.12   Who children lived with prior to their present care episodes   52

2.13   Evidence of serious family problems   53

2.14   Nature of home ownership or tenancy of children's families of origin   54

2.15   Truancy rates for sample children prior to their present placements   56

2.16   Sex of foster parents and residential staff   58

2.17   Ages of foster parents and residential staff   58

2.18   Total numbers of natural children of caretakers   59

2.19   Numbers of natural children of caretakers (a) under 16 years and (b) 16 years and over   59

2.20   Social class of foster parents   60

2.21   Type of occupations undertaken by staff immediately prior to obtaining employment in residential child care field   60

2.22   Length of time for which caretakers had occupied their roles/ posts   61

3.1   Care practice scores for foster homes and Children's Homes   71

3.2   ICM items in relation to which differences between foster homes and Children's Homes were found to be statistically significant   72

3.3   RICI items in relation to which differences between the means of scores for foster homes and Children's Homes were statistically significant   81

3.4   Overnight visits by children to their natural parents homes within the fortnight preceding data collection   82

3.5   Children's holidays with natural parents within the year preceding data collection   83

3.6   Visits by natural families to children's placements within the month preceding data collection   83

3.7   RIPE items in relation to which statistical significance was obtained for differences between the means of scores for foster homes and Children's Homes   85

4.1   Observed role activities of caretakers - King *et al* (1971) categories   104

4.2   Observed role activities of caretakers - Cawson (1978) categories   106

4.3   Location of observations   108

4.4   Caretaker perceptions of their actual roles   111

4.5   Caretaker perceptions of their ideal roles   113

4.6   Type of speech used by caretakers towards children   118

4.7   Tone of voice used by caretakers towards children   118

4.8   Bodily expressions used by caretakers towards children   119

4.9   Physical gestures by caretakers involving bodily contact with children   120

4.10   Initiation of interaction   121

4.11   Reliability coefficients for ST/FPAS subscales   123

4.12   ST/FPAS items in relation to which differences between the scores of foster parents and residential staff were found to be statistically significant   125

5.1   General activities of foster and residential children compared   134

5.2   Physical gestures used by foster and residential children, involving bodily contact with caretakers   135

5.3   Bodily expressions manifested by foster and residential children   136

5.4   Language used by foster and residential children   136

5.5   Reliability coefficients for RSCS subscales   141

5.6   RSCS items for which differences between foster and residential children's scores were found to be statistically significant   143

5.7   Mean ranks awarded by foster and residential children when asked to state who they would most prefer to consult over a personal problem   144

5.8   Natural mothers' views of children's placements   147

5.9   Natural fathers' views of children's placements   147

5.10   Proportions of foster and residential children reported as cheeky, abusive or disobedient towards their caretakers   150

5.11   Proportions of foster and residential children reported as having manifested physical violence prior to and during their present placements   152

5.12   Proportions of foster and residential children who made court appearances as alleged offenders prior to and during their present placements   152

5.13   Proportions of foster and residential children who had truanted prior to and during their present placements   153

Preface

What follows is an account of an attempt to compare care practice in foster homes and Children's Homes (capitals are used in the latter term throughout the text in order to avoid possible ambiguity when comparing the two forms of provision concerned) for older children in local authority care. Findings reported are based on a lengthy period of fieldwork in substitute care provisions supervised and administered by two local authorities. This venture was embarked on with some trepidation owing, first, to the technical difficulties of the task in hand; second, to the often acrimonious debate associated with the respective merits or otherwise of the two forms of substitute child care in question; and, third, to the constraints placed on the research by the relatively meagre resources available.

The first source of apprehension issued from the difficulty of comparing two types of care which involve very different social phenomena: the family, on the one hand, and the residential institution, on the other. It is for the reader to assess how well this problem was dealt with, but a few comments on the overall approach followed are appropriate here. The general method adopted was essentially sociological in orientation. However, as Mishra (1981, pp. 3-4) relates, in Britain ..." the systematic study of discrete social problems and their solution by way of piecemeal reforms has come to be known - and institutionalised academically - as social administration"... The author identifies the following as the major features of this discipline:" a focus on national policies and problems; a focus on state-provided welfare; an interventionist and prescriptive approach; a field rather than a disciplinary orientation; and, finally, empiricism, or concern largely with the facts of welfare. Each of these features is, to some degree, reflected in the work undertaken.

Although the notion of a completely value-free social science has been strongly challenged, one of the dangers associated with the interventionist approach of social administration is that a particular value position may be so much taken for granted that its implications are not appreciated (Mishra, 1981, p.12). This brings us to the second cause of initial anxiety. It seemed that certain commentators are strongly committed to particular forms of care rather than others. Given that the issues involved are complex, and that the research literature on the consequences of different types of substitute care contains important inconsistencies, the adoption of dogmatically held views often appears to owe more to value judgements than to empirical evidence. Accordingly, an objective approach to the task of comparing foster and residential care was consciously sought through appropriate use of the tools and techniques of social research.

The third reason for disquiet resulted from the ambitious nature of the fieldwork planned. The severe logistical problems of the project were compounded by the fact that, compared to the sums usually allocated to applied research of this sort, the study was undertaken on a very stringent budget. That the work was completed on schedule owed a great deal to financial help from several quarters, which supplemented an award made by the Economic and Social Research Council. Here, special thanks are due to Professor A.H. Halsey, for his efforts in ensuring that the study was adequately funded; to the Violet Butler Bequest, from which £250.00 was gratefully received; to Mrs. J. Brock and students of Fielden Park College, who raised £350.00 on behalf of the research; and, to Nuffield College, Oxford, which gave substantial direct and indirect financial help. A considerable debt is also owed to the children, foster parents, residential staff, administrators, fostering officers, and social workers who participated in the study. In this context, the assistance given by the following persons merits citation: Mr. R. Collier, Mr. B. Maher and Mrs. A.E. Williams. Finally, thanks must go to Professor A.H. Halsey, Dr. K. Sylva, Dr. E.V. Batstone and Dr. A.J. Crowle for the advice and encouragement which they provided throughout; and to Mrs. K. Walker for her help in preparing this manuscript for publication.

Chapter 1 opens with a discussion of services for children in care. Previous research on substitute child care and related fields is then reviewed; this is followed by a statement of the research and method of approach. The second chapter introduces the research settings (foster homes and Children's Homes), children, and caretakers (foster parents and residential staff). Chapters 3 - 5 report findings concerning care practice and the responses of children. Four aspects of care practice are examined in Chapter 3. Chapter 4 concerns the roles of caretakers, and their behaviour and attitudes towards the children, whilst the responses of the latter are considered in Chapter 5. The final chapter begins with a summary of major findings. Factors which help to define care practice are then discussed as a prelude to a statement on the implications of the findings for policy and practice in the field of substitute child care. Research instruments used for the purpose of data collection are presented in the Appendices.

1 Background to study

Introduction

The subject of children in local authority care is unfamiliar territory for most of us. Just who are the children *in care* ? Why do children go into care? Who does the caring, and how much does it cost? The first section of this chapter attempts to answer such questions; it opens with a brief discussion of the numbers of children in care and the expenditure devoted to the area of social policy in question. This is followed by a consideration of the major legal routes by which children enter care and recent changes in this process and in the nature of the children in care population. Statutes which govern the treatment of children in care are then examined, along with the provisions made for such children. The opening section concludes with a brief review of the development of children's services in the post-war period.

   The second part of this chapter reviews the research on substitute child care and related fields, beginning with the work of writers who, in the period since the Second World War, have greatly influenced our conception of residential institutions. Attention is then directed to research specifically concerned with the residential care of children. Although my empirical research centred on older children, studies of younger children are also reviewed because a good deal of the earliest work on the consequences of residential care concerned this group; hence, these studies are of considerable import. Several, mainly sociological, studies on the family are then considered. These show that although some writers hold a generally favourable view of the family others are distinctly hostile towards it. Thus, as would appear to be the case in relation to residential institutions, the family is supported by some and attacked by others, with ideology seemingly playing an influential role. A similar point can perhaps be made with respect to residential and family placement for children in care, and the section ends with a review of the research literature on family placement - foster care and adoption - for children who enter local authority care.

It is important to stress that the review of the research literature on substitute child care (and, indeed, the account of the relevant literature in general) is not intended to be exhaustive; the constraints of space would not permit such an undertaking. However, whilst decisions about what to include and what to omit were inevitably somewhat arbitrary, the overall impression conveyed of inconsistent, contradictory and, thus, inconclusive, findings appears to reflect accurately our rather confused current state of knowledge in this field. A second point that should, therefore, emerge from the review of research literature on substitute child care is that there are very compelling reasons for increasing our knowledge in this field. The account which follows in subsequent chapters is offered as a contribution towards this task, and the subject and method of research undertaken are discussed in the final section of this chapter.

1. Services for Children in Care

Numbers of children in care

Children in care (apart from a relatively small number who are cared for by voluntary organisations) are the responsibility of local authorities and their Social Services Departments which operate under the general direction of the Secretary of State for Social Services. In 1973, there were an estimated 89,000 children in the care of local authorities in England - approximately 1 child in 150. During the following four years this proportion increased to 1 in 130. Thus, by 1977 just over 96,000 children were in care. Since 1977, however, the proportion has remained fairly steady, with the number of children in care falling by 1981 to 92,000 in line with the fall in the child population (Social Services Committee, session 1982-83, p.1).

Expenditure

Approximately one third of local authority social services net current expenditure is devoted to services for children, representing some 4 per cent of all local authority net current expenditure (Social Services Committee, Session 1982-83, p.1). Table 1.1 illustrates fairly recent trends in expenditure on various provisions for children. It can be seen that residential care is by far the most costly of the services involved. Indeed, nearly half of all expenditure on personal social services is allocated to residential care. Hallet (1982, p.28) notes that the average figure for all local authorities in 1979, with respect to spending on residential care, was 47.7 per cent. Factors such as the labour intensive nature of the service (some 80,000 people are employed by Social Services Departments in residential care establishments, of whom approximately 60,000 are ancilliary staff), and the capital costs which have to be added to current expenditure on salaries and running costs, result in high costs for each resident accommodated. Not surprisingly, therefore, as Walton and Elliot (1980, pp.1-3) observe, cost-benefit arguments have been used as a

2

means of questioning the continuing provision of residential care at present levels, particularly in the present period of severe economic stringency.

Table 1.1
Gross revenue expenditure on personal social services for children

England					£m at Nov 80 prices	
	1975-76	1976-77	1977-78	1978-79	1979-80	1980-81
Residential Homes	273.0	279.9	275.6	282.0	287.0	290.5
Hostels and other residential accommodation	6.8	7.0	8.0	10.0	13.4	12.8
Boarding out	29.9	35.5	38.5	44.0	45.5	47.4
Intermediate treatment	1.7	1.9	3.2	4.2	4.9	6.0
Day nurseries	51.6	55.6	56.3	57.6	57.3	62.1
Other day service	5.6	6.0	6.2	7.1	7.8	8.1
Total PSS expenditure (inc Joint Finance)	1,671.8	1,718.0	1,760.0	1,836.9	1,906.5	1,956.1

Source: Social Services Committee, session 1982-83, p.30.

Routes into care

In the context of local authority social services, child care means looking after children who are temporarily or permanently deprived of normal home life. Duties are imposed on social workers by the Child Care Act 1980 (CCA 1980), and the Children and Young Persons Act 1969 (CYPA 1969) [1]. At national level, the DHSS (for England), the Scottish Office and the Welsh Office are responsible for ensuring that local authorities carry out their legal duties.

The general aim of the legislation referred to is that of preventing (where possible) the need for a child to leave home or to encourage (where appropriate) arrangements for a child to be cared for by relatives or friends. Section 1 of the CCA 1980 confers on local authorities their main preventive powers. However, irrespective of the fact that the concept of prevention has been expressed in legislation for some twenty years (the notion appeared first in S.1 of the Children and Young Persons Act 1963, which later became part of the CCA 1980), each year some 40,000 children go into care with roughly the same number discharged from care (Social Services Committee, session 1982-83, p.31).

Two major legal routes into local authority care may be distinguished:
(1) a child may be *received* into care under S.2 of the CCA 1980, where it appears to a local authority that his/her parents cannot look after him/her or that he/she is an orphan or has been abandoned and that his/her welfare requires intervention; this is usually referred to as *voluntary* care;

3

(2) a child may be *committed* to care by an order or interim order of the court as a result of care proceedings, criminal proceedings or domestic proceedings; in cases of emergency (e.g., instances of child abuse) a child may be removed to a place of safety for up to 28 days on the order of a magistrate.[2]

On 31 March 1981, approximately 40,200 children had been received into care in England under S.2 CCA 1980 - 43.6 per cent of the total number of children in care (Social Services Committee, session 1982-83, p.34). A significant proportion of such children required care as a consequence of short-term family crisis, and over half of all children received into care under the 1980 Act are likely to leave care within six months. Parents retain their *parental rights* and may remove the child from care. However, if the child has been in care for six months, the local authority may require 28 days notice of the parents' wish to remove the child. Moreover, in specified circumstances, the local authority is empowered to pass a resolution, assuming parental rights over a child, under S.3 of the CCA 1980 (Hoggett, 1981; Pearl and Gray, 1981). In 1981, some 17,300 children in care were subject to a parental rights resolution under S.3 CCA 1980. This procedure has been heavily criticised for failing adequately to safeguard the rights of natural parents.

Moreover, certain commentators have strong reservations about whether the term voluntary care is an appropriate one. Section 2 of the CCA 1980 implies that parents make a positive choice to place their children in care. Taylor *et al* (1979, pp.12 -17), however, argue that care as a chosen option may apply to fewer children than is generally supposed. The authors draw attention to the work of Holman (1976) who has shown that poverty is a major factor in determining the reception of children into care. That structural factors such as poverty, homelessness, inadequate income-maintenance provision, etc., appear to be a necessary condition underlying the reception of many children into care cautions against viewing such receptions as indicative of personal failure or inadequacy or maladjustment on the part of natural parents.

With respect to the second major route into care identified above, local authorities have a statutory duty to protect children from ill treatment and neglect, and a responsibilty to investigate any circumstances in which a child may be at risk. Moreover, where necessary, local authorities have a duty to initiate proceedings under S.1 of the CYPA 1969. In 1981, about 28,100 children were in care under S.1 CYPA 1969 - 30.4 per cent of all children in care (Social Services Committee, session 1982-83, p.34). In order to make a care order under S1 CYPA 1969, the court must be satisfied that one of the grounds for a care order exist and also that the child is in need of care and control which he/she would not otherwise receive. The most usual ground for the making of a care order under S.1 CYPA 1969 concerns neglect and ill treatment (Social Services Committee, session 1982-83, p.5). Where children of 10 years and over are found guilty of an offence punishable in the case of an adult with imprisonment, the court may make a care order under S.7 (7) of the CYPA 1969. An estimated 13,300 children were in care under this provision in 1981 - 14.4 per cent of the total number of children in care (Social Services Committee, session 1982-83, p.34). During the same year, approximately 1,900 children were in care after either being committed under an interim care order, or remanded to care, or detained in care after arrest (2.1 per cent of children in care in 1981).

The powers and duties of local authorities in relation to children who are committed into their care are set out in S.10 of the CCA 1980. The local authority may restrict the child's liberty. It has the same powers as a parent, but must not cause the child to be brought up in a religious creed different from that in which he/she was being brought up prior to the care order. Further, the natural parents retain the right to agree, or refuse to agree, to the making of an adoption order with respect to the child (Freeman, 1981; Hoggett, 1981).

It may be noted that in the post-war period (both at home and abroad - particularly in the USA), the juvenile justice system has been the subject of considerable debate around which a substantial body of literature has developed. The controversy may, in large part, be attributed to the fact that the juvenile justice system comprises multiple functions and competing aims. It attempts to protect society and serve the interests of children, meet children's needs whilst also trying to safeguard their rights. This complexity is compounded because society is concerned with controlling behaviour in children extending far beyond the commission of criminal acts (Parsloe, 1978). Throughout the course of this century child care legislation, culminating in the CYPA 1969, has increasingly blurred the distinction between offenders and children deemed in need of care for other reasons, on the assumption that the underlying difficulties of both groups are essentially similar and should be dealt with under the same system. The CYPA 1969 has been the subject of much criticism, and this will be returned to later.

A relatively small, but increasing (see below), number of children enter care each year through matrimonial and other domestic proceedings because the courts consider there are exceptional circumstances making it undesirable or impractical for the child to be under the care of either parent or any other person (Hoggett, 1981).

Recent changes in the ways that children enter care and in the children in care population

According to a Social Services Committee report on children in care (Social Services Committee, session 1982-83, p.16), the last decade or so has witnessed changes in the ways that children arrive in care. First, the number of children received into care under S.2 CCA 1980 has decreased, whilst there has been a rise in the number of children committed to care by the courts under the CYPA 1969. As stated, in 1981 43.6 per cent of children in care had been received into care under S.2 CCA 1980, against 47.2 per cent in 1977. Moreover, whilst 30.4 per cent of children in care in 1981 had been committed to care by the courts via proceedings under S.1 CYPA 1969, in 1977 the figure was 24.6 per cent. However, the number of children committed to care in criminal proceedings under the CYPA 1969 declined from roughly 18.6 per cent of the total number of children in care in 1977 to the 14.4 per cent reported for 1981. The proportion of children in care through matrimonial proceedings increased from 4.1 per cent of children in care in 1977 (in 1973 the figure was just 1.9 per cent) to 6.7 per cent in 1981 (Social Services Committee, session 1982-83).

Second, numbers of children under 5 years of age have fallen, whilst remaining stable as a proportion of all under 5's (1 in 300 children under 5 were in care in 1981). By contrast, the number of 16 - 17 year olds has risen

5

(although falling as a proportion of all 16 - 17 year olds) - 1 in 70 of children between 16 and 17 years of age are in care. Table 1.2 shows these trends in more detail.

Table 1.2
Children in care of local authorities (1977-1981) by age group

England	Percentages				
	1977	1978	1979	1980	1981
Under 5 years	11.7	10.8	10.4	10.6	10.4
5-9 years	19.4	19.2	18.9	19.0	18.6
10-15 years	45.8	45.9	45.7	46.3	46.3
16 years and over	23.1	24.0	24.8	24.1	24.6
Total	100	100	100	100	100

Source: Social Services Committee, session 1982-83, p.35.

Third, the average age of children in care is increasing. Over a 10 year period between 1966 and 1976, proportions of children below school leaving age fell from 22 per cent to 12 per cent, while proportions over school leaving age rose (Fuller and Stevenson, 1983, p.89).

Finally, children are remaining in care longer. Considerable numbers of children in care have been there for lengthy periods. The *care episode* (defined as the length of time during which a child is continuously in the care of a local authority without a change in legal status) of approximately 80 per cent of children in care on March 1981 had commenced more than a year before, and for 30 per cent it had begun more than five years earlier. The proportion of children whose current care episode began over 5 years before 31 March 1981 was highest for children received into care under S.2 CCA 1980. Some 17,000 children in care for 5 years or over on 31 March 1981 were in care under S.2 CCA 1980 against roughly 10,000 children committed to care under the CYPA 1969 who had also been in care for 5 or more years (Social Services Committee, session 1982-83).

Parker (1978) considers that the sorts of changes referred to will have important implications for placement policies; especially, for groups traditionally regarded as difficult to foster. He also comments that an older in care population will comprise more children with their own views about placement.

Treatment of children in care

The CCA 1980 stipulates the ways in which all children in care should be treated (i.e. regardless of the legal route into care). In arriving at any decision concerning a child in care, local authorities must give first, and paramount, consideration to the welfare of the child throughout his/her childhood and, so far as is practicable, ascertain the wishes and feelings of the child and give them due consideration having regard to his/her age and understanding. This is referred to as the welfare principle (S.18 CCA 1980). In broad terms, the local authority's responsibilities towards a child in care are those of a natural parent.

Section 21 of the CCA 1980 permits local authorities wide discretion in choosing the most suitable placement for a child in care. A local authority may place a child in a residential home administered by the authority itself or by a voluntary organisation, or in a privately run home (S.21 CCA 1980). Alternatively, children can be boarded out with foster parents. Or, a child may be permitted to live with a parent, relative or friend; or, the authority may make whatever other arrangements seem best for the child (S.2 CCA 1980). Authorities must review the case of each child in care at not less than 6 monthly intervals (S.20 CCA 1980), are empowered to provide financial help to parents, relatives or friends to enable them to visit a child in care (S.26 CCA 1980), and may ask the parents of a child in care (or the child if the latter is 16 years of age and in full-time employment) to contribute towards maintenance costs (S.45-46 CCA 1980). A child in care may be adopted, but the local authority cannot agree on behalf of parents or guardians to the making of an adoption order.

Local authorities also have duties in relation to young people who have left care and are empowered to assist them. This may include help with further education and training (S.27-28 CCA 1980). Parents of children in care are required to maintain contact with local authorities, and local authorities have a statutory duty to work towards the child's return to his/her parents, relatives or friends. However, if all attempts to rehabilitate the child and his/her family fail, a local authority must consider long term plans for the child with a view to providing him/her with a stable and secure upbringing. Some parents of children in care and groups which represent them have, however, criticised the lack of opportunity for challenging the decisions made by local authority social services departments. They argue that the courts have no powers over important decisions such as where a child is placed or access by natural parents, which are by statute the sphere of local authorities.

Types of provision

Table 1.3 shows the proportions of children accommodated in the various types of provision for children in care on 31 March 1981. Some of the provisions concerned are discussed below, along with adoption.

Family placement: foster care and adoption

As indicated, a child may be boarded out with foster parents who care for the child as a member of the family. Whilst a child may stay for a long period with foster parents, no formal legal relationship is established: the local authority continues to be ultimately responsible for the child throughout his/her time in care. Children who are considered to require permanent new families may, however, be found an adoptive home and in law become the child of the adoptive parents, ceasing to be under the care of the local authority.

Table 1.3 shows that the proportion of children in care boarded out is rising; an increase which includes a growth in the numbers of older children fostered. On 31 March, 1981, an estimated 35,700 children were boarded out. Many local authorities have introduced special schemes in recent years for the

Table 1.3
Manner in which children in care are accommodated

England	Percentages				
	1977	1978	1979	1980	1981
Boarded out [Fostered]	33.8	34.6	36.0	36.9	38.7
In community homes provided, controlled or assisted by LA with observation and assessment facilities	4.9	4.9	4.8	5.2	5.1
With education on the premises	6.2	5.9	5.8	5.5	5.0
Other community homes	20.7	20.0	19.2	18.9	18.1
Voluntary homes	3.7	3.4	3.3	3.3	3.0
Under charge of parent, guardian, relative or friend	17.7	18.5	18.4	18.2	18.5
Others	13.2	12.5	12.4	12.0	11.4
Total	100	100	100	100	100

Source: Social Services Committee, session 1982-83, p.36.

fostering of *hard to place* children (i.e. children who were previously regarded as unsuitable for fostering, or for whom it was believed that foster homes would be difficult to find - for example adolescents who were considered too old or too difficult/disturbed, handicapped children, sibling groups, black children). The publication of Rowe and Lambert's (1973), *Children Who Wait*, has been influential in stretching ideas about which children in care can be fostered. Local authorities are empowered to set the rates of allowances paid to foster parents to suit local circumstances. However, projects which involve the fostering of hard to place youngsters provide higher rates, which normally include a reward element. In 1980-81, the Department of Environment Audit Inspectorate concluded that foster care could be some £50.00 per week cheaper than residential care - even where the cost of preparation and support, vital to any fostering scheme, are taken into account (*The Provision of Child Care: A study of 8 local authorities in England and Wales - final report, HMSO, 1982*). This view depends, however, on the recruitment of sufficient numbers of foster parents to facilitate the closure of residential homes and involves the assumption that the children concerned are suitable for fostering.

The late 1960's and early 1970's saw increasing recognition that many of those children in care with no hope of being reunited with their natural parents would benefit from placement in a permanent adoptive home. The Houghton Committee (set up in 1967) report recommended reforms that would focus adoption law on the needs of the child and promote more effective planning to achieve security for children whose parents could not care for them (see Social

Services Committee, session 1982-83). Many of the Committee's proposals were given legislative expression by the Children Act 1975. The Act included measures to encourage and aid the adoption of children who would otherwise remain in care (e.g., older children and handicapped children). Moreover, it provided for custodianship orders to enable courts to confer legal custody on any person caring for a child on a long-term basis, thus offering an alternative to adoption, particularly for children who would benefit from maintaining links with their natural families (Social Services Committee, session 1982-83).

Residential care

On 31 March, 1981, approximately 29,200 children were accommodated in local authority or voluntary residential homes - community homes. Numbers of children in residential care have been declining since 1976. Whilst this partly reflects attempts to find more appropriate or effective community alternatives, it is clear that the relatively high cost of residential care has also been a major factor. Community homes include the following types of provision: residential nurseries; homes with observation and assessment facilities (O and A centres); homes providing education on the premises (CHE's - known as Approved Schools prior to the CYPA 1969); other community homes where children typically attend local schools - Children's Homes. Given that this thesis concerns older children, nothing will be said here about residential nurseries (although reference will be made to this form of provision later, when studies on the consequences of residential care for younger children are briefly discussed).

For certain children who enter care, O and A centres are intended to provide a sophisticated assessment of their needs and the placement that will best meet them. Two projects undertaken in the Wessex region (SSRIU, 1976; Wessex Regional Planning Committee, 1976), however, cast doubt on the rationale of a would be sophisticated and expensive assessment process. First, there appeared to be a lack of coherent policy as to which children were to undergo residential assessment. Second, however, once admitted to an O and A centre, a child's chances of remaining in residential care were high. Third, there was a general failure to give due consideration to home background so as to balance observations undertaken in the more artificial environment of the O and A centre. Fourth, decisions with respect to type of placement mirrored a "common-sense" view of the sorts of provisions available. Thus, allocation to placements might be made not so much on the basis of sophisticated analysis, but more on such self-evident criteria as sex, age, "offender-or-not", and geographical location. Taylor *et al* (1979) list other shortcomings associated with the operation of O and A centres, including the fact that only some 20 per cent of residential staff held any kind of relevant qualification, which further undermines the idea of sophisticated assessment in residential settings. In 1981, a DHSS report argued for less reliance on residential assessment (DHSS, 1981). Accordingly, some local authorities have developed assessment services on a day basis, or using community based assessment teams. Multi-purpose community homes with an assessment base have also been developed in some localities (DHSS, 1981).

Like O and A centres, community homes providing education (particularly for young offenders) have been much criticised in recent years. Numbers of children placed in CHE's have fallen sharply. In the West Midlands Regional Planning Children's Area, for example, numbers decreased by one half between 1978 and 1981. Those who determine policy at central government level are well aware of the high costs of accommodating youngsters in CHE's (estimated in 1979 as £220 per week per child) and of the research evidence on their ineffectiveness (Fuller and Stevenson, 1983).

Cornish and Clarke (1972) attempted to compare the effects on later delinquency of two contrasting care regimes - one therapeutic, the other traditional - operating in different houses of a CHE. On the basis of random allocation and measurement of reconviction rates over a period of two years following discharge from the CHE, Cornish and Clarke (1972) concluded that the two distinctive care regimes were equally ineffective. Moreover, for only about 20 per cent of the 280 children admitted to the CHE could it be claimed that residential placement had provided more than a temporary interlude with respect to their offending behaviour. The authors acknowledge that the controlled trial in penal research is unlikely to produce unambiguous findings given the multivariate nature of causation. But they defend their results with the following arguments. First, the prevention of reconvictions (rather than, say, changes in attitude) is of paramount import, for it was delinquent activity which resulted in institutionalisation in the first place and it is the least that could be expected of residential treatment. Second, the difficulties associated with the control of variables is less significant in view of the fact that no important differences in outcome were found between the two groups.

Millham *et al* (1975) examined the effects of different care regimes in 18 CHE's, involving 1,000 boys. Their findings are somewhat less discouraging for advocates of residential treatment than those reported by Cornish and Clarke (1972). Whilst the overall reconviction rate was high, there were small, but significant differences between schools. Such differences, however, were between individual schools rather than between types of school classified in terms of training model and therapeutic community. Factors associated with reduced levels of later delinquency included high scores on attempts to foster staff-child relationships; high commitment on the part of boys to expressive goals; and, high levels of enjoyment derived from stay, as rated by the boys themselves.

Over 1,600 ordinary community or Children's Homes in England and Wales, accommodate some 18,000 children or roughly 20 per cent of all children in care. Yet surprisingly little is known about their operation. For the most part, the youngsters accommodated in Children's Homes have tended to be long stay children whose difficulties were not considered to warrant specialised residential provision.

Since 1948, certain trends can be discerned with respect to the nature of Children's Homes, but the speed and extent of their development is variable. Fuller and Stevenson (1983, p.110) relate that in... "the wake of social concern about the ill effects of large isolated institutions and grouped 'cottage homes', which, while more personal in their care, still created a ghetto of children in care, strenuous efforts were made to create more 'homely' environments. These were epitomised by the large numbers of very small homes, usually located on small housing estates and typically staffed by a married couple and an assistant"... However, the authors report that difficulties were encountered in running such homes, including the fact that the family group home, as it was called, was not in fact a family and..."there was an element of hypocrisy... in the name. There were age restrictions; not all took children under five and very few children were allowed to stay beyond school-leaving age. The mixture of eight to ten children, often emotionally disturbed and frequently clustering in age, did not look like a family and integration in the local community was variable... [Staffing] of such small homes posed grave problems. In the interests of a family model, it was assumed that the male partner would go out to 'ordinary' work. Yet few 'ordinary' men have the energy and commitment after a day's work to cope with the demands of such children, many of whom were difficult and unhappy. The role of the assistant was often a lonely one - 'three's a crowd' "... (Fuller and Stevenson, 1983, pp.110-111).

The problems referred to resulted in a movement towards somewhat larger groups, in which ... "there was less attempt to emulate the external characteristics of family life but rather to identify its essential components and reproduce them in a setting designed to meet the needs of children and staff"... (Fuller and Stevenson, 1983, p.111).

Berridge (1985) offers a three-fold classification of such provision based on the administrative criteria of size and leadership style: (1) family group - small, matriarchal, establishments, which shelter a wide range of children, including many adolescents; few of their staff have undergone professional training and their approach to care is one of intuitive tending; (2) hostel style - medium sized and characterised by the head of home operating as part of a wider staff team; they usually accommodate older adolescents, and often perform specialist functions such as helping to equip youngsters with the practical and social skills necessary for independent living, accommodating adolescents with schooling problems and diverting budding delinquents, (3) multi-purpose style - relatively large; they perform varied functions and provide services for the local community including day and respite care; their staff are more professional and treatment-oriented in relation to children and place greater emphasis on developing relationships with outside professionals (e.g., social workers, teachers, psychologists, etc.) than do staff in the family group and hostel style Children's Homes (Berridge, 1985).

Berridge (1985) considers that Children's Homes perform an essential function, for the most part well, and that the standards of individual care provided for children are generally satisfactory. This view seems broadly consistent with the findings of the London Region of the DHSS Social Work Service survey of residential care for children, which included an investigation of 30 Children's Homes. The majority of the Homes were felt by social work advisors to be adequately meeting children's needs, although some were poorly integrated with their neighbourhoods. A study of residential establishements by Berry (1975), however, found that Children's Homes were better integrated into their neighbourhoods than other types of provisions studied (e.g., O and A Centres, and CHE's). But, the quality of daily care in the Children's Homes varied considerably. Lasson (1980) studied a sample of long stay youngsters in Children's Homes in which she focused on their family links. She found that natural parents remain important to children who live in residential settings. Youngsters who were visited by their parents were more settled in their placements, and better able to develop and maintain relationships with staff and friends, than those who were not. While staff claimed to support natural parents, this was often not borne out in their actual behaviour towards them.

The author concluded that despite high levels of physical care, the Homes were failing to meet the emotional requirements of a significant number of their long-stay children and that they were often too isolated from the communities in which they were located.

Studies which have examined the experience of individuals who have spent periods in Children's Homes (e.g., Kahan, 1979; Page and Clarke (eds), 1977) reveal considerable variation in the quality of care provided. Some are portrayed as offering stability and security for children whilst others are depicted as insensitive and uncaring. Three major points emerge from these consumer studies. First, children stress their experience of stigma associated with living in Children's Homes and how they feel different from other children. Second, the instability of many children's lives in care - consequent upon factors such as multiple caretakers, the absence of a parent substitute, and the continual turnover of staff and peers - is highlighted. Third, adolescents emphasise the anxiety and problems surrounding discharge from residential care: many young people leaving care feel ill-equipped to cope with adult life (Berridge, 1985, p.7).

The development of children's services

Whilst the origins of public provision for deprived children lie in the Poor Law, the development of our present day statutory services in this field can be traced from the Children Act 1948 (which, as noted, was to become part of the CCA 1980). The Act was based on the recommendations of the *Report of the Care of Children Committee* (1946) - the Curtis Committee. The latter recommended the establishment of a new and unified system for the reception and care of children deprived of a normal home life. Accordingly, the 1948 Act required each local authority to set up a Children's Committee and appoint a Children's Officer to direct the work of a Children's Department which would have undivided responsibility for children whose parents were unable to look after them, and local authorities thereafter had a statutory duty to receive children into care. If high standards of child care were to be achieved, the Committee considered that training in child care was a necessity. Hence, the Central Council in Child Care was established in 1947 (subsequently to become the Central Council for Education and Training in Social Work - CCETSW). The committee emphasised the role of foster care as the preferred form of substitute care and recommended that local authorities make vigorous efforts to extend it. The committee argued that the small, mixed, family group homes referred to earlier represented the ideal, and also advocated the introduction of reception centres which would serve to provide observation and more informed understanding of the child in order to plan his/her appropriate placement (now known as O and A Centres).

However, beyond the rather drastic step of receiving children into care, the 1948 Act offered no means of helping families. Whilst a Home Office circular in 1948 emphasised the notion of maintaining families intact where possible, thus reflecting a shift in philosophy towards the idea of prevention, it was not until the Children and Young Persons Act 1963 (CYPA 1963) that social workers were given formal powers to assist families through the provision of material aid (S.1 CYPA 1963, subsequently S.1 CCA 1980). This followed a recommendation contained in the *Report of the Committee on Children and Young Persons* (1960) - the Ingleby Committee.

The Children Act 1948 was concerned with the provision of substitute care for children whose parents had requested their reception into care or for children without parents. At that time children who were ill treated, or neglected, or in moral danger could be brought before the courts under the Children and Young Persons Act 1933 as being in need of care and protection. The courts were empowered to place such children under supervision or commit them to an approved school or to the care of a fit person (which usually meant the local authority). Young offenders could also be committed to an approved school or to the care of a fit person.

Amidst concern about rising levels of officially recorded juvenile delinquency, the Ingleby Committee was established to consider the powers and procedures of juvenile courts, possible means by which to help young offenders, and whether local authorities should be given new powers and duties to prevent or forestall the suffering of children through neglect in their own homes. The Ingleby Committee acknowledged the conflict between *welfare* and *justice* in the juvenile court. Paragraph 60 of the Committee's report states: "the court remains a criminal court ... Yet the requirement to have regard to the welfare of the child and the various ways in which the court may deal with an offender suggest a jurisdiction that is not criminal. It is not easy to see how the two principles can be reconciled"... The Ingleby Committee's main recommendation that criminal proceedings for all children under 12 years of age, regardless of offence committed, should be replaced by welfare-oriented care and protection proceedings was not given legislative expression.

However, the Government White Paper, *The Child, the Family and the Young Offender* (Home Office, 1965) - based on the recommendations of the Longford Committee - went further than Ingleby in calling for the abolition of the juvenile courts and their replacement by family courts that would remove the social stigma associated with criminal proceedings. This suggestion engendered considerable controversy. Consequently, modified proposals were presented in a subsequent White Paper, *Children in Trouble* (Home Office, 1968), in an attempt to arrive at a more acceptable compromise between the principles of welfare and justice. This entailed the retention of the juvenile courts and it was this second White Paper that provided the basis for the CYPA 1969.

Although the CYPA 1969 has failed to resolve the tension between welfare and justice in the juvenile court, and whilst the crucial section relating to the age of criminal responsibility was not implemented [3], the CYPA 1969 did initiate significant changes, including: first, responsibility for delinquents was transferred from central government under the Home Office to local government in the form of newly created Social Services Departments (see below). Second, the Act (Part 1) gave local authorities increased responsibility and discretion *vis a vis* young offenders, and the juvenile courts lost their power to make an approved school order or a fit person order; these were replaced by the more general care order with the forms of care left unspecified by the court and decided by the local authority. Third, twelve regional planning committees were established in England and Wales to plan community home provision in their areas; the latter were created out of the Approved school system, and responsibilty for such provisions was removed from central government under the Home Office to local authorities. Finally, the newly created supervision order, which replaced the probation order, was a responsibilty to be shared initially by local authorities and the probation service; closely related to the supervision order was the notion of intermediate treatment (a service aimed specifically at preventing children from entering care, involving supervision and a range of community-based activities for young people deemed to be at risk of trouble with the law), which was also to involve local authorities in establishing schemes for its administration.

The welfare approach to juvenile justice has been subject to much criticism in recent years. In the USA there has been a distinct move towards a return to a justice approach and, indeed, even in the "half-hearted" form in which the welfare approach exists in England and Wales, in the shape of the CYPA 1969, it is attacked on all sides: by conservatives, because it insufficiently embraces punishment and social control; by liberals, because the legal rights of the individual are undermined; and, by radicals, because it is premised on spurious assumptions concerning the aetiology of delinquency, paying too little, if indeed any, attention to causes at the level of social structure [4]. Of these groups the Criminal Justice Act 1982, which represents a shift away from the welfare-oriented CYPA 1969 towards a more rigid, judicial model of juvenile justice, has been most favourably viewed by the first; a group which includes magistrates and the police. Tutt (1982, p.10) reports: "Whereas the decade started with a formally expressed faith in the 'welfare' approach with arrangements made for professional social workers to decide on the treatment of delinquent children, for treatment programmes to be indeterminate and flexible in order to respond to the changing and developing needs of the child, and for the child to be protected from the stigma of contact with adult offenders, the decade has concluded with an almost complete reversal in formal policy with a return of power to the magistracy, determinancy of sentencing, diversion away from social work agencies and less differentiation between children and adult offenders"... Provisions in the Criminal Justice Act 1982 for 14 - 17 year olds, for example, include the following: (a) retention of the detention centre order, but with shorter maximum and minimum periods of detention; (b) powers for the courts to impose medium term sentences of Youth Custody on offenders between 15 and 16 years of age, who were formerly liable to be sentenced to Borstal training which the Act abolished; and, (c) power for the juvenile courts to impose community service orders on offenders aged 16 years (Justice of the Peace, 1982, p.726).

The question of juvenile justice was influential in shaping our present day local authority Social Services Departments. Throughout the 1950's and 1960's, support for the family - then increasingly provided by the Curtis Committee inspired Children's Departments - was considered a central element in the attempt to prevent juvenile delinquency. In contemplating whether new powers should be given to local authorities, the Ingleby Committee received evidence indicating the need to widen the scope of the Children's Department into a family service, and urged further study of this question in its report. The White Paper, *The Child, the Family and the Young Offender* (Home Office, 1965) took up the call and announced the government's intention to ..." appoint a small independent committee to review the organisation and responsibilities of the local authority personal social services and to consider what changes are desirable to ensure an effective family service"... Hence, the *Committee on*

Local Authority and Allied Personal Social Services - the Seebohm Committee -
was appointed later that year (25 December, 1985) in order to carry out this
task.

The Committee's findings were published in July, 1968, and stimulated a
debate throughout (and beyond) social work circles, which culminated in the
Local Authority Social Services Act 1970. The Seebohm report recommended
..." a new local authority department, providing a community based and family
oriented service which will be available to all. This department will, we
believe, reach far beyond the discovery and rescue of social casualties; it will
enable the greatest possible number of individuals to act reciprocally, giving and
receiving service for the well-being of the whole community. The new
department will have responsibilities going beyond those of existing local
authority departments"... (Report of the Committee on Local Authority and
Allied Personal Social Services, p.11, paras.2 and 3).

Thus, the image created by the Seebohm Committee's report was that of a
unified Department, outgoing in nature (in the sense of encouraging people to
make use of its services), and strengthened by community support and
participation. The committee was confident that its proposals would lead to a
marked improvement in the efficiency and effectiveness of the personal social
services. Five major changes would contribute to this outcome: integration,
increased resources, higher professional standards, decentralisation and the
involvement of the community. The integration of the previously separate
social work services - children's, welfare, and mental health - would allow the
needs of clients to be treated as a whole and thus make the service more readily
intelligible to consumers. The new Departments would be considerably larger,
wield more influence and attract increased resources. Organisational change
would improve the standing of the social work profession and attract staff of
high calibre. The decentralisation of field social work services to area offices
vested with a substantial degree of autonomy would facilitate policies shaped to
local needs and ensure the involvement of the community in the delivery of
services (Hadley and Mcgrath, 1980, p.4).

Whilst a detailed treatment of the difficulties faced by local authority Social
Services Departments (SSD's) would take us too far beyond the subject of
interest - children's services - one may note the widespread view that SSD's
have failed to live up to the Seebohm Committee's vision. Hadley and Mcgrath
(1980, p.5) argue that SSD's manifest ..."the worst characteristics of
bureaucracies... ; they are hierarchic, rule bound, and slow to respond to
changes. Professionalism tends to imply a one-to-one helping relationship with
individual clients, and community involvement, if present at all, is usually
relegated to individual workers operating separately from the area team. The
overall style of the departments is defensive and reactive rather than preventive.
Major categories of clients, including the elderly, the handicapped and the
mentally ill are inadequately helped and supported"... The authors consider that
the major shortcomings of the present system issue from assumptions
concerning the centrality of the statutory service in the overall provision of care
and failure on the part of SSD's to relate to the actual caring systems of the
community. To be sure, although effectiveness is notoriously difficult to
measure, as a means of preventing the reception of children into care and
reducing recorded delinquency, the SSD's appear to fall some way short of
being an effective family service.

However, viewing the problems experienced by SSD's as being mainly due to a mechanistic conception of organisations is perhaps not altogether satisfactory, for SSD's do not operate in a socio-economic vacuum, nor are the problems of clients unrelated to the structures - socio-economic and political - of the wider society. Other factors which have played a part in frustrating the aspirations of the Seebohm Committee include the present economic recession and associated attacks on state welfare [5]. In this context, the conclusions of the more recent Barclay Committee Report (National Institute for Social Work, 1982) are perhaps surprising. They amount to a reassertion of the Seebohm vision. In his dissenting note Pinker is, unfortunately, probably correct when he argues that SSD's do not have the resources to seek out needs in the community, and in the present economic climate SSD's must be content to perform a reactive, rather than preventive, role. The structural problems - poverty, bad housing, poor health, and so on - which impinge upon the lives of social work clients are typically beyond the scope of SSD's. Moreover, the notion of community-based social work may become somewhat romantic when applied to inner-city areas which provide a disproportionately large number of the children in local authority care [6].

2. Previous Research on Substitute Child Care and Related Fields

Studies of residential institutions

The origin of our present system for dealing with the various forms of deviance and dependency can be traced to the revolution in social practice which occurred at the end of the 18th and beginning of the 19th centuries. As Cohen (1979, p.609) notes: "a centralised state apparatus was developed to control crime and take care of people in need of help. The deviants and dependents were segregated into asylums - mental hospitals, prisons, reformatories and other such closed purpose-built institutions for treatment and punishment"... Accounts differ as to why this transformation occurred; though none doubt that an extraordinary change in social practice took place. Rothman (1970), Foucault (1977), Melossi and Pavarini (1981) and Scull (1984), for example, all attempt to show how institutions [7] moved from being places of last resort at the end of the 18th century to places of first resort by the middle years of the century which followed.

Yet, by the end of the 1960's, institutions seemed once again to have become places of last resort. The idea of abolition, rather than mere reform, became prominent and ..."with varying degrees of enthusiasm and actual measurable consequences, officials in Britain, the United States and some Western European countries, became committed to the policy labelled decarceration: the state sponsored closing down of asylums, prisons and reformatories"... (Cohen, 1979, p.609). Ironically, the expectations engendered by the prospect of abolishing institutions are as great as those which greeted their adoption. Like the nineteenth-century institutions, community care/control tends [8] to be regarded as a panacea for certain social problems.

Cohen (1979) distinguishes a number of beliefs which drive the community care/control movement. First, institutions are considered ineffective in terms of failing to achieve their formal objectives; they neither deter nor rehabilitate. This claim is based on evidence such as the reconviction rates for persons discharged from institutions. An example here would be the previously mentioned very high reconviction rates for children discharged from CHE's. Equally high reconviction rates have been recorded with respect to persons discharged from prisons [9]. Second, institutions are considered more costly than community alternatives. It was earlier reported that just such a conclusion was reached by the authors of a DHSS study comparing the costs of foster and residential care [10]. Third, theories of stigma and labelling suggest that the further the deviant or dependent person is processed into the care/control system, the more difficult it becomes to facilitate his/her rehabilitation into normal life. The influence of this notion is evidenced in the policy of diversion from the juvenile justice system. Fourth, advocates of community alternatives to segregative modes of care/control argue that the causes of most forms of deviance and dependency are rooted in the structures of society (family, school, community, economic system). Hence, care/control can only be undertaken in the community and not in artificially created agencies premised on a model of individual intervention. Fifth, it is claimed that liberal measures such as the juvenile court, reformatories and, indeed, the whole rehabilitative model are politically suspect, irrespective of whatever benevolent motives underpin them. The state should be committed to doing less harm rather than more good. Hence, policies of decriminalisation, diversion and decarceration are advocated. Sixth, institutions are considered less humane than community alternatives. Rather than improving matters, it is argued that institutions may exacerbate, and can even create, the very problems that they are intended to resolve.[11]

The final criticism of institutions listed above has derived support from the work of social scientists (mainly psychologists and sociologists) who, although approaching the subject from differing theoretical perspectives and with differing interests (e.g., children, mental patients, prisoners), have focused primarily on the adverse effects of residential institutions *vis a vis* inmates or residents. The work of Erving Goffman (*Asylums: Essays on the Social Situation of Mental Patients and Other Inmates*, 1961) has been particularly influential in alerting us to the potentially negative features of life in residential institutions.

Goffman (1961) terms organisations such as mental hospitals, prisons, concentration camps, orphanages, monasteries and army barracks *total institutions*. A total institution is a place of residence and work where a large number of individuals, isolated from the wider society for an appreciable period of time, together lead an enforced, formally administered round of life. According to Goffman (1961), total instititions are forcing houses for changing persons. Because inmates are largely cut off from the outside world and from long-standing relationships with family, friends and work groups, they are separated from the social contexts in which an individual's self-concept is sustained. An individual's view of self is also rooted in his name, appearance, clothes and personal possessions. However, admission procedures in total institutions entail the removal of many items from this identity-kit.

On this view, admission procedures and future interactions within the total institution not only change, but also mortify the self. The inmate may be searched, undressed, bathed, disinfected, fingerprinted and be forced to submit himself before superiors. Permission may be required to perform the most basic human functions, and in some instances the inmates' humiliation is increased by an absence of privacy. Such experiences tend to break the inmates' former self-concept. Subsequently, the self is slowly rebuilt, partly by means of rewards and punishments administered by those in authority. Goffman (1961) claims that many of the actions of inmates can only be understood with reference to the strict supervision and mortification of self that occurs in many total institutions.

Goffman (1961) identifies the following five types of inmate adaptation: (1) situational withdrawal (the inmate withdraws attention from everything except events immediately surrounding his body and minimizes his interaction with others); (2) the intransigent line (the inmate flatly refuses to cooperate with staff and manifests sustained hostility towards the institution); (3) colonisation (the inmate becomes institutionalised, and regards life in the institution as preferable to life on the outside); (4) conversion (the individual adopts the staff's definition of the model inmate and acts out the part); and, (5) playing it cool (the inmate attempts to stay out of trouble and alternates between the other types of adaptation depending on the situation). Playing it cool offers the inmate the best chance, in the particular circumstances, of eventually getting out physically and psychologically undamaged. Despite the sustained assault on the self in total institutions, Goffman (1961) argues that for most inmates a radical and permanent change of self does not occur, partly because inmates are able to defend themselves from the mortification process by playing it cool. Thus, Goffman (1961) concludes that rather than offering cure and rehabilitation, etc., many total institutions, most of the time, seem merely to function as storage dumps for inmates [12].

Some of Goffman's (1961) ideas are echoed by the work of writers whose intentions have been mainly reformist rather than analytical. Russell Barton's book, *Institutional Neurosis* (1959), provides one of the best known examples. Barton (1959) employs the term institutional neurosis to denote a condition which is characterised by apathy, lack of initiative, loss of interest, submissiveness, apparent inabilty to make plans for the future, lack of individuality, and sometimes a characteristic posture and gait. In Barton's (1959) view, institutional neurosis may be superimposed upon the original ailment in a mental hospital and can remain long after the original illness has been alleviated or cured. Barton (1959, p.77) lists the factors which contribute to institutional neurosis. These are very similar to the features of institutional life identified by Goffman (1961), and include: loss of contact with the outside world, enforced idleness and loss of responsibility; brow-beating, brutality and teasing; bossiness of medical and nursing staff; loss of personal friends, possessions and personal events; use of drugs; ward atmosphere; and loss of prospects outside the institution. That these sorts of treatment may exist in residential settings is corroborated, for example, by a series of public inquires into psychiatric and subnormality hospitals (Walton and Elliot, 1980, p.8).

Students of prisons - notably Terence and Pauline Morris (1963) - have written about prisonisation; a somewhat different process to institutional neurosis in that it involves working the system, rather than succumbing to it. In their study of Pentonville, the Morris's (1963) observed signs of prisonisation, which may be defined as the continuous and systematic destruction of the psyche as a consequence of the experience of imprisonment, and the taking on of new attitudes and behaviours which, in addition to being unsuited to life outside the walls of the prison, often make it impossible for the individual to act successfully in any normal or conventional social role. Whilst similar to institutional neurosis, the process of prisonisation entails an element of adaptation to circumstances. Like institutional neurosis, prisonisation involves the erosion of the personality, but does not necessarily represent a retreat into an apathetic state of a-sociality. Rather, it may produce a distinctive type of prisonised man whose behaviour constitutes the hard core of inmate culture, which can influence other prisoners and play a major role in the formation of a distinctive sub-culture of the prison.

By no means all students of residential institutions have confined their interest to mental hospitals and prisons: less controversial settings have also proved a fertile ground for research. Peter Townsend (1962), for instance, carried out a survey of residential institutions for the elderly. In a chapter on *The Effects of Institutions*, Townsend attacks batch living, observing that although people live communally with a minimum of privacy, their relationships with each other are tenuous. Many residents exist in a sort of defensive shell of isolation, and they are subtly oriented towards a regime which requires submission to an orderly routine that facilitates neither creative occupation nor the exercise of self-determination. Whilst it might be argued that Townsend's survey is somewhat dated, a collection of readings edited by Jerome (1984) shows that residential provision for the elderly in contemporary Britain often remains ill-designed to meet the needs of many residents.

Perhaps the most impressive attempt to investigate the relationship between institutional environment and inmate behaviours is Wing and Brown's (1970) study of the adverse effects on schizophrenic patients of a prolonged stay in mental hospital. The authors were able to demonstrate a close association between the clinical condition of patients and the social condition of the different wards in which they lived. Thus, their original hypothesis that patients living in widely differing social environments would manifest different symptoms was confirmed. Wing and Brown's (1970) research involved a general method of approach which might have much to offer in terms of helping to expand our knowledge in the field of substitute child care. Unlike the ethnographic method of Goffman (1961), Wing and Brown's approach was quantititive. In addition to its technical merit, Wing and Brown's work is also valuable from a policy viewpoint for, having identified problems associated with the treatment of schizophrenia they were able to show how these could be resolved.

Wing and Brown's (1970) work - particularly their success in developing quantitative scales by which to measure the severity of schizoprenic patients' handicaps and their skill in measuring the social poverty of the environment in which the patients lived - had a profound influence on King *et al's* (1971) exemplary attempt to test for crucial factors in the provision of child-oriented care in residential institutions accommodating mentally retarded children. So too did the work of Goffman (1961). However, King *et al* (1971) found Goffman's (1961) ideas difficult to use in empirical research ..."for although he shows in a graphic way that similarities may exist between what hitherto had been regarded as quite disparate institutions, he does so by the use of an 'ideal type' construct which does not have the flexibility required for comparative and empirical investigations...With Goffman's concept as it stands, one is presented with the problem that when looking at any particular institution, one can say little more than it is, or it is not, total - according to how well it conforms to the ideal type. But what if some institutions are more total than others? What if an institution has only some of the features which are said to characterise the total institution?"...(King *et al*, 1971, pp.46-47).

Writers such as Jones (1967), Plowman (1967), Walton and Elliot (1980) and Jones and Fowles (1984) have considered the variation which may exist between residential institutions and which may be of consequence for inmates or residents. Jones (1967, p.17), for example, argues that it is erroneous to treat the subject of residential institutions as though all inmate populations have the same attitudes and motivation; as though all were confined against their will, and for no useful purpose; as though all shared indefinite or life-long confinement. An unfortunate result of the application of theory to practice is that it may become distorted or oversimplified in the transfer. Goffman's (1961) writings have tended to be misinterpreted to become: "all residential institutions are punitive, humiliating and harsh to experience".

However, the value of Goffmans (1961) work should not be underestimated. King *et al* (1971) were able to operationalise concepts derived from Goffman (1961) in developing a scale to measure child-management practice in different residential settings for mentally handicapped children, thereby making possible a more refined analysis of institutional life than that offered by Goffman's (1961) ideal-type concept of the total institution.

Research on the consequences of residential child care

For ease of presentation, a number of studies concerning particular forms of residential care have been discussed already (i.e. when the various types of provision for children in care were discussed). The focus in what follows will be on research into the consequences of residential care for children's development and competencies, beginning with studies pertaining to infants and younger children.

Another writer whose work has sometimes been misrepresented is John Bowlby (1951; 1953). Bowlby's maternal deprivation thesis is often grossly oversimplified, thus: "any family home in the community is better than institutional care". The literature on the effects of deprivation of mother love in early infancy is too well known to require extensive rehearsal here. The literature has been summarised by Bowlby (1951) and reassessed by Ainsworth (1962) and Rutter (1972). Reviewing the evidence concerning the relationship between early maternal care and subsequent mental health, Bowlby concluded that maternal deprivation (the term denotes long separation, inability to form bonds, or repeated changes of mother figure) during the first three years of life has a detrimental effect on personality development. Whilst Bowlby acknowledged that a mother substitute might provide a child with a relationship conducive to mental health, he also postulated that children tend to be monotropic (i.e. that they form the key emotional bond with one person only). Moreover, he reported that research suggested that the effects of maternal deprivation (e.g., inability to establish affectionate relationships, retarded development, and the formation of a psychopathic character) were irreversible. Bowlby's work had a profound effect on policy and practice in the field of child-rearing and, since much of the associated research had concerned the effect of maternal deprivation on young children living in institutions (e.g., Goldfarb, 1943; Spitz, 1949), led to the closure of many residential nurseries.

Ainsworth (1962) concurred that the evidence cited by Bowlby in support of his thesis was impressive, but considered the task of interpretation far more complex than it had appeared ten years earlier. Whilst accepting the notion that bad care has bad effects, Rutter (1983) insists on the need for a more accurate description of both. He argues that the experiences covered by the term maternal deprivation are too heterogeneous, and the effects too varied, for the term to have any further usefulness and proposes that the concept be abandoned. Further, a collection of readings edited by Clarke and Clarke (1976) challenge the belief that the child's social experiences in the first few years of life exert a disproportionate influence on later development. To be fair, Bowlby himself has indicated that the investigators who first drew attention to the adverse effects of maternal deprivation tended to overstate their case. However, he remains unrepentant that the roots of our emotional life lie in infancy and early childhood [13]. Also, it should not be thought that the early deprivation studies were of no value. One of the main achievements of these studies seems to have been that they exposed the deplorable conditions in many institutions and the indifference of many hospitals to children's sensibilities. Moreover, reviewing later research, Prosser (1976) found no new evidence to counter the view expressed by Dinnage and Pringle (1967) that prolonged institutionalisation during the early years of life leaves a child very vulnerable to later stress.

However, while earlier studies emphasised the impaired language, poor intelligence and disturbed behaviour, discovered among children reared in institutions, Prosser (1976) suggests that more recent work appears to indicate that these are not found in all children brought up in residential care. Research in Britain seems to show that, as far as cognitive development is concerned, the quality of care experienced by children is more important than the fact of institutionalisation *per se*. Children reared in the best residential nurseries, where there are adequate levels of care and cognitive stimulation, do not appear to manifest any significant intellectual retardation. However, the social development of such children may be retarded; a finding which may be related to discontinuities in the staffing of residential nurseries (e.g., high rates of staff turnover and relatively large numbers of different caretakers) [14].

The findings of Dinnage and Pringle (1967) and Prosser (1976) concerning the shortcomings of research on children in residential care in failing (a) to disentangle the effects of various aspects of institutional life, (b) to trace the influence on outcomes of different styles of residential care, and (c) to compare residential experience with other forms of experience, perhaps apply with greatest force to research on older children. Also worth highlighting is that whilst a good deal of research effort has been focused on institutions accommodating delinquent children, such as CHE'S, ordinary community or Children's Homes have been virtually neglected (some of the very few studies of Children's Homes have already been reviewed).

Equally regrettable is the fact that although research on foster care has expanded considerably in recent years, there seems to have been a lack of interest in comparing fostering with residential care. The following passage from Dinnage and Pringle (1967, p.35) draws attention to one of the major difficulties traditionally associated with such an undertaking: "even if it were substantiated that children in foster homes do better than those in Children's Homes, this would inevitably reflect to some extent the factors which determine selection for one or other type of substitute care; foster care may tend to be chosen for the less disturbed, less backward, and thus more acceptable and responsive child". However, the development of special foster schemes for children previously considered unsuitable for fostering might well render this sort of argument untenable. Triseliotis and Russell (1984) have recently attempted to compare the outcome of late adoption and residential care. The authors report that the material, social and personal circumstances of a group of adults who had grown up in residential care were generally found to compare unfavourably with those of a group of adults who had been adopted at a relatively late stage in their childhood.

Turning to research exclusively concerned with the effects of residential care on older children, several early studies suggest an association between lengthy periods in residential care and later maladjustment or inability to make use of family life (e.g., Trasler, 1955; Conway, 1957; and Pringle and Bossio, 1960). Long-term institutional living was also found to impair children's intellectual and educational development. Dinnage and Pringle (1967) note: "the ill-effects of long-term institutional life have been found to be very similar in the United States, in the Western European countries ..., and in Israel (except... for Kibbutz-reared children). The ill-effects manifest themselves in relatively low scores on intelligence tests, poor educational progress and deficiencies in emotional and social development, when compared to children in their own families. The two potentially most damaging aspects of residential care are that a psychologically, culturally and emotionally restricted, impoverished or, at worst, even depriving substitute environment may unintentionally be provided; secondly, that unless special steps are taken, children may grow up without a personal sense of identity"...(Dinnage and Kellmer Pringle, 1967, pp.34-35).

It would appear that more recent research concerning the consequences of residential care for older children has concentrated on children's social and emotional development, rather than on their intellectual and educational development. Pappenfort and Kilpatrick (1969), reporting a national survey of over 2,000 institutions in the USA, assert that three-quarters of all institutionalised children were considered to be emotionally disturbed. Rosen (1971) argues that youngsters in long-term care are retarded in both their emotional and social development. Yule and Raynes (1972) found that children in care are more likely to be maladjusted than those growing up in their own homes. However, Wolkind and Rutter (1973) suggest that children experiencing short-term residential care are susceptible to anti-social disorder, not so much because of the effect of the care *per se* , but rather because they are likely to come from disturbed families. Wolkind (1974) also found important sex differences in the development of anti-social disorders among children in institutions.

Thus, whilst more recent studies, on the whole, seem to confirm that children in residential care are more likely to manifest behavioural disorders and emotional disturbance than children living in their own homes, the possible differential effects of variables such as age, sex, period spent in care, age on first admission, family background, etc., should not be overlooked. Moreover, it might be that to attempt at all costs to keep a child with his/her own family may not always be the most appropriate means to prevent the development of psychiatric disorder, since the child might be severely damaged prior to his/her entry to care (Prosser, 1976). If this point is valid, then it appears imperative that factors within the residential environment likely to cause further damage to the child following admission be identified, in addition to factors likely to facilitate some measure of recovery.

Research on the residential treatment of identified delinquents was previously commented upon. Given that the evidence appears to suggest that residential treatment of young offenders fails to achieve its aim in terms of preventing subsequent delinquent behaviour following discharge, perhaps some attempt to explain this is required here. Clarke and Martin (1975, pp.247-274) argue that it is not possible to deal directly with most forms of delinquency in an institutional setting, simply because they are unable to manifest themselves: their occurrence depends upon unrestricted movement in the community. For this reason, the authors assert that..."in dealing with delinquency the emphasis should be shifted to the modification of the social and economic conditions in the community which establish and maintain delinquent behaviour, or at least to more intensive work in families/schools and workplaces"... In short, the focus of action should be shifted from the individual child to his/her environment.

Finally, certain commentators (e.g., Kadushin, 1971, Prosser, 1976, Aldgate, 1978, Berridge, 1985) stress positive aspects of residential child care. Aldgate (1978) and Berridge (1985), for example, draw attention to the fact that for certain youngsters, residential care may be preferred to family placement (see Chapter 6 for a more detailed consideration of the sorts of factors which are are held to constitute the strengths of residential care). The Barclay report (1982) argues that there should be no presupposition that residential care is inferior to family care; indeed, the report even goes so far as to suggest that foster care ought to be seen as a variant of residential care. Berridge (1985) urges that Children's Homes be regarded as a vital element in a comprehensive package of services for children at risk. Such statements seem intended to rescue residential care from blanket hostility and counter dogmatic views about the respective merits or otherwise of family and residential placement. Accounts have been presented by those who have sought to create specialist therapeutic milieux for the treatment of severely disturbed children (e.g., Docker-Drysdale, 1968; Wills, 1970). These have had an important impact on what may be termed the progressive element in residential child care. Equally, work by writers such as Beedell (1970) and Berry (1975) is held by many social work tutors to exemplify what residential care ought to entail.

The family

Before reviewing research on family placement, it would appear appropriate to clarify the meaning of the term *family* and to discuss competing conceptions of this social institution, with particular reference to the tasks performed by families in relation to child rearing.

There is increasing acknowledgement of the diversity of family types. In the forward to a collection of readings on families in Britain, for example, Laslett (1982) argues that..." *The British Family* is not the phrase to use, but a phrase consciously to abandon. For there is now no single British family, but a rich variety of forms, states, traditions, norms and usages...[The] stereotype family group consisting of father, mother and at least two residing children, is entirely misleading in contemporary Britain. A majority of our households now consist in solitaries, people living with persons not their relatives, couples (married or unmarried) without accompanying offspring, or single parent households"... [15]

In recognition of the diversity of family types, Close (1985, pp.9-10) conceives the term family as referring to..."that area of social life covering and circumscribed by kinship (blood or consanguinal relationships) and marriage (conjugal and other affinal relationships)"... He considers that..." the application of the term in this sense does not presume that in practice there will necessarily be an area of social life which is exclusive to the family. The term 'a family' then refers to any social group based on consanguinal and/or affinal relationships...Any instance of a family ...[therefore]... will be at the same time an instance of one or more 'family types', depending on its composition, content or character. Thus a family may belong to the 'nuclear family' type, if it is composed of a man and a women and their dependent offspring; to the 'one-parent family' type; to the 'child centred family' type, and so on. In addition, a range of families and of family types may belong to the same 'family form' in so far as they display a similar overall shape or outward appearance in relation to the rest of society. For example, a set of nuclear families and one-parent families may be similarly 'closed' in relation to external kin and community; they may exhibit similar degrees of 'relative autonomy' in relation to other families; their relationship with the economy may be similarly dependent upon the supply of wage labour, and so on. Moreover, it may be argued that there is in any particular society a family form which is dominant. This may be done on various grounds, including the discovery that most families belong to this family form, that all families are converging towards it; that the dominant economic structures and processes are best 'articulated' with it. Thus it has been widely argued (albeit...in the face of some notable opposition) that modern societies tend to be characterised by a distinctive, dominant family form whereby the 'conjugal family of procreation' is prominent"...

Many sociologists believe that the family has lost several of its functions in modern industrial society. Social institutions such as businesses, political parties, schools and welfare organisations now perform functions previously undertaken by the family. However, the importance of the latter has not declined in a general sense. Rather, the family has become more specialised, and the loss of certain functions make its remaining functions more important (Haralambos, 1980, pp.355-358). Talcott Parsons (1980, pp.192-197), for instance, claims that the American family retains two basic and irreducible functions which are common to all societies; namely, the primary socialization of children and the stabilization of the adult personalities of the population of the society.

The primary socialisation of children involves two basic processes: the internalisation of society's culture and the structuring of the personality. Parsons affirms that the continued existence of society depends on the internalisation of culture, for without shared norms and values social life would not be possible. Culture is not simply learned. Rather, it is internalised as part of the personality structure. The child's personality is shaped in terms of the the central values of the culture to the point where they become part of him/her. With respect to American society, Parsons claims that the child's personality is moulded in terms of independence and achievement - the two central values of American culture. Families, in Parsons view, are "factories" which produce human personalities. They are essential for this purpose because primary

24

socialisation requires a context which provides warmth, security and mutual support. He can conceive of no social institution other than the family that could provide this context. Once produced, the stability of the individual's personality is ensured by marriage and the emotional security couples provide for each other, which serves to counter the stresses and strains of everyday life. This is especially important in modern industrial societies given that the nuclear family is largely isolated from kin and, hence, lacks the security hitherto provided by the close-knit extended family. The parent role in the socialisation of children also contributes to the stabilisation process by allowing adults to act out childish aspects of their own personalities which they have retained from childhood but which cannot be indulged in adult society.

Parsons' thesis has been criticised on several grounds. It is argued that he idealises the family in presenting a picture of well-adjusted children and sympathetic spouses caring for each others every need. Second, his view is based in large part on middle class American families; variations associated, for instance, with different socio-economic classes, regions, religions, ethnic groups, are not fully considered; third, he does not examine functional alternatives to the family; and, finally, he conceives socialisation as a oneway process whereby parents shape the personalities of children and tends to ignore the two-way interaction process which occurs between parents and children. (Haralambos, 1980, pp.332-333)

Contrary to the view expounded by Parsons, certain commentators argue that it may be the case that the family is dysfunctional both for its individual members and society. The anthropologist Edmund Leach (1967) holds a pessimistic view of the modern industrial family. According to the author, isolated from kin and the wider community and thus deprived of an important source of moral support, the family looks inward upon itself. This involves an intensification of emotional strain between husband and wife and parents and children greater than most of us are able to tolerate. The result is conflict: parents fight; children rebel. The isolation and close-knit nature of modern family life breeds hate which leads to conflict in the wider community. Far from being the basis of the good society, Leach argues that the family with its narrow privacy and tawdry secrets is the source of all our discontents. For Leach, the ills of society will not be ameliorated until individuals can escape from the prison of the nuclear family, rejoin their fellows, and give and receive support.

The phenomenological pyschiatrist, R.D.Laing (1976), offers a second radical alternative to Parsons' view of the family. Laing is concerned with interaction within the family and the meanings that develop in that context. He conceives the family in terms of sets of interactions and refers to the family group as a nexus. From interaction within the nexus, what Laing calls reciprocal interiorization develops; viz., family members become a part of each other and the family as a whole; they interiorise or internalise the family. In Laing's view, the interiorization process is pyschologically damaging, for it inhibits the development of the self. Because the individual carries the blue-print of the family with him/her for the rest of his/her life, this vitiates any real autonomy or freedom of self. Echoing Leach, the author holds that problems in the family cause problems for society. The nature of the nexus and its associated interiorisation process results in the erection of a defensive barrier between the family and the outside world. Family members, especially children, perceive the world in terms of harmful and dangerous distinctions and stereotypes - Black and White, Protestent and Catholic, etc. Moreover, patterns of obedience laid down in early childhood within the family form the basis for obedience to authority in adult life. Without family obedience training, people would question orders, follow their own judgement and arrive at their own decisions and we might no longer inhabit a society which Laing believes is, in many respects, insane.

The work of Leach and Laing is open to several criticisms. For example, neither has undertaken detailed fieldwork on the family in contemporary industrial society. Laing's research is restricted to his study of families in which one member has been diagnosed schizophrenic. Both discuss the family without reference to its position in the social structure. Laing's work lacks a historical perspective. Both begin with a view of society which subsequently helps to style their accounts - the view that society has got out of hand underpins Leach's work, whilst Laing goes even further in conceiving modern society as largely insane (although a conservative bias can be discerned in the view expounded by Parsons; for example, Parsons stresses the universality and inevitability of the family which serves to justify its existence; and, his preoccupation with the positive aspects of the family could be said to legitimate it).(Haralambos, 1980, pp.335-337)

Despite Laing's assault on family life, he stated in an interview in 1977: "I enjoy living in a family. I think the family is still the best thing that...exists biologically as a natural thing. My attack on the family is aimed at the way I felt that many children are subjected to gross forms of violence and violation of their rights, to humiliation at the hands of adults who don't know what they're doing"...(Haralambos, 1980, p.337)

The revival of Marxian approaches to the family that appeared in the late 1960's and 1970's [16] owed much to the Women's Liberation Movement. A number of feminist writers utilised Marxian concepts in their criticism of the family. Here the family is regarded as a unit which produces one of the fundamental commodities of capitalism: labour. This is produced cheaply from the viewpoint of capitalists because they are not obliged to pay for the production or maintenance of children. Women are not paid for producing and rearing children. Benston (1972) considers that a massive redistribution of wealth would be necessary to pay women for their work - even at minimum wage levels. Currently, the support of the family is a hidden tax on the wage earner whose earnings purchase the labour power of two people. That the husband is required to pay for the production and upkeep of future labour means that he cannot easily withdraw his labour from the market. Thus, as an economic unit, the nuclear family is an important stabilising force in capitalist society (Benston, 1972).

In addition to the production and rearing of cheap labour, the family also maintains the latter in good order at zero cost to the employer. The woman's role as housewife entails attending to her husband's needs so that he may perform his role as a wage labourer. Parsons' view that the family functions to stabilise adult personalities is reinterpreted as follows: the emotional support provided by the wife operates as a safety-valve for the frustration which working in a capitalist system engenders in the husband. This frustration is soaked up by the comforting wife instead of being turned against the capitalist system which produced it (Ansley, 1976).

26

According to Marxian approaches, the social reproduction of labour power does not merely entail the reproduction and maintenance of children: it also involves the reproduction of the attitudes essential for an efficient workforce under capitalism. Hence, Cooper (1972) regards the family as an ideological conditioning device in an exploitative society. Within the family children learn to submit to authority; to conform. Thus, the foundation is laid for the obedient and submissive workforce required by capitalism. Similarly, Feeley (1972) asserts that the structure of family relationships socialises children to accept their place in a class stratified society.

Marxian perspectives on the family are handicapped by some of the shortcomings distinguished in relation to the other approaches previously outlined. Above all they lack comparative and historical perspective. They fail to give due consideration to possible variations in family life between types of society, social classes and over time. Further, as Haralambos (1980, p.368) notes, many feminist writers appear to ..."begin with two value judgements. First, capitalism is an evil and exploitative system. Second, women are oppressed and exploited, particularly within the family. They put these two value judgements together and from then on their analysis of the family follows a predictable pattern. Everything they dislike about the family is blamed on capitalism. Everything that is bad about the family is seen to support the capitalist system"...Inevitably, this leads to a narrow view of the family. A broader perspective would show that many of the aspects of family life perceived as exploitative are not restricted to capitalist society (Haralambos, 1980, p.368).

Research on family placement

The two forms of family placement - adoption and fostering - have very different roots and traditional functions. Adoption, for the greater part of its relatively short history (it has been a legal process since the first Adoption Act in 1926), has primarily been regarded as a means of providing children for childless couples (often middle class), rather than as a response to the needs of deprived children (Tizard, 1977; Aldgate, 1982), with consequent stress in the placement process on meeting the wishes of infertile couples. By contrast, the social policy of boarding out or fostering children deprived of their own families originated in the seventeenth century under the auspices of the Poor Laws (Aldgate, 1982), and is traditionally a lower status activity that has fluctuated in esteem as a means of providing substitute care.

Adoption

Reviewing American research on adoption, Kadushin (1971) concludes:
> (1) the largest proportion of children available for adoption are illegitimate children of unmarried parents;
> (2) adoptions are generally successful for 70-80 per cent of families (including hard to place children);
> (3) successful adoption can reverse the effects of earlier deprivations and traumas; family and developmental history do not appear to influence outcome (whilst placement under two months may be

particularly favourable, age at placement has generally not been found to be significant);

(4) the major factors which influence outcome are parent variables: attitudes to children, child-rearing practices and marital relationship are significantly related to outcome; however, the age of parents, their income, education, socio-economic status, religion, and motivation are not; neither is the matching of the physical characteristics of parents and children;

(5) adopted children are over-represented among psychiatric referrals, though not strongly and the majority of adoptees are not referred;

(6) most adoptees prefer to be given some information about their natural parents, but this appears to owe more to curiosity rather than to a desire to initiate contact with their natural parents.

The congruence between these findings, Kellmer Pringle's (1967) earlier British review, and later studies discussed by Fuller and Stevenson (1983) would appear impressive. Adoption has also been compared favourably with long-term fostering by Tizard (1977) on the grounds that the former involves a greater sense of security for parents and children than the latter. Moreover, as reported above, Triseliotis and Russell (1984) show that adoption compares favourably with residential care in relation to long-term outcome; and, Triseliotis (1983) found that young adults who had grown up in long term foster homes were, overall, less secure and confident than those who had been adopted. He concludes that the ambiguous nature of fostering relationships appeared to have had a qualitative impact on the foster children's sense of identity.

Given the generally very favourable impression of adoption, the question arises as to why it is not practised more widely. As a form of placement for children in care, adoption has accounted for only roughly 3 per cent of all discharges from care in recent years. Although there have been calls for higher priority to be given to adoption as a form of placement for children in care (see, for example, Tizard, 1977), Fuller and Stevenson (1983, p.108) doubt whether there can be a large scale shift from fostering to adoption because of..." the enormity of the decision for a natural mother to release her child permanently, the enormity of the judgement that would be required of a social worker to work towards that end. Clearly also the possibilities of a return to an adequately functioning natural family will remain 'live' in a large number of cases"...

With respect to the question of whether research evidence warrants increased emphasis on adoption at the expense of fostering, Fuller and Stevenson (1983, p.108) note two caveats. First, the difficulty associated with comparing the outcomes of adoption and fostering. Because foster children remain in public care, their progress is subject to social worker and research scrutiny, and the ready-made criterion of placement breakdown represents strong evidence of failure. No such criterion is available in relation to adoption, except in the small number of cases where the children concerned come to the notice of the authorities because of delinquency or emotional disturbance. The authors suggest that greater research attention to the subsequent careers of adopted children could reveal more disquieting evidence about adoption than that collected hitherto.

The second, and perhaps more compelling, caveat relates to the possible consequences for natural families if an interests of the child policy was rigorously pursued. Fuller and Stevenson (1983) invoke the concept of filial deprivation (Jenkins and Norman, 1972) and argue that parents deprived against their wishes of a child suffer considerable distress. The authors are not aware of any study that has examined the effects of such an event in terms of the social and emotional adjustment of natural parents, but suggest that it is likely that in some cases there are consequences for the health and personal social services. Fuller and Stevenson (1983) believe that although such considerations must not affect the planning for individual children at specific times, they do perhaps indicate the need for more skilled help to natural parents.

Fostering

As Table 1.3 shows, the proportion of children in care who are fostered increased during the late 1970's. Yet, it would appear that this expansion was not grounded in any body of empirical research demonstrating the success of fostering, but rather owed much to the assumption that family placement was a more appropriate form of substitute care than residential care. By contrast with adoption, as one of the most influential advocates of foster care, Rowe (1983, p.13), frankly concedes,..."the theoretical base for work in foster care is still rather thin"...

Prosser (1978), who carried out a fairly recent review of fostering in Britain, laments the state of knowledge about this form of substitute care. Little appears to be known about the long-term effects of foster placement on different groups of children; the majority of studies are small in scale and associated results mirror local factors of dubious generalisability; experimental schemes await adequate evaluation; insufficient basic information is routinely recorded. Evaluative researchers have been obliged to adopt somewhat arbirtary indicators of success such as measures of adjustment, discharge to natural parents, stability of long-term foster placement - each of which is capable of positive or negative interpretation on the basis of what may subsequently happen to the child - which renders the dearth of longitudinal studies especially regrettable.

Whilst placement breakdown may not necessarily constitute failure, fostering breakdowns have nonetheless long been a source of considerable concern. Rowe (1983, p.9-10) reports that careful examination of a number of small recent studies indicates that between 20 and 40 per cent of all foster placements end in an unplanned way (although rates as high as 47 per cent and as low as 11 per cent have been reported). However, Rowe (1983) considers that there has been a degree of improvement on the 50 per cent breakdown rates revealed by earlier studies undertaken by Parker (1966), George (1970), and Napier (1972).

Studies of fostering have, according to Cooper (1978), reported success rates of 40-50 per cent. As the author complains, this state of affairs can be used to argue for or against fostering and provides fertile ground for ideological loyalty rather than empirical support for an extension of foster care provision.

Holman (1975) has examined the effects of contact between foster children and their natural parents. Although conceding the complexity of the evidence, Holman (1975) discerns a developing consensus that the *inclusive* model of fostering (which encourages contact between foster children and their natural parents, and attempts to ensure that the foster child understands his/her situation) is associated with fostering success whether conceived in terms of stability of placement or foster children's adjustment. Although Holman's (1975) work was generally welcomed as a clarification of concepts, it has not been followed by any official commitment to the inclusive model. A study by Shaw and Lebens (1976) indicates that, in practice, what Holman (1975) terms the *exclusive* model of fostering (which discourages contact between foster children and their natural parents, with foster families approximating natural families) predominates.

During the 1970's and 1980's fostering has been in a state of transition. Rowe (1983, p.6) relates that the traditional definition of fostering as "bringing up someone else's child" is appropriate only for a proportion of foster placements. The author conceives a continuum of family placement running from short term fostering (which can offer, for example, emergency care, assessment, placement prior to rehabilitation, respite care, and treatment) through to long term foster care (either with or without contact between children and their natural families) and on to adoption [17]. Rowe discusses the schemes (referred to earlier) which were first established in the 1970's by a number of authorities and voluntary societies for the fostering of hard to place children. Rather than being asked to bring children up as though they were their own, the foster parents involved were required to provide a professional caring service for which they would receive payment in excess of the normal boarding out allowances (Rowe, 1983, p.19).

Whilst not the first specialist fostering scheme, the Kent Special Family Placement Project for difficult and delinquent adolescents is the best known and has been the most influential of the intiatives concerned. This scheme is based on the Swedish model of community care for adolescents and emphasises normalisation, individualisation and participation. Many authorities now have specialist schemes. The majority of these entail family placements for adolescents. Shaw and Hipgrave (1983) relate that of 67 local authorities outside London who responded to a postal questionnaire, 50 had at least one specialist scheme, and of these some 42 included delinquent or disturbed adolescents. Rowe (1983, p.20) reports that most schemes do not entail more than 10 - 12 foster placements, and numbers of placements are often fewer.

Those responsible for the schemes are inclined to be enthusiastic about their operation. Shaw and Hipgrave (1983), for example, found that 75 per cent of those canvassed believed their success rate high or very high. This impression appears to be supported by an independent evaluation, undertaken by Yelloly (1979) of the first 25 placements made by the Kent scheme which suggested that three-quarters of the adolescents concerned had improved. Whilst the scheme has not been wholly unproblematic - for example, not all the placements lasted as long as had been envisaged - its progress is generally seen as encouraging in the light of the difficult backgrounds of the youngsters involved.

The special foster care initiatives referred to concern short or medium length placements. Special schemes have also been set up to provide children with permanent substitute families. Among the most well known of these are Barnardo's New Families Projects, Parents for Children, The Children's Society's, The Child Wants a Home and the Independent Adoption Service. The majority of such initiatives stress adoption as offering the greatest security. However, where adoption is not possible or appropriate a number employ what they term permanent fostering. Here the aim is to ensure a feeling of security and mutual commitment on the part of child and family. Though small in scale, such projects represent an alternative to traditional, open-ended, long term fostering, and it might be that the stress on permanence sharpens thinking with respect to what can and ought to be done to provide security within the framework of fostering as well as adoption (Rowe, 1983, p.20).

3. Subject of Research and Method of Approach

As stated, my research entailed a comparative study of care practice in special foster homes and Children's Homes for older children in local authority care. The approach adopted was essentially sociological in orientation and, in addition to its comparative nature, featured the application of a range of quantitative research instruments.

A comparative study of foster homes and Children's Homes seemed of value from both a sociological and social policy/social work viewpoint: from the former, because comparing residential care with family placement appeared a useful means of gaining insights about the nature of daily life in family and residential settings; from the latter because, as noted, Children's Homes had hitherto received scant attention from evaluative researchers who have elected to confine their interest to the more controversial residential provisions accommodating delinquent (though not exclusively) youngsters; moreover, we have seen that the comparative study of foster and residential care is another neglected topic. This is surprising given the long running debate about the respective merits or otherwise of family and residential placement, and in view of the evidence that there is a degree of interaction between fostering and residential care in two senses. First, any one child in care may experience a variety of placement types. Second, there are well known and considerable regional variations in the proportions of children placed in different types of provision. Thus, children fostered in one area would be quite likely, if they lived in another area, to be placed in a residential setting. The proportions of children fostered have been estimated to range from 22 per cent (Wandsworth) to 65 per cent (Warwickshire). Whilst this may mean that the preferred placement is simply not available, it also appears to indicate that the notion that there is an appropriate type of child, or child problem, on which there would be general agreement for each placement type is fallacious (Fuller and Stevenson, 1983, p.94). Whatever the case, it would seem that children and placements are not matched according to children's needs and characteristics; a point which is bolstered by the previously reported developments in specialist fostering and by the knowledge that in certain European countries such as Sweden, the majority of children who come to the notice of the authorities as offenders are placed with families rather than in residential provisions (Elliot, 1981).

Limiting the focus of the study to older children and to special (rather than orthodox) foster placements ensured that the foster and residential children involved in the study would share broadly similar characteristics. The value of the specialist foster schemes in this respect was, of course, that they reflected attempts on the part of the local authorities concerned to provide children who were previously considered too difficult, handicapped, old and so on with family care. Thus, given that the children placed in special foster homes would, until recently, have been accommodated in residential settings such as Children's Homes, it seemed reasonable to suppose that a sample of these children would not differ greatly from a sample of youngsters placed in Children's Homes. As will be seen from the chapter which follows, this assumption was subjected to fairly rigorous scrutiny via the collection of detailed information on the histories of a sample of foster and residential children. A major purpose of establishing the extent to which the foster and residential children studied shared broadly similar histories, etc., was to ascertain how far findings associated with care practice could be said to reflect the nature of the children accommodated in the settings visited.

The decision to carry out a comparative study rather than a case study was dictated by the need to take account of possible variation within and between the two forms of substitute care. A comparative study of a relatively small number of cases was preferred to the large scale survey method of data collection because the latter would have precluded the sort of intimacy with individual cases (i.e. substitute care settings) which the problem required. A further advantage of the comparative study is that it usually facilitates generalisations of a kind which are not possible on the basis of a single case study.

In addition to its comparative nature, the study reveals some preference for quantitative techniques because, to borrow a phrase from Wing and Brown (1970), it did not seem that ..."the most animated and evocative description by the most perceptive participant observers could possibly answer the questions"...set. The study was also characterised by a multi-method approach (sometimes referred to as methodological triangulation) to data collection. The main value of using multiple methods is that it helps to counter arguments that findings are artefacts of a particular method (Smith, 1975, pp.271 - 296).

Perhaps the most important conclusion drawn from the research literature on children in care at the outset of this study was that there seems to have been an over-emphasis on the measurement of children's development and competencies, with insufficient attention devoted to the systematic study (as distinct from the anecdotal and impressionistic accounts typically undertaken) of the child's environment. This is regrettable given the literature in social psychology which points to the importance of situational determinants of behaviour (e.g., Mischel, 1973; Milgram, 1974). Although it is plain that factors other than care practice (e.g., family history, age of child on admission to care, length of stay in care, etc.) may have an important influence on outcome, the detailed study of the care experienced by children is germane to debate about the consequences of different forms of substitute care and to questions such as which children are likely to benefit from which type of care, the appropriate balance between foster and residential care in terms of the number of placements offered by each, the strengths and weaknesses associated with each form of care and how identified shortcomings might be ameliorated. Clearly, it is impossible to discuss these issues intelligently without detailed knowledge of one of the critical variables - care practice. This is not, of course, to suggest that the account which follows is considered definitive. However, it may be seen as an exploratory attempt to clarify what foster and residential care actually entail.

Several dimensions or aspects of care practice in the foster homes and Children's Homes were compared through the use of additive scales. These were: the management of recurrent (mainly daily) social events; children's involvement in community activities; the provision of physical amenities; and, the methods used by foster parents and residential staff to maintain control over children. The research instruments used are detailed in the Appendices. The main method of data collection employed in relation to the four instruments referred to was the closed interview, although use was also made of simple structured observation in relation to the first and third aspects of care practice listed. The behaviour of foster parents and residential staff towards children was also studied by structured observation; a technique that also served as one means to examine the role activities of caretakers. This topic was further explored during interviews with foster parents and residential staff undertaken in order to gather data on the role perceptions of the two caretaker groups. These interviews yielded data on the attitudes of staff and foster parents towards children, which were compared by means of an additive scale.

Originally, it was intended that the responses of children to the care practice they experience would be examined exclusively in terms of their directly observable behaviour, in view of the dearth of empirical research on this topic. Few studies of children in care have undertaken systematic observations of the behaviour manifested by children and related these to features in the children's social environment. Tizard (1975) regrets this in relation to research on children in residential care and urges further study of the subject. Data on children's behaviour were collected by way of structured observation. However, resource constraints did not allow observation of children's behaviour in the manner, and to the extent, initially envisaged (see Appendix (i)). This meant that although worthwhile data were collected on children's behaviour, additional ways by which to study children's responses were sought. First, foster and residential children's perceptions of their social environments were compared. This mainly involved the use of a further additive scale which was applied during individual interviews with a sample of foster and residential children. Second, an attempt was made to gain some idea of the respective progress made by foster and residential children during the course of their placements. This information was collected during interviews with children's social workers, as were data about children's histories.

The overall research objectives were:
(1) to delineate and compare care practice in special foster homes and Children's Homes for older children in local authority care; and,
(2) if possible, ascertain whether the responses manifested by children (defined in terms of children's directly observable behaviour, children's perceptions of their social environments and children's progress during their placements) in such settings can be related to the care practices they experience.

These objectives were translated into two working hypotheses that provided a loose but useful point of departure for empirical research:
(1) there are characteristic variations between the care practices in special foster homes and Children's Homes for older children in local authority care;
(2) the responses manifested by the children studied will vary according to the care practice they experience.

Turning now to the related problems of selecting and negotiating access to research settings, as previously mentioned the comparative approach usually seeks generalisations about social phenomema. However, generalisation can, strictly speaking, only be made on the basis of probability sampling (i.e. random selection of cases), irrespective of the fact that innumerable studies in the field of social research violate this rule - often with good reason. Unfortunately, it was not possible to apply probabilistic sampling procedures owing to very severe financial constraints [18]. The costs of travel to and from research venues, and accommodation and maintenance for the duration of fieldwork, meant that the selection of cases had, of necessity, to be determined by geographical convenience - in order to minimise costs, and by the degree of cooperation likely to be extended by those responsible for the operation of the substitute care settings concerned (i.e. administators, foster parents, residential staff, fostering officers, social workers, and so on). The importance of the latter criterion should not be underestimated in relation to a study which, from the point of view of those concerned, addressed many sensitive issues.

Permission was obtained to study the substitute care provisions of two local authority Social Services Departments in my home region of North West England. Authority A - a city Social Services Department and the larger of the two authorities - consented to the study of 12 of its special or contract [19] foster homes. Authority B - the Social Services Department of a Metropolitan Borough - agreed to make its five Children's Homes available for study. In the event only four of the five Authority B Homes were studied owing to the closure of one of the Homes (see Chapter 2). However, having gained entry, it was later possible to obtain access to an additional eight Children's Homes administered by Authority A (the authority's full complement of Children's Homes) and a further seven special foster homes. Five of the latter were administered by authority A, with the remaining two representing part of Authority B's attempt to establish a special foster scheme.

It may be noted that other local authorities were approached, but were either inconveniently situated geographically or appeared defensive with respect to the prospect of having their substitute care settings studied - as evidenced by the manner in which they seemed to stall attempts to negotiate access. By contrast, although Authorities A and B did require considerable reassurances that the research would be carried out in the strictest confidence and would not adversely affect the functioning of their foster homes and Children's Homes, key senior figures in both authorities seemed genuinely interested and enthusiastic about the nature of the research which appeared to augur well for its successful completion. These individuals served as liaison officers for the project and their support was invaluable.

Also worth mentioning is that Authority A was very satisfied with its special foster scheme and, overall, morale associated with the operation of the residential provisions of both authorities appeared good. Hence, one of my associates at the University of Oxford has suggested that the quality of the Children's Homes visited might be superior to those administered by the authorities who appeared reluctant to participate in the study. Unlike Authority A, Authority B was located in a generally affluent part of the region concerned; although both authorities embraced areas of inner-city deprivation. Local government in Authority A is traditionally controlled by the Labour Party, whilst the Conservative Party appeared an equally dominant force in the local politics of Authority B. These points are made because they convey something about the nature of the two authorities and, as such, may perhaps be felt to have a bearing on the issue of how representative of the general case the settings studied can be considered.

34

Having resolved the question of access to research settings, fieldwork commenced with a six week pilot study (18 June - 27 July, 1984). This involved trials of the research instruments earmarked for use. Most of the research instruments were tested at a community home situated near to the City of Oxford (and which was not included in the subsequent research) where I spent a week in residence. Trials which eventually produced a structured observational instrument that was used for observing the behaviour of caretakers and children were carried out in two of the Authority B Children's Homes. During the pilot period a week was spent at one of these Homes; the second Home was used between the six week pilot study and the beginning of the data collection period (see below) to conduct further trials of the instrument concerned. Pilot work also involved visits to several Authority A foster homes with a view to gaining insights as to how certain research instruments, which had originally been designed for application in residential settings, could be modified for use in family settings.

Because the study concerned many delicate issues, the major period of fieldwork was divided into two phases. The purpose of Phase 1 (20 August - 12 October, 1984) was to familiarise myself with all the research settings to which access had been gained - at that time, this meant the twelve Authority A foster homes and five Authority B Children's Homes mentioned earlier - and to establish relationships with administrators, residential staff, foster parents, children, fostering officers and social workers of a kind that would ensure the successful completion of Phase 2 - the period of data collection. One full week was spent at each of the five Children's Homes and a full day of fieldwork time was allocated to visiting each of the twelve foster homes. That Phase 1 proved worthwhile is evidenced by the fact that, despite a degree of apprehension on my part, the collection of data during Phase 2 was completely problem free in the sense that those concerned extended their full cooperation.

As reported, whilst one of the five Authority B Children's Homes closed between Phase 1 and Phase 2, eight Authority A Children's Homes and an additional number of foster homes were recruited to the study during this period. Although I only managed to gain access to these extra venues after arrangements for the in-depth study of the 12 original Authority A foster homes and 4 Authority B Children's Homes had been finalised (something which I was exceedingly reluctant to attempt to alter because making the necessary arrangements had been a tricky business in terms of synchronising the timing of the diverse elements of data collection to minimise the costs and time involved), as will be seen, the additional provisions enabled me to enhance the quality of my work considerably.

Between 3 December, 1984 and 29 March, 1985 one week of field work time was devoted to the study of each of the 12 Authority A foster homes originally recruited. This involved the succesful application of all research instruments. From 1 - 23 April, 1985, a survey of the 8 Children's Homes administered by the same authority was carried out. The survey involved the application of the research instruments associated with the following areas: the management of recurrent social (mainly daily) events; children's community contacts, the provision of physical amenities and the controls and sanctions employed by caretakers in order to maintain control over children. Approximately two full days were spent at each setting, and the purpose of the survey was to collect data that would provide some indication of the degree to which care practice at the 4 Authority B Children's Homes was typical of Children's Homes generally. Between 29 April and 7th July, 1985, two and a half weeks of fieldwork time was allocated to the study of each of the 4 Authority B Children's Homes. As already implied, this involved the application of all research instruments.

Throughout the time that I spent at Authority B during the two major phases of fieldwork - a period totalling some 18 weeks - I was kindly provided with accommodation and maintenance at the largest of the Authority's Children's Homes (later referred to as CH1), and received generous hospitality at all the settings visited. The lengthy period which I spent in residence at the Authority B Home provided me with insights into the nature of family and residential life that I could not have gained otherwise. Although I had substantial previous experience as a member of staff in residential child care settings, the perspective of the neutral observer is a markedly less restricted one.

The additional foster homes were visited between 8 and 24 July, 1985, in order to increase the number of foster children and foster parents included in the study. Rough parity had already been obtained with respect to the numbers of foster homes and Children's Homes in relation to which data on care practice had been collected. Thus, only those research instruments concerned with the following were used: children's histories, children's progress during their placements, children's perceptions of their social environments (placements), caretakers perceptions of their roles, and caretakers attitudes towards children.

Notes

1. The Child Care Act 1980 represents the first major consolidation of the law relating to children; it places together statutory provisions derived mainly from the Children Act 1948, the Children and Young Persons Act 1963, the Children and Young Persons Act 1969, and the Children Act 1975. The legislation contains many inconsistencies and gaps; some of which are, however, deliberate. Thus, although the Child Care Act 1980 deals with the effects of a care order, the grounds for making a care order are still found in the Children and Young Persons Act 1969. Given that care orders may be a consequence of criminal conviction, it was considered necessary to retain the grounds in a separate statute (Freeman, 1981).

2. Whilst commentators such as Taylor *et al* (1979) attack local authorities for failing to give sufficient consideration to the interests of children's natural parents, the recent well publicised report on the tragic death of Jasmine Beckford, for example, highlights (among other things) the sorts of counter pressures experienced by social workers of children in care, and why local authorities must give paramount consideration to the welfare of children. It has been estimated that between 150 and 200 deaths are caused by child abuse annually (*Social Work Today*, 16 December, 1985).

3. Although the intention of the framers of the CYPA 1969 was that criminal jurisdiction should only apply to young people of 14 years of age and over (except for cases of homicide), this provision - Part 1, Section 4 CYPA 1969 - has never been implemented.

4. For an informative summary of the controversy surrounding the CYPA 1969 see Elliot (1981).
5. See, for example, Gough (1979) and Mishra (1984).
6. See, for example, Taylor *et al* (1979, p.13).
7. The term institution is ambiguous: sociologically, it may denote any organised set of procedures or ways of doing things. Business, sport, religion, marriage, the family are all social institutions. However, the kinds of institutions which concern us, residential institutions, were delineated as an organisational type and established as a field for sociological enquiry by Goffman (1961) - see main text (below).
8. The concept of community care is nebulous. Does community care mean care in the community (e.g., day care and small residential homes, such as Children's Homes) or care by the community (i.e. care by families, relatives or friends)? Official policy appears to orientate towards the former definition, reflecting attempts to develop comprehensive and integrated networks of care, which span the continuum from institutional to independent or family living. Some writers, however, show a clear preference for the latter usage, and the phrase true community care is sometimes employed to convey this.
9. The observation that residential institutions often fail to achieve their stated goals is as old as the institutions themselves. Rothman (1970), for example, relates that the asylums erected in Jacksonian America were forced, by the 1870's, to settle for a purely custodial, rather than a curative, role. In one sense, what perhaps requires explanation, therefore, is not so much the reasons underlying the failure of institutions, but rather their continued existence despite knowledge of such failure for so long. Indeed, perhaps terms such as success and failure are inappropriate in this context. It may be that success in the ordinary sense is not the object, and that social control is an exercise which largely justifies itself; for, as Foucault (1977) speculates with respect to the foundation of the 18th century prison system, the point of the latter was to classify, order, regulate. Moreover, according to Foucault, the prison and the legal system more generally is not primarily a means by which to eliminate crime. Instead, what prison and its associated disciplinary mechanisms have achieved over the last century and a half is the creation of an autonomous sub-class of delinquents, or habitual offenders, recruited mainly from, but no longer members of, the working class. By concentrating illegalities which threatened to spread amongst the masses into one, relatively small, group it was possible to contain them. See Melossi and Pavarini (1981) for an alternative, Marxian, account of the rise of the prison. See also Ignatiev (1978) and Scull (1984).
10. Scull (1984) affirms that what is interesting about recent critiques of institutions is that they, unlike their predecessors, fall on such willing ears. Scull's explanation for this is that decarceration only became possible in the second half of the 20th century with the development of a welfare infrastructure which made segregative forms of care/control far more costly, in relative terms, and hence considerably more difficult to justify. Moreover, the more or less simultaneous development of a fiscal crisis of the state in the post-war period compelled policy makers to introduce less costly means of dealing with deviance and dependency. In

short, Scull argues that economic factors have driven an increased substitution of community initiatives for traditional institutional methods of dealing with certain social problems: the expansion of the former made possible and desirable the contraction of the latter.

11. Cohen (1979) argues that we should be sceptical about the community control movement on the following grounds.

  (1) It is by no means clear that decarceration has been taking place as rapidly as the ideology would have us believe. The establishment of various supposed alternatives to incarceration does not necessarily decrease imprisonment rates, nor have beneficial effects on the rest of the system.

  (2) It has not been established that any community alternative is more effective in reducing crime (through preventing recidivism) than traditional imprisonment.

  (3) Nor are these new methods always dramatically cheaper.

  (4) The humanitarian rationale for a move from imprisonment may be unfounded in two entirely opposite ways. First, it may indeed lead to something like a non-interventionist policy - and this ends up as a form of benign neglect, with groups like the old, the mentally ill, the inadequate dumped back into communities unable to look after them. For fiscal and other pragmatic reasons welfare state services are withdrawn from those who need them most. Second - the more likely route for criminals and delinquents - new and more extensive forms of intervention result. These may be hard to distinguish from the old institutions and may reproduce in the community the very practices they were designed to replace.

However, as Cohen (1979, p.611) also states, to ..."be aware of the dangers is not to defend the old system. Nor - even less - is it to argue that no reforms should ever be contemplated on the grounds that they inevitably lead to disaster. This is a recipe for political nihilism, and there is no inexorable logic that things always get worse"...

12. Goffman (1961) approaches his subject from what sociologists term an interactionist perspective (i.e. he attempts to investigate and interpret the meanings which actors assign to objects, events and activities). The author believes that an individual's name, his clothes and possessions, for example, are symbols - that they are impregnated with meaning. By interpreting such meanings he claims to be able to assess the significance of the removal of these symbols. However, given that we are unable to enter the consciousness of others, it is impossible to be certain that the meanings identified by the observer are those employed by the actors.

The interactionist perspective is also frequently criticised for its narrow focus. That is, it tends to concentrate on small-scale interaction contexts and ignores the wider society. Goffman (1961) devotes little attention to the experiences of inmates in the outside world prior to their entry to total institutions. Thus, because pre-institutional experience may have an important influence on modes of adaptation within the total institution, analysis which is limited to the confines of the latter may prove inadequate for understanding inmate behaviour (Haralambos, 1980, pp.316-319).

Goffman (1961) argues that the secondary adjustments (e.g., withdrawal, colonisation, rebellion, etc.) manifested by inmates are not merely incidental mechanisms of defence, but rather are essential constituents of the self. The individual, claims Goffman (1961), is a stance taking entity that adopts a position somewhere between identification with an organisation and opposition to it, and at the slightest pressure regains its balance by shifting its involvement in either direction. According to Goffman (1961), it is thus only against something that the self can emerge (Goffman, 1961, pp.279-280). However, what is Goffman (1961) really saying about the self here? Is there nothing at the centre of the individual save that which takes reactive stances against the stances of others? Should we not attend to the possibility that the actor brings something to the encounter derived from outside the encounter? In the case of substitute care settings, for example, the real difficulties/sufferings of children?

Finally, the interactionist perspective focuses on meanings in the context of interaction situations. Consequently, it has also been attacked for failing to consider the possibility that these meanings may be generated by the wider society. Definitions of criminality and mental illness, for example, may have their origins in the structure of society. In particular, they may be related to the nature and distribution of power in society. Powerholders may define activities which threaten their interests as criminal or a product of mental illness. In turn, these definitions may guide the actions of staff in prisons and mental hospitals (Haralambos, 1980, p.320).

13. See Bowlby's three volume work *Attachment and Loss* (1969, 1973 and 1980).

14. See, for example, Tizard and Joseph (1970), Tizard and Tizard (1971), Tizard, B. (1975) and Tizard and Hodges (1978); also, Prosser (1976) and Fuller and Stevenson (1983).

15. Note Laslett's potentially misleading shift of reference from the family *to households*.

16. With the exception of Friedrich Engels, who wrote an important work entitled, *The Origin of the Family, Private Property and the State* (first published in 1884), until the 1960's few writers applied Marxian theory to the family. Briefly, Engels considered that throughout history increasing restrictions were placed on sexual relationships and the production of children. Marriage and the family evolved through a series of stages (including polygymy) from the promiscuous horde to the monogamous nuclear family. For Engels, the monogamous nuclear family is based on the supremacy of men *vis a vis* women and evolved with the emergence of private property - in particular, the private ownership of the forces of production - and the advent of the state, which instituted laws to safeguard the system of private property and enforce the rules of monogamous marriage. The latter was the most efficient means by which to solve the problem of the inheritence of private property. Property was owned by males who had to be sure about the legitimacy of their heirs. This necessitated greater control over women in order to produce children of undisputed paternity.

17. Rowe (1983, pp.32-33) defines short-term fostering as between eight and ten weeks in legal terms, but in practice it is considered to be up to six or eight months. Medium-term fostering is defined as longer than short-term

placement but not having permanence as its objective. Long-term fostering denotes placements where permanence is intended, but where legal adoption is either not desired or cannot be achieved.

18. Strictly speaking, the statistical procedures used for analysing the data collected require the application of random sampling. This rule is also violated by innumerable social researchers, and often without trace of explanation. My justification for using the statistical tests concerned is that they provide an invaluable guide to the importance that may be attached to observed differences - particularly, overall differences found between the foster homes and Children's Homes studied.

19. Rowe (1980, pp.22-23) relates that the ..."use of written agreements or contracts between all parties to the placement was seen from the first as the cornerstone of the Kent special family placement scheme and has spread from this to other schemes, especially those for adolescents. These contracts are not ... binding in the legal sense but are seen as a means of sharing information and making plans clear to everyone"...

2 Characteristics of research settings, children and caretakers

Introduction

Having reported the background to the study and outlined my research strategy, this chapter introduces the research settings, children and caretakers, and is divided into three main parts. The opening section compares the foster homes and Children's Homes visited in terms of their size and social composition, whilst the second section examines the characteristics of the foster and residential children under five sub-headings: age and sex of children; children's care careers; children's natural families; behavioural characteristics of children; and, other characteristics. The final part discusses the personal and professional characteristics of the foster parents and residential staff.

1. The Research Settings

The material presented in this section has its origins in a simple research question. How do foster homes and Children's Homes compare with respect to size, as measured by numbers of adults and children, and social composition? The notion of size has a common-sense appeal as a possible determinant of resident- management in institutions, and numerous commentators (e.g., Street *et al*, 1966) have conceived it thus. Moreover, Berridge (1985) identifies size of Home as a major characteristic by which different Children's Homes may be distinguished.

Data collection associated with my attempt to answer the question noted above involved the construction and application of a research instrument which I termed the IOSIQ (*Internal Organisation of Settings Interview Questionnaire*) -

see Appendix (a). As its title indicates, this questionnaire was used during interviews with foster parents and residential staff. Interviews in the foster homes involved either one or both foster parents (or the lone foster parent), while IOSIQ interviews in the Children's Homes were conducted with either the person in charge or a senior member of staff. All together, the IOSIQ was applied in twenty four different research settings - twelve foster homes and twelve Children's Homes. The foster homes were drawn exclusively from the substitute child care provisions of Authority A, as were eight of the Children's Homes. The remaining four Children's Homes are administered by Authority B.

In the interests of confidentiality, the twelve foster homes shall hereafter be referred to by codes ranging from FH1 to FH12. The four Children's Homes administered by Authority B will be denoted by the codes CH1 to CH4, and the eight Children's Homes of Authority A will be coded CH5 to CH12. The foster homes and Children's Homes concerned are those in relation to which data pertaining to care practice were collected. The following tables, which give the total numbers of residential staff (including domestic and ancilliary staff), foster parents and children (including natural children of foster parents living at foster homes) in each of the twenty four substitute care settings where the IOSIQ was applied, convey an immediate impression of the varying size of the research settings.

Table 2.1
Total numbers of foster parents and children living at foster homes where data on care practice collected

Foster Homes:	FH1	FH2	FH3	FH4	FH5	FH6	FH7	FH8	FH9	FH10	FH11	FH12
F. parents:	1	2	2	2	2	2	1	2	2	2	2	2
Children:	1	1	4	4	2	1	6	6	1	2	4	8

Table 2.2
Total numbers of staff and children at Children's Homes

Children's Homes:	CH1	CH2	CH3	CH4	CH5	CH6	CH7	CH8	CH9	CH10	CH11	CH12
Staff:	27	8	12	22	20	16	6	8	5	15	7	6
Children:	21	10	11	26	17	13	6	9	7	13	6	8

It is clear that the total number of adults employed in the Children's Homes generally far exceeded the number of foster parents in each foster home. Moreover, the numbers of children accommodated in the larger Children's Homes easily outstripped the numbers of children living in each of the foster settings. However, the numbers of children in some of the smaller Children's Homes and in the larger foster homes were very similar. Indeed, the number of children in the largest foster home (FH12) actually exceeded the numbers of children in three of the Children's Homes (CH7, CH9 and CH12). It may be noted that none of the staff at the Children's Homes visited actually lived at the homes when off-duty.

In terms of the three ideal-type categories of Children's Homes distinguished by Berridge (1985), and reported in Chapter 1, it may be said that CH1, CH4, CH5, CH6 and CH10 were multi-purpose Children's Homes. CH2, CH7 and CH9 can be placed in the hostel category, and CH3, CH8, CH10, CH11 and CH12 approximate the family group style of provision. Hence, the Children's Homes studied comprised representatives of each of the three categories identified by Berridge.

Also worth highlighting is the fact that two of the foster homes were headed by a lone foster parent. In the case of FH1, the foster parent was an unmarried middle-aged man and the foster child an adolescent boy. FH7 was headed by a middle aged widow with a relatively large number of grown up children of her own and two foster children - both boys, aged 12 and 15 years. Several other lone foster parents (all women, usually with grown up children) were also encountered during the course of the study. Parenthetically, some idea of the relatively generous fees received by the special foster parents studied is provided by the following. The boarding out allowance received each week by ordinary foster parents of youngsters between 13 and 15 years of age in Authority A was, at the time of writing, £36.19p. Authority A's special foster parents of hard to place youngsters falling within the same age range received the ordinary weekly boarding out allowance, plus £59.69p. per week. The latter represents the reward element of the special fostering allowance.

With respect to the issue of caretaker-children ratios, table 2.2 is misleading because, as already reported, it includes domestic and ancilliary staff. This is not to suggest that such staff do not have contact with, or do not take an interest in, the children concerned. However, child care is not their primary task; and, given that domestic and ancilliary staff - excluding teaching staff for present purposes - are not free to organise their work, their contact with children is sporadic. Moreover, with the exception of some cooks, domestic and ancilliary staff are usually not present during the evening after school and at weekends. In view of these points, along with the time constraints associated with fieldwork, it was decided to exclude domestic and ancilliary staff from the study.

Table 2.3 shows the composition of the staff groups at the twelve Children's Homes. It can be seen that two of the larger Homes each had an administrative assistant. CH1 also had three night care staff and three teaching staff, and was the only Home with a school on site - partly a legacy of its days as an Observation and Assessment Centre (although some of the children at CH1 did attend schools in the community). However, children at CH6 attended a school attached to a larger residential provision (not studied) for children, situated in adjoining grounds and so, in effect, also attended school on site. All the Homes visited had domestic staff - cooks, cleaners, laundry workers etc. The senior staff category includes all staff above the basic houseparent or residential social worker level; for example, senior houseparent/senior residential social worker, team leader, third-in-charge, deputy-officer-in-charge, officer-in-charge, unit leader, and so on. The titles given to residential staff vary between local authorities and, as the reader will have gathered, they sometimes have an institutional connotation.

Table 2.3
Composition of staff groups

Children's Homes:	CH1	CH2	CH3	CH4	CH5	CH6	CH7	CH8	CH9	CH10	CH11	CH12
Sen. care staff:	5	2	3	6	5	3	2	3	2	5	2	1
Jun. care staff:	9	3	5	8	6	6	3	3	2	5	4	3
Night staff:	3	-	-	-	-	-	-	-	-	-	-	-
Teaching staff:	3	-	-	-	-	-	-	-	-	-	-	-
Domestic staff:	6	3	4	8	8	7	1	2	1	5	1	2
Admin. staff:	1	-	-	-	1	-	-	-	-	-	-	-

Having distinguished child care staff from other grades of staff, we are now able to compare the ratio of caretakers to children in the foster homes and

Table 2.4
Ratio of foster parents to children living at foster homes where data on care practice collected

Foster Homes:	FH1	FH2	FH3	FH4	FH5	FH6	FH7	FH8	FH9	FH10	FH11	FH12
	1.1	2.1	1.2	1.2	1.1	2.1	1.6	1.3	2.1	1.1	1.2	1.4

Table 2.5
Ratio of residential child care staff to children

Children's Homes:	CH1	CH2	CH3	CH4	CH5	CH6	CH7	CH8	CH9	CH10	CH11	CH12
Total staff (halved):	1.3	1.4	1.3	1.4	1.4	1.3	1.2	1.3	1.4	1.3	1.2	1.4
Jun. staff (halved):	1.5	1.7	1.4	1.7	1.6	1.4	1.4	1.6	1.7	1.5	1.3	1.5

N.B. Ratios in tables 2.4 and 2.5 are rounded to the nearest whole number

Children's Homes. Two sets of staff-children ratios are presented in Table 2.5. First, a total care staff (halved) to children ratio. Second, a junior care staff (halved) - only - to children ratio. Numbers of staff must be divided by two in order to take account of the shift systems that operate in Children's Homes with respect to hours worked by care staff. Given factors such as staff leave, sickness, the knowledge that senior staff are often preoccupied with administrative tasks and the supervision of junior colleagues, and the knowledge that shifts are not necessarily manned by as many as half the total complement of care staff, it would appear that the ratio comprising junior staff (halved) - only - is the most accurate measure of staff-children ratios in the Children's Homes visited. It is evident from tables 2.4 and 2.5 that, overall, the staff-residential children ratios compare unfavourably with the ratios of foster parents to children (including natural children of foster parents) living at the foster homes. However, FH7, FH8 and FH12 were no more well endowed with respect to number of caretakers relative to numbers of children than some of the Children's Homes. Indeed, FH7 compares unfavourably with all twelve Children's Homes if the total care staff (halved) to children ratios are used.

Table 2.6 resolves the ambiguity created by preceding tables concerning the foster homes in distinguishing numbers of foster children from natural children of foster parents living at the foster homes. Five sets of foster parents had natural children of adult age not living with them. In six of the twelve foster

Table 2.6
Numbers of foster children and natural children of foster parents living at foster homes where data on care practice collected.

Foster Homes:	FH1	FH2	FH3	FH4	FH5	FH6	FH7	FH8	FH9	FH10	FH11	FH12
Foster children	1	1	2	2	2	1	2	3	1	2	2	2
Natural children:	-	-	2	2	-	-	4	3	-	-	2	6

homes concerned, there were no children other than the foster children, and in only two of the foster homes did the natural children of foster parents outnumber foster children. Except in the cases of FH3, FH8 and FH12, foster children were either considerably older or younger than the natural children of foster parents living at the foster homes. One of the foster children at FH7, another at FH8 and a third at FH12 were not designated hard to place children, but rather were ordinary foster children (hence they were excluded from study) who were all younger than the hard to place foster children with whom they were living.

2. The Children

Data on the characteristics of foster and residential children were primarily collected with a view to testing the assumption that the children placed in the special foster homes would, prior to the inception of the two special fostering schemes concerned, have been placed in residential settings. Questions concerning the characteristics of children are clearly of great importance in relation to examining the determinants and outcomes of different forms of child-management practice.

A study by Cawson and Martell (1979) on children referred to closed or secure units was helpful in suggesting an appropriate means by which to gather data about the characteristics of children. The authors designed a questionnaire and used it to collect information on children in secure units from D.H.S.S. and social work records (the advantages and disadvantages associated with collecting data from official records are well known, and are rehearsed in some detail by Cawson and Martell, 1979, pp.235-237). Owing to the need to safeguard the identity of the children and other persons involved, Cawson and Martell's (1979) questionnaire was particularly suited to my requirements because it concentrated on the deviant characteristics of children. Any such characteristic, for example, not mentioned in the records kept on a child was assumed by the authors not to be present to any important degree. Moreover, most items could be completed simply by marking the appropriate code. This approach would, it seemed, allow me to build up a profile of each child's characteristics relatively quickly and without collecting unnecessarily detailed information of a kind which could result in the identification of those concerned.

However, the original questionnaire required substantial modification in order to tailor it to the demands of my research. Further, in an attempt to overcome some of the disadvantages associated with the collection of data from official records, the *Children's Characteristics Questionnaire* (CCQ) - see Appendix (b) - was applied during interviews with children's Social Workers who referred to their records on the children where necessary. These interviews were conducted at various social work offices of the two local authorities involved in the study.

I was able to collate data on the characteristics of all special foster children; a group comprised of 27 children from Authority A and 2 children from Authority B. However, time constraints meant that such data could only be gathered on a sample of children from each of the four Children's Homes administered by Authority B. The fact that many residential placements for children are currently relatively short in duration complicated the task of selecting residential children. Initially, it was envisaged that the selection of such children would be limited to youngsters who had been placed at the four Authority B Children's Homes for a minimum period of six months, and who were 12 years of age and over. This was because I had elected to interview - see chapter 5 - only children about whom I had previously obtained CCQ data, and it seemed appropriate to ensure that these children had (a) been living at their placements for a reasonable period of time, and (b) would be able to understand the questions put to them at interview. Whilst it was possible to apply the criteria referred to with respect to CH4, the six-month criterion had to be relaxed to one of three months in the cases of CH1, CH2 and CH3. However, all residential children chosen were at least 12 years of age.

Eleven children were selected from CH1, six from CH2, six from CH3, and eleven from CH4. Thus, as Table 2.2 verifies, data were collected on the characteristics of approximately half of the children in each of the four Authority B Children's Homes. Because they were relatively few in number, foster children had to be included in the exercise concerned simply on the basis of being available for study. However, I did insist that my access to foster children should not be limited to only those whose placements were considered successful and/or unproblematic. The personnel responsible for the special foster schemes cooperated fully in this respect, and the problems associated with certain of the foster placements studied (see Chapters 4 and 5) would seem to corroborate this view.

Age and sex of children

Table 2.7 compares the ages of the foster and residential children on whom data were collected.

Table 2.7
Ages of foster and residential children on which CCQ data collected

	Foster Children		Residential Children		ROW TOTAL	
	%	(N)	%	(N)	%	(N)
6 - 11 years	10.3	(3)	-	(0)	4.8	(3)
12 - 15 years	51.7	(15)	50.0	(17)	50.8	(28)
16+ years	37.9	(11)	50.0	(34)	44.4	(28)
COLUMN TOTAL	46.0	(29)	54.0	(34)	100.0	(63)

CHI-SQUARE = 4.03933 SIGNIFICANCE = 0.1327 [1]

Most of the children studied were concentrated within the 12-17 years age band. Roughly equal proportions of foster and residential children were between 12 and 15 years of age. However, a higher proportion of residential than foster children were aged 16 years and over, whilst a number of foster children occupied the 6-11 years of age group. The three young foster children concerned - a sibling group - were included to increase the numbers of special foster children studied. In retrospect, it would have been prudent to exclude these children in order to minimise differences between the foster and residential children selected for study. But it should be pointed out that CH3 and CH4 accommodated children under 12 years of age. Hence, the age differences between the two groups should not be overestimated.

Table 2.8 shows that the two sets of children can be said to have constituted a fairly homogeneous group in relation to the variable, sex. Two-thirds of the children comprising the overall sample were male, with females under-represented in both the foster and residential groups. Berridge (1985) also found that boys outnumbered girls in the Children's Homes which he studied.

Table 2.8
Sex of foster and residential children studied

	Foster Children		Residential Children		ROW TOTAL	
	%	(N)	%	(N)	%	(N)
Male	62.1	(18)	70.6	(24)	66.7	(42)
Female	37.9	(11)	29.4	(10)	33.3	(21)
COLUMN TOTAL	46.0	(29)	54.0	(34)	100.0	(63)

CHI-SQUARE = 0.19967 SIGNIFICANCE = 0.6550 (AFTER YATES CORRECTION)

Almost half of the residential children were in care under Section 2 of the Child Care Act 1980, as Table 2.9 shows. This means that *parental rights* remained vested in their natural parents. By contrast, parental rights had been transferred to the local authority with respect to over 70 per cent of the foster children. A good deal of the difference found between the two groups is attributable to the fact that the local authority had assumed parental rights, by way of a resolution under Section 3 of the 1980 Act, in relation to 27.6 per cent of foster children. These children's initial reception into care will have been under Section 2 of the Child Care Act 1980. I reported in the previous chapter that the voluntary status of such receptions contrasts with admissions to care under the Children and Young Persons Act 1969 and Matrimonial statute, which involve children being committed to care by the Courts.

Table 2.9
Legislation in force with respect to foster and residential children

	Foster Children		Residential Children		ROW TOTAL	
	%	(N)	%	(N)	%	(N)
S2 CCA 1980	27.6	(8)	47.1	(16)	38.1	(24)
S3 CCA 1980	27.6	(8)	5.9	(2)	15.9	(10)
CYPA 1969	37.9	(11)	32.4	(11)	34.9	(22)
Matrimonial statute	6.9	(2)	-	(0)	3.2	(2)
Ward of court	-	(0)	14.7	(5)	7.9	(5)
COLUMN TOTAL	46.0	(29)	54.0	(34)	100.0	(63)

CHI-SQUARE = 12.95142 SIGNIFICANCE = 0.0115 [2]

It should be noted that where a child is made a ward of court, parental rights and duties, except for the right to refuse consent to adoption or custodianship, are transferred to the court. The court determines the allocation of care and control; it will make arrangements for parental access and schooling and, most importantly, it will decide whether the child should be committed to care under Section 7 of the Family Law Reform Act 1969. Although such a committal means that the child is under the care of the local authority, the authority may not assume parental rights by a resolution under Section 3 of the Child Care Act 1980. This is because the child is not in care under Section 2 of the 1980 Act but rather, as was noted, by virtue of a Section 7 order under the Family Law Reform Act 1969 (Pearl and Gray, 1981, pp.37-38).

Table 2.10
Reasons associated with children's latest admissions to care [3]

| | Foster Children | | | | Residential Children | | | |
| | Primary | | Secondary | | Primary | | Secondary | |
	%	(N)	%	(N)	%	(N)	%	(N)
Neglect or injury	6.9	(2)	13.8	(4)	2.9	(1)	2.9	(1)
Behaviour problems at home	13.8	(4)	17.2	(5)	23.5	(8)	14.7	(5)
Marital breakdown or problems	-	(0)	10.3	(3)	2.9	(1)	2.9	(1)
Mental illness of parents	13.8	(4)	-	(0)	2.9	(1)	2.9	(1)
Homeless (excluding eviction)	17.2	(5)	6.9	(2)	20.6	(7)	5.9	(2)
Non-school attendance	-	(0)	-	(0)	2.9	(1)	5.9	(2)
Delinquency	-	(0)	-	(0)	14.7	(5)	5.9	(2)
Physical illness of parents	3.4	(1)	6.9	(2)	2.9	(1)	-	(0)
Death of parent	17.2	(5)	-	(0)	8.8	(3)	-	(0)
Family homeless	-	(0)	-	(0)	2.9	(1)	-	(0)
Behaviour problems at school	-	(0)	-	(0)	-	(0)	5.9	(2)
Other reason	24.1	(7)	-	(0)	8.8	(3)	8.8	(3)
No reports	3.4	(1)	44.8	(13)	5.9	(2)	44.1	(15)
COLUMN TOTALS	46.0	(29)	46.0	(29)	54.0	(34)	54.0	(34)

However, Table 2.9 tells us little about the reasons underlying the children's admission to local authority care. Whilst it must be emphasised that children seldom enter care for a single reason, and that their entry is often precipitated by a multiplicity of complex reasons, Table 2.10 shows the factors which, according to the social workers interviewed, resulted in the children's admission to care. Although differences were found between the two groups in this respect, overall, perhaps they are not too dissimilar [4].

One of the noticeable general differences between the foster and residential children, however, is that the behaviour of the residential children appears to have been more instrumental in the admission to care process than that of foster children. But six of the seven residential children for whom delinquency was said to have been a factor in their entry to care were accommodated at CH1, as were the two residential children whose school behaviour had contributed to admission to care. Two of the three residential children for whom non-school attendance had played a part in entry to care were also placed at CH1. Behaviour problems at home were said to have contributed to the admission to care of some 31 per cent of foster children (N = 9). This compares with 63.7 per cent of CH1 children (N = 7), 33.3 of children at CH2 (N = 2), 33.4 of CH3 children (N = 2) and 18.2 of children at CH4 (N = 2). Thus, closer inspection of the data demonstrates that, except for CH1 youngsters, the differences between foster and residential children with respect to proportions of children for whom behavioural problems had helped to determine admission to care were not great.

Moreover, although the foster children seem to have experienced more unfortunate home circumstances than their residential counterparts, perhaps caution is required in drawing conclusions about causal relations since the sorts of factors identified are frequently interrelated. For example, there is a well established association between problem behaviour in children and adverse family circumstances.[5]

Also worth underlining is the point that Table 2.10 concerns children's latest admissions to care. In the case of the majority of foster children this occurred some time ago. The present stay in care (which may have involved several different placements) of only 6.9 per cent of foster children began within the 12 month period preceding data collection. This compares with a considerably larger 44.1 per cent of residential children. Indeed, over 75 per cent of residential children against less than 35 per cent of foster children commenced their present stay in care within the two years preceding data collection. An estimated 5.9 per cent of residential children had begun their current stay in care six years prior to my study. However, 17.2 per cent of foster children had been in care for at least 8 consecutive years prior to fieldwork being carried out. This would appear to suggest two conclusions: first, a greater proportion of residential, than foster, children entered care during their adolescence; and, second, that the care careers of the foster children group generally exceeded those of the residential children group in duration.

Both the above points seem to be supported by the data concerning the ages of sample children reported earlier, along with data collated with respect to the purpose of children's placements and the number of previous placements in local authority care experienced by children.

As few as 23.5 per cent of residential children, against an overwhelming 96.6 per cent of the foster children studied, were reported to be staying at their current placements until their discharge from care at 18 years of age. The present placements of most of the residential children were, by contrast, regarded as being of a temporary, short-term, nature. An estimated 2.9 per cent of residential children were placed on an emergency basis; 2.9 per cent for assessment only; 8.8 per cent owing to the breakdown of their previous placement; 20.6 per cent were awaiting rehabilitation with their natural families; 11.8 per cent were awaiting a further residential placement; 2.9 per cent were placed for other reasons; and, the future was uncertain for the remaining 8.8 per cent. One of the foster children was placed on a temporary basis for assessment, but with a view to a subsequent, albeit different, long-term foster placement.[6]

Only 6.9 per cent of foster children, compared with as many as 41.2 per cent of residential children had not been previously placed in local authority care. However, roughly equal proportions of foster and residential children (48.2 per cent and 53 per cent, respectively) had experienced between two and four previous placements. But 44 per cent of foster, compared with only 5.8 per cent of residential, children had experienced five or more previous placements; and, one of the foster children had experienced eighteen previous placements in local authority care. All except five of the foster children had spent periods, sometimes a considerable number of years, in residential care.[7]

Table 2.11 reveals that the duration of the present placements of the foster and residential children was relatively short. Whilst this observation applies with somewhat greater force to the residential children, differences between the two groups were not statistically significant [8]. The length of many residential children's placements was sufficient to undermine their purportedly temporary status.

Table 2.11
Duration of sample children's placements

	Foster Children %	(N)	Residential Children %	(N)	ROW TOTAL %	(N)
Less than 12 months	44.8	(13)	64.7	(22)	56.6	(35)
12 months - 2 years	44.8	(13)	29.4	(10)	36.5	(23)
3 - 5 years	10.4	(3)	5.9	(2)	16.3	(5)
COLUMN TOTAL	46.0	(29)	54.0	(34)	100.0	(63)

Children's natural families

In view of what has been said so far about the children's backgrounds, it will not surprise the reader that half of the residential children last lived at home on a full-time basis within the 12 month period preceding data collection. This compared with only 13.7 per cent of foster children. Some 41.4 per cent of foster children, against 29.4 per cent of residential children, had last lived with their natural families within two years of my research. An estimated 44.8 per cent of foster, compared with only 20.6 per cent of residential, children had not lived with their natural parents for three or more years.[9]

Table 2.12 shows the parental figures with whom the children lived prior to their current care episodes, and thereby clarifies the term natural family (or families), which is used merely to distinguish natural and adoptive families from foster families. One of the most striking points which emerges from Table 2.12 is that relatively few children from each group had lived with both their natural mothers and fathers prior to their entry to care [10]. The CCQ, in fact, collected much data suggesting that some of the children studied had

Table 2.12
Who children lived with prior to their present care episodes

	Foster Children %	(N)	Residential Children %	(N)	ROW TOTAL %	(N)
Father and mother	13.8	(4)	14.7	(5)	14.3	(9)
Father only	13.8	(4)	14.7	(5)	14.3	(9)
Father and stepmother	-	(0)	14.7	(5)	7.9	(5)
Mother only	44.8	(13)	26.5	(9)	34.9	(22)
Mother and stepfather	13.8	(4)	5.9	(2)	9.5	(6)
Mother and cohabitee	-	(0)	2.9	(1)	1.6	(1)
Adoptive parents	-	(0)	2.9	(1)	1.6	(1)
Grandparents or other relatives	3.4	(1)	17.6	(6)	11.1	(7)
Other	10.3	(3)	-	(0)	4.8	(3)
COLUMN TOTAL	46.0	(29)	54.0	(34)	100.0	(63)

experienced repeated changes in parental figures. Moreover, 79.3 per cent of foster, and 73.5 per cent of residential, children were reported to have been separated from one or both of their natural parents for a period of more than two months, and for reasons other than admission to care. In some cases, repeated separations of this kind had been experienced.[11]

Further evidence of the troubled family histories of the children studied is provided by CCQ data which reveals the numbers of children from each group who had suffered rejection by their natural parents. Sadly, only 10.3 per cent of foster, and 32.4 per cent of residential, children were reported as not having experienced any such rejections. This reinforces the view that the young lives of many of the children studied have been ones of extreme personal tragedy. Some 48.3 per cent of foster, and 41.2 per cent of residential, children had been rejected by both their natural father and mother; and, 27.5 per cent of foster, and 23.5 per cent of residential, children had been rejected by one of their natural parents.[12]

Aside from the trauma of outright rejection, the family backgrounds of the children studied were discovered to have been afflicted by numerous problems. Some of these problems were touched on when the reasons underlying the children's admissions to care were discussed. Table 2.13 shows the proportions of residential and foster children from natural families in relation to which evidence of one or more of three serious family problems was found to exist. The table below demonstrates that, whilst the natural families of foster children were, overall, somewhat more affected than the natural families of residential children, relatively few of the sample children's natural families were

Table 2.13
Evidence of serious family problems

	Foster Children %	(N)	Residential Children %	(N)	ROW TOTAL %	(N)
Neglect/cruelty only present	31.0	(9)	26.5	(9)	28.6	(18)
Mental illness only present	10.3	(3)	23.5	(8)	17.5	(11)
Criminality only present	-	(0)	8.8	(3)	4.8	(3)
Neglect/cruelty and mental illness present	13.8	(4)	8.8	(3)	11.1	(7)
Neglect/cruelty and criminality present	3.4	(1)	-	(0)	1.6	(1)
Mental illness and criminality present	10.3	(3)	-	(0)	4.8	(3)
All three problems present	20.7	(6)	8.8	(3)	14.3	(9)
None of problems present	10.3	(3)	23.5	(8)	17.5	(11)
COLUMN TOTAL	46.0	(29)	54.0	(34)	100.0	(63)

completely free of the problems in question.[13]

However, one of the shortcomings of Table 2.13 is that it fails to distinguish between the natural parents and siblings of the children studied. All but 3.4 per cent of foster, and 11.8 per cent of residential, children had one or more siblings. Indeed, 37.9 per cent of foster children and 26.4 per cent of residential children had four or more siblings. Yet, despite evidence suggesting that many of the sample children were members of sibling groups, it was also found that a large number of such groups had been fragmented. For example, 69 per cent of foster, and 38.2 per cent of residential, children had siblings who no longer lived with their natural parents; a finding which cannot be explained in terms of siblings leaving home on attaining maturity, etc. Some 37.9 per cent of foster, and 8.8 per cent of residential, children had one or more sibling(s) who were also in care and who were placed with them. However, over half (55.1 per cent) of foster, and 14.7 per cent of residential, children had one or more sibling(s) who were also in care but who were not placed with them. These figures include individual children sharing the same placement in care with some siblings, but not others - who had been placed elsewhere by the local authority. Clearly, admission to care may involve even more than the disruption or severance of relationships with natural parents: relationships with brothers and sisters may also be impaired or ruptured. Although children from both groups had experienced this, once again it appears that, overall, the foster children had suffered more than their residential counterparts[14].

53

In closing this account of sample children's natural family backgrounds, some idea of the social class of the families concerned can be derived from Table 2.14, which shows the nature of their home ownership or tenancy. The table suggests that the great majority of sample children were from working class families, and other data established that most of these families can be more accurately described as lower working class[15].

Table 2.14
Nature of home ownership or tenancy of children's families of origin

	Foster Children		Residential Children		ROW TOTAL	
	%	(N)	%	(N)	%	(N)
Owner occupied	13.8	(4)	26.5	(9)	20.6	(13)
Standard council house/ flat etc.	58.6	(17)	47.1	(16)	52.4	(33)
Private rented accommodation	10.3	(3)	17.6	(6)	14.3	(9)
Other	17.2	(5)	8.8	(3)	12.7	(8)
COLUMN TOTAL	46.0	(29)	54.0	(34)	100.0	(63)

Behavioural characteristics of children

As stated earlier, the CCQ tends to focus on what might be described as children's deviant characteristics. Where no record of a given deviant characteristic could be found it was assumed not to be present to an important degree. The behavioural characteristics examined in this part of Chapter 2 may be loosely separated into three broad areas: children's psychiatric histories, records of delinquent type activity and their educational records.

With respect to the first of the above categories, we may begin by noting that 79.3 per cent of foster, and 91.1 per cent of residential, children had no record of psychiatric treatment or oversight. Three of the foster children (or 10.3 per cent) had received psychiatric treatment mainly on an out patient basis; one had undergone observation as an inpatient; and another had been recommended for psychiatric oversight, only. One of the residential children had received psychiatric treatment as an inpatient, a second had been treated on an outpatient basis and a third had been recommended for treatment [16]. Some 86.2 per cent of foster, and 67.7 per cent of residential, children had not been to a child guidance clinic or accepted or recommended for placement at a special school for so-called maladjusted children [17]. Moreover, there was no evidence of brain damage with respect to approximately 95 per cent of children from each group [18].

No record of active physical violence towards people or animals prior to their present placements was found in relation to approximately 80 per cent of children from each group. Where evidence of such attacks did exist, these mainly involved other children and adult members of the public, including residential staff and foster parents. Two violent assaults - one by a foster child, the other by a residential youngster, were perpetrated against animals [19]. An estimated 65.5 per cent of foster and 73.5 per cent of residential children were said not to lack guilt about their anti-social acts. Some 27.6 per cent of foster, and 8.8 per cent of residential, children were considered to clearly lack such guilt by their social workers; however, contradictory reports existed with respect to 6.9 per cent of foster, and 17.6 per cent of residential, children [20].

Over two-thirds of the children from each group were reported as not being sexually at risk or a risk to others. Approximately 17 per cent of children from each group were, however, said to be at risk. One of the foster children - an adolescent boy - was considered by his social worker as a potential risk to others, and a further male foster child was said to be both sexually at risk and a risk to others [21].

No evidence was found to suggest that roughly 80 per cent of foster, and 90 per cent of residential, children had ever threatened or attempted to commit suicide. However, just over 10 per cent of foster, and approximately 3 per cent of residential, children had threatened to kill themselves at some time. About 7 per cent of foster against 3 per cent of residential children had inflicted injury to themselves. One child from each group was reported to have made a serious attempt to commit suicide [22].

Moving on now to the second behavioural area distingiushed - children's delinquent type activities, some 93.1 per cent of foster children, compared with a a much smaller 67.7 per cent of residential children, had no record of court appearances as alleged offenders prior to their present placements [23]. However, all but two of the residential children who were found to have made such appearances were placed at CH1. Over 80 per cent of sample children from this Home had been before the courts at least once as offenders [24], and approximately two-thirds of these children had made two such court appearances. But, only one of the children involved had been found guilty of an offence which could be described as dangerous. The offence concerned was that of wounding, and involved another child [25].

It has been pointed out that the children at CH1 were somewhat different to the foster children's group with regard to court appearances made as alleged offenders prior to their present placements. However, these residential children were also different to their counterparts in CH2, CH3 and CH4 [26] in this respect. Moreover, some of the foster children had also appeared before the courts and been found guilty of offences. Hence, the difference identified presents no threat to the notion that but for the inception of the special foster schemes concerned, the foster children would have been living in residential settings [27].

With respect to the third, and final, behavioural area - children's educational records, Table 2.15 offers a necessarily crude comparison of the truancy rates for foster and residential children prior to their current placements [28] and reveals that the differences found between the two groups were not statistically significant at the 0.05 level. No evidence of school behaviour problems prior to children's present placements existed in relation to 79.3 per cent of foster, and 73.5 per cent of residential, children. An estimated 17.2 per cent of foster, against 14.7 per cent of residential, children were reported to have exibited such behavioural problems; and, for 3.4 per cent of foster and 11.8 per cent of

Table 2.15
Truancy rates for sample children prior to their present placements

	Foster Children		Residential Children		ROW TOTAL	
	%	(N)	%	(N)	%	(N)
Frequently truanted	17.2	(5)	23.5	(8)	20.6	(13)
Occasionally truanted	24.1	(7)	14.7	(5)	19.0	(12)
Never truanted	41.4	(12)	44.1	(15)	42.9	(27)
No reports	17.2	(5)	17.6	(6)	17.5	(11)
COLUMN TOTAL	46.0	(29)	54.0	(34)	100.0	(63)

CHI-SQUARE = 1.05973 SIGNIFICANCE = 0.868

residential children the reports obtained were contradictory [29]. However, as many as 40 per cent (approximately) of children from each group were reported to have performed less than satisfactorily with respect to their school work prior to their current placements. Contradictory reports were obtained for 2.9 per cent of residential children, whilst the educational performance of 48.3 per cent of foster and 44.1 per cent of residential children was said to have been satisfactory. No reports were available for 13.8 per cent and 11.8 per cent of foster and residential children, respectively [30].

Other characteristics of children

The CCQ also attempted to collect data on the IQ's of children. However, no reports were available for 90 per cent of the children from each group. Where reports were obtained they were either incomplete and/or referred to tests undertaken some years previous to the research being carried out. Hence the exercise was abortive. Some 10 per cent of foster, against roughly 3 per cent of residential, children were reported to be mentally handicapped, and about 6 per cent of residential children were physically handicapped. Approximately 90 per cent of children belonging to each group were not handicapped [31]. Finally, some 17 per cent of foster, compared with roughly 3 per cent of residential, children were reported to have suffered traumatic illness resulting in separations from parents during childhood. However, no evidence of such illness was found in relation to some 80 per cent of foster, and 90 per cent of residential, children. Moreover, the significance of the presence of the variable in question is perhaps made negligible by the other discontinuities which had characterised the lives of the sample children [32].

The major points which emerge from this section may be summarised as follows. Prior to their entry to care, proportionately more CH1 youngsters than foster children had engaged in delinquent type activities and manifested other behavioural problems. But little difference was found between the foster children and youngsters living at CH2, CH3 and CH4 with respect to the areas in question. Further, overall, the foster children seemed to have suffered greater trauma in relation to their past experiences than the residential children. Hence, it seems reasonable to conclude that, but for the inception of the special foster schemes, the foster children would have been placed in the Children's Homes studied. Finally, differences between the foster and residential children with respect to the duration of their present placements were not statistically significant.

3. The Caretakers

Having examined the characteristics of the type of children accommodated in the foster homes and Children's Homes visited, we now turn to the characteristics of the caretakers - foster parents and residential staff. This third section of Chapter 2 addresses the following questions: first, what were the personal and professional characterstics of the foster parents and residential staff studied? Second, did the personal and professional characteristics of foster parents and residential staff vary and, if so, how?

The data that will be reported in attempting to answer these questions were collected via the application of the ST/FPIQ (*Staff/Foster Parent Interview Questionnaire*) - see Appendix (g). In designing this research instrument, I drew on work carried out by King *et al*, (1971), Cawson, (1978) and Raynes *et al*, (1979) in related fields. The ST/FPIQ was applied at individual interviews with the 22 foster parents from the twelve Authority A foster homes where care practice was studied, plus an additional 11 foster parents. That is, from the foster homes recruited in order to increase (a) the number of children on whom CCQ data were collected and who would be interviewed, and (b) the number of foster parents interviewed. Three of the additional foster parents were from Authority B foster homes. The remainder were from Authority A foster homes. All available residential child care staff from the four Authority B Children's Homes - CH1, CH2, CH3 and CH4 - were interviewed. In sum, interviews were conducted with 33 foster parents, 4 Heads of Children's Homes, 12 other senior residential staff, and 24 junior residential staff.

The following table compares the sex of foster parents and residential staff and, shows that observed differences between the two groups were not statistically significant at the 0.05 level. Table 2.16 also demonstrates that female foster parents outnumbered their male counterparts [33]. But the trend is reversed in the Children's Homes where, overall, male staff were more numerous than female staff. It should be pointed out, however, that this owes much to the fact that male staff outnumbered female staff by 6.1 at CH1. Conversely, at CH4 numbers of male and female staff were equal, and female staff exceeded male staff by 3.2 at CH2 and by 5.2 at CH3.

Most of the foster parents (93.9 per cent) were, or had been, married, compared with only 62.5 per cent of residential staff. Clearly, this represents an important difference between the two caretaker groups [34], in view of which it was not surprising to also find significant differences between the ages of foster parents and residential staff [35]. Exactly half of the staff interviewed were aged between 20 and 30 years. By contrast, almost the same proportion of

Table 2.16
Sex of foster parents and residential staff

	Foster Parents %	(N)	Residential Staff %	(N)	ROW TOTAL %	(N)
Male	45.5	(15)	57.5	(23)	52.1	(38)
Female	54.5	(18)	42.5	(17)	47.9	(35)
COLUMN TOTAL	45.2	(33)	54.8	(40)	100.0	(73)

CHI-SQUARE = 0.62398 SIGNIFICANCE = 0.4296 (AFTER YATES CORRECTION)

foster parents (48.5 per cent) were aged between 31 and 40 years. Table 2.17 compares the ages of the two groups in more detail.

Table 2.17
Ages of foster parents and residential staff

	Foster Parents %	(N)	Residential Staff %	(N)	ROW TOTAL %	(N)
21 - 30 years	9.1	(3)	50.0	(20)	31.5	(23)
31 - 40 years	48.5	(6)	30.0	(12)	38.4	(28)
41 - 50 years	33.3	(11)	15.0	(6)	23.3	(17)
51 years and over	9.1	(3)	5.0	(2)	6.8	(5)
COLUMN TOTAL	45.2	(33)	54.8	(40)	100.0	(73)

Given the major differences between the two caretaker groups with regard to age and marital status, predictable major differences were also uncovered in relation to the numbers of caretakers with children of their own (i.e. natural or adoptive children). Over half (57.5 per cent) of residential staff, against only 15.2 per cent of foster parents, were without such children. Table 2.18 compares the total numbers of natural children of foster parents and staff, with Table 2.19 showing the numbers of such children who were (a) under the age of 16 years and (b) 16 years and over. Both tables reveal very clear differences between the two caretaker groups [36]. In view of the fact that nearly half of the foster parents had reared children from birth to adulthood (or thereabouts it is plain that, overall, the foster parent group was vastly more experienced in relation to child-rearing children from birth than the residential staff group.

Table 2.18
Total numbers of natural children of caretakers

	Foster Parents %	(N)	Residential Staff %	(N)	ROW TOTAL %	(N)
None	15.2	(5)	57.5	(23)	38.4	(28)
One	3.0	(1)	10.0	(4)	6.8	(5)
Two	45.5	(15)	17.5	(7)	30.1	(22)
Three	27.3	(9)	7.5	(3)	16.4	(12)
Four or more	9.1	(3)	7.5	(3)	8.2	(6)
COLUMN TOTAL	45.2	(33)	54.8	(40)	100.0	(73)

Table 2.19
Numbers of natural children of caretakers (a) under 16 years and (b) 16 years and over

	Foster Parents				Residential Staff			
	Under 16 %	(N)	16+ %	(N)	Under 16 %	(N)	16+ %	(N)
None	42.5	(14)	54.5	(18)	62.5	(25)	82.5	(33)
One	12.1	(4)	15.2	(5)	20.0	(8)	7.5	(3)
Two	33.3	(11)	-	(0)	12.5	(5)	5.0	(2)
Three	12.1	(4)	21.2	(7)	2.5	(1)	2.5	(1)
Four or more	-	(0)	9.1	(3)	2.5	(1)	2.5	(1)
COLUMN TOTAL	45.2	(33)	45.2	(33)	54.8	(40)	54.8	(40)

The following table provides some idea about the social class of foster parents, based on the occupation of major wage-earners (in all but 3 cases this was the male foster parent) and uses the Registrar General's five social classes [37]. It can be seen that the families concerned tend to be concentrated in Social Class 3 (Skilled occupations) - some 63.15 per cent of total families, with the Skilled Manual category holding more families than the Skilled Non-manual category. None of the foster families belonged to Social Class 1 (Professional and Managerial occupations) [38].

Table 2.20
Social class of foster parents

	Foster Homes	
	%	(N)
SOCIAL CLASS 1: Professional and Managerial	-	(0)
SOCIAL CLASS 2: Intermediate occupations	15.79	(3)
SOCIAL CLASS 3: Skilled occupations:		
Non-manual	26.31	(5)
Manual	36.84	(7)
SOCIAL CLASS 4: Partly skilled occupations 10.53		(2)
SOCIAL CLASS 5: Unskilled occupations 10.53		(2)
TOTAL	100.00	(19)

By virtue of their present occupations, residential staff would be placed in Social Class 2 (Intermediate occupations) of the Registrar General's classificatory system. However, this tells us little about the sort of people who occupy staff roles. Table 2.21 again makes use of the Registrar General's five social classes, and reveals the sorts of occupations undertaken by staff immediately prior to their move into residential child care/social work. The *other* category contains staff who went into residential child care immediately

Table 2.21
Type of occupations undertaken by staff immediately prior to obtaining employment in residential child care field

	Residential Staff	
	%	(N)
Professional and Managerial	-	(0)
Intermediate occupations	7.5	(3)
Skilled occupations:		
Non-manual	27.5	(11)
Manual	12.5	(5)
Partly skilled occupations	15.0	(6)
Unskilled occupations	12.5	(5)
Other	25.0	(10)
TOTAL	100.00	(40)

on terminating full-time education. Table 2.21 allows only imperfect comparison with the social class of foster parents for various reasons, one being that the social class of female staff will, in some cases, have been defined by major wage-earners such as husbands and fathers. However, Table 2.21 is able to show quite plainly that for the majority of staff obtaining employment in residential child care involved a significant improvement in occupational status (even though for some staff their change of occupation may have resulted in a reduction in income).

However, high occupational status is normally conditional on a fairly lengthy period of formal training and the acquisition of some kind of qualification, which is intended to attest an individuals competence in his or her chosen vocation. As one might expect, most of the foster parents (90.9 per cent) held no formal qualifications pertaining to child care. Equally unsurprising, (at least to those with a knowledge of this field) was the finding that 72.5 per cent of the residential staff interviewed also lacked any kind of formal training relevant to their work [39]. Only 5 per cent of staff held a qualification recognised as being genuinely appropriate for those working in the residential child care field [40]. However, length of time spent working in a given field is also regarded as an index of competence, and is one means by which career advancement can be achieved. Overall, residential staff were found to have had more previous experience of looking after other people's children than the foster parents. For example, residential staff had generally occupied their present roles/posts somewhat longer than foster parents had theirs, as Table 2.22 shows [41]. It was also established that over 50 per cent of staff, compared with 33.3 per cent of foster parents, had gained over 5 years experience in the same or a related field

Table 2.22
Length of time for which caretakers had occupied their roles/posts.

	Foster Parents %	(N)	Residential Staff %	(N)	ROW TOTAL %	(N)
Less than 12 months	33.3	(11)	30.0	(12)	31.5	(23)
12 months - 2 years	42.4	(14)	27.5	(11)	34.2	(25)
3 - 4 years	24.2	(8)	27.5	(11)	26.0	(19)
5 years and over	-	(0)	15.0	(6)	8.2	(6)
COLUMN TOTAL	45.2	(33)	54.8	(40)	100.0	(73)

of child care prior to undertaking their present roles/posts [42]. Finally, 80 per cent of residential staff had previous experience in residential child care prior to commencing their present roles/posts, compared with a significantly smaller 45.4 per cent of foster parents with previous experience of fostering [43].

Notes

1.   As indicated, Table 2.7 has a chi-square of 4.03933 and an associated significance of 0.1327, which shows that observed differences between foster and residential children are fairly close to being statistically

significant at the customarily adopted 0.05 level. However, two of the cells have expected frequencies (E.F.) of < 5, which means that the statistics concerned may be somewhat unstable.

Many of the crosstabulations undertaken with respect to comparing the characteristics of the inhabitants of foster homes and Children's Homes have cells with E.F.< 5 . This problem results from the small numbers of cases - in this instance, children - involved in the study, relative to the number of values assumed by row variables. One solution to the problem would have been to collapse or reduce the number of such values. Unfortunately, the results obtained for most (if not all) crosstabulations would have been rather meaningless had such a procedure been adopted, and information of much interest and considerable relevance would have been forfeited. Accordingly, although I have excluded them from the main text, I elected to make use of the statistics associated with such crosstabulated data in their original form (although some of the crosstabulations were modified for the purposes of presentation) in these notes, and to indicate where they involve cells with E.F.< 5. At worst, these statistics provide a rough idea of the importance or significance that should be attached to observed differences between the populations of foster homes and Children's Homes. It may also be noted that Norusis (1983) comments that although it has been recommended that all expected frequencies be at least 5, recent studies indicate that this is probably too strict and can be relaxed.

Returning to Table 2.7: prior to being collapsed the data concerned had an associated chi-square of 4.60913 and significance of 0.7984 (cells with E.F.< 5 = 13 of 18), which is obviously a long way from statistical significance at the 0.05 level. Thus, as stated in the preceding text, it seems reasonable to conclude that observed differences between foster and residential children with respect to the variable in question were not significant.

2.   Table 2.9 - cells with E.F.< 5 = 5 of 10.

3.   Some of the categories for Table 2.10 were derived from Berridge (1985). I noted in Chapter 1 that structural factors such as poverty are known to be associated with entry to care. These factors were not adequately addressed by Table 2.10. However, it must also be pointed out that poverty was given little attention when examining children's background characteristics because of my wish to focus on deviant characteristics, and irrespective of how one chooses to define poverty it is clearly too widespread to be regarded as a form of deviance (see, for example, Townsend, 1979, for a discussion of the major competing definitions of poverty). Veitch (1986) reports that there are currently more than 19 million people (1 in 3 of the population) in Britain living on or just above the official poverty line.

4.   Table 2.10 - the crosstabulation regarding primary reasons had a chi-square of 13.92421 and significance of 0.2372 (cells with E.F.< 5 = 19 of 24), while that pertaining to secondary reasons had a chi-square of 14.63646 and significance of 0.1459 (cells with E.F.< 5 = 19 of 20). Both significance levels, therefore, fail to attain statistical significance at the 0.05 level.

5.   For example, see Rutter (1975) regarding the aetiology of problem behaviour in children, and Elliot (1981) for a concise summary of competing theories concerning delinquency causation.

6.   The crosstabulation concerning the purpose of children's placements produced a chi-square of 35.94066 and significance of 0.0001 (cells with E.F.< 5 = 16 of 18). Therefore, observed differences between the two groups were very large.

7.   The crosstabulation regarding number of previous placements in care experienced by children had a chi-square of 21.4145 and significance of 0.0061 (cells with E.F.< 5 = 12 of 16). Hence, differences between the two groups were significant at 0.01 level. The previous placements of both groups of children included foster placements, placements in Children's Homes, O and A centre, CHE'S, Special residential schools, residential nurseries, secure residential provisions, hostels, and so on. However, the main point to note is simply that the majority of foster children had, prior to their special foster placements, been accommodated in Children's Homes. Indeed, the very Children's Homes administered by Authority A and Authority B (depending, of course, on which of the two authorities individual foster children belonged to) that were studied.

Unfortunately, it is not possible to accurately report the number of stays in care experienced by children. However, it can be said that many of the children studied from both the residential and foster groups had experienced repeated admissions to (and discarges from) local authority care. Often these periods in care were relatively short, with children returning to their natural families within days or weeks of their entry to care (such stays in care were typically associated with family crises).

Some children, on the other hand, had experienced relatively few stays in care but a considerable number of different placements in care. One reason for this was the breakdown of placements. Certain youngsters had, at various times, lived in each of the major types of provisions comprising the substitute care continuum (see the section on the types of provisions for children in care in Chapter 1), shuttling back and forth between provisions as a purported consequence of being difficult to manage, and with each placement failure moving closer to the custodial end of the scale. For example, O and A centre to foster home, back to O and A centre, on to small Children's Home, back to O and A centre, on to large Children's Home, back to O and A centre, on to CHE, etc.

A noteworthy point to emerge from this is that whilst much is made of the disturbingly high breakdown rate of foster care (see the review of the research literature on foster care in Chapter 1) it may be that residential placements also breakdown with greater frequency than is generally supposed. Moreover, from reading the social work files kept on the children studied, it was clear that it is not unsual for certain children to begin their care careers in foster homes in their early childhood and progress successively nearer the custodial end of the scale as they grow up (indeed, some of the youngsters encountered during the course of the study had spent periods in placements outside the aegis of local authority Social Services Departments - e.g., Detention Centres and Youth Custody Centres). However, it seems that the transition from family placement to the custodial end of the continnum can be made within a very much

63

shorter period. This is perhaps not surprising given that many first admissions to care now involve adolescents.

Finally, over the last few years, the closure of residential provisions such as Children's Homes seemed to have been an important source of discontinuity in the care histories of a number of children in the care of both Authority A and Authority B.

8. The original crosstabulation for the data reported in table 2.11 produced a chi-square of 3.49911 and significance of 0.4780 (cells with E.F. < 5 = 4 of 8). Thus, differences between the two groups were not significant at 0.05 level.

9. Original data on when children last lived at home resulted in a chi-square of 10.8312 and significance of 0.0548 (cells with E.F. < 5 = 6 of 12), which shows that differences between the two groups of children were significant at 0.05 level.

10. Table 2.12 has an associated chi-square of 11.36728 and significance of 0.1817 (cells with E.F. < 5 = 14 of 16), which fails to obtain statistical significance at 0.05 level.

11. The crosstabulation regarding children's separations from natural parents for reasons other than admission to care had a chi-square of 1.84096 and significance of 0.398 (cells with E.F. < 5 = 2 of 6). Hence, observed differences between the two groups concerned were not significant at the 0.05 level.

12. Data concerning rejections by parents had an associated chi-square of 12.40192 and significance of 0.0146 (cells with E.F. < 5 = 6 of 10). Therefore, differences between the two groups were found to be significant at the 0.01 level.

13. The crosstabulation relating to evidence of serious family problems had a chi-square of 12.36940 and significance of 0.0890 (cells with E.F. < 5 = 10 of 16), which shows that differences between the groups are very close to being significant at 0.05 level.

14. Although differences between the two groups regarding total numbers of siblings were not found to be statistically significant at the 0.05 level (chi-square = 5.44701; significance = 0.4879; cells with E.F. < 5 = 8 of 14), differences concerning numbers of siblings living with natural parents were close to being significant at 0.05 level (chi-square = 8.00191; significance = 0.1561; cells with E.F. < 5 = 8 of 12). As noted in the main text, considerably more residential children than foster children had siblings who lived with their natural parents, and the low number of foster children's siblings living with natural parents could not be explained in terms of siblings leaving home on attaining maturity, etc.

15. Table 2.14 is based on one used for similar purposes by Millham *et al* (1975) in studying the characteristics of boys in CHE's. The CCQ did collect data on the occupations of children's natural parents; however, this proved inadequate as a means of determining the social class of children's natural families because the whereabouts of both natural parents was unknown or uncertain with respect to some foster children, and the whereabouts of natural fathers was too often unknown or uncertain in the case of residential children. However, on the basis of the data collected, it was clear that the majority of the children comprising each group came from lower working class families, and that natural parents tended to

work in partially skilled or unskilled occupations. But, a considerable number of natural fathers were reported as unemployed.

Table 2.14 has an associated chi-square of 3.07593 and significance level of 0.3801 (cells with E.F. < 5 = 4 of 8), which shows that observed differences between the two groups in relation to the home ownership/tenancy of their families of origin were not statistically significant at the 0.05 level.

16. The data on children's records of psychiatric treatment had a chi- square of 6.56908 and significance of 0.3624, indicating that differences between the two groups were not statistically significant at the 0.05 level.

17. Data on child guidance clinics, etc., produced a chi-square of 3.11270 and significance of 0.2109 (cells with E.F. < 5 = 2 of 6), demonstrating that differences between foster and residential children were not significant at the 0.05 level.

18. Data on brain damage, etc. had an associated chi-square of 0.71293 and significance of 0.7001 (cells with E.F. < 5 = 4 of 6); hence, differences between the groups were not significant at the 0.05 level. There was evidence of brain damage vis a vis two of the residential children; however, their social workers were unable to specify the precise nature of the conditions involved.

19. Data regarding violent assaults by children prior to their present placements had a chi-square of 7.73523 and significance of 0.3565 (cells with E.F. < 5 = 14 of 16). Thus, differences between the two groups were not statistically significant at the 0.05 level.

20. Data concerning whether children lacked guilt about their anti-social acts had an associated chi-square of 5.49189 and significance of 0.139 (cells with E.F. < 5 = 4 of 8), which indicates that differences between the two groups failed to obtain statistical significance at the 0.05 level.

21. The data relating to whether children were considered to be sexually at risk or a risk to others produced a chi-square of 3.22460 and significance of 0.5210 (cells with E.F. < 5 = 6 of 10). Thus, differences between the two groups were not significant at the 0.05 level.

22. Data on suicide, etc., showed that observed differences between the two groups were not significant at the 0.05 level (chi-square = 3.48677; significance = 0.4799; cells with E.F. < 5 = 8 of 10).

23. The number of court appearances made by children is not a particularly satisfactory means by which to measure children's participation in delinquent type activities. For one thing, it only shows offences that children have been charged with and taken to court over (though not the actual number of such alleged offences). However, a considerable amount of additional data were collected on the area in question (as the reader will gather from examining the CCQ) and this facilitated a cross check on the value of N court appearences as a crude indicator of participation in delinquent type activities. Moreover, statements made by social workers in relation to children's offending behaviour could be tested to some extent by documents contained in children's social work files (e.g. charge sheets, etc.). It should also be mentioned that although the differences between the proportions of foster and residential children who had made court appearances appeared high, they just failed to obtain

statistical significance at the 0.05 level (chi-square = 7.9734; significance = 0.0926; cells with E.F. < 5 = 8 of 10).

24. At the time of research, CH1 seemed to be accommodating some children who, prior to cutbacks in Authority B's spending on residential placements outside the authority, would have been sent to CHE's (Authority B had no such provision of its own). It may be noted that although a few children of a similar type were found in the special foster homes of Authority A, the latter Authority generally reserved three large residential provisions for such children that, as indicated in the main text, were not studied because they did not fall within the Children's Home (or ordinary community home) category.

25. Of course, this is not intended to minimise the nuisance associated with offences committed by CH1 children. Rather, simply to draw a distinction between offences which involved either danger to the children themselves or to others (or both) and the sorts of offences typically committed by youngsters at the Home (e.g. petty theft - for example, shoplifting - and, at the more serious end of the continuum, offences such as burglary). As would be expected, the difference between the two groups regarding dangerous offences was not statistically significant (chi-square = 0.000; significance = 1.0000 (after Yates correction); cells with E.F. < 5 = 2 of 4).

26. And also different from at least the majority of children in Authority A Children's Homes, given what has already been said in 24 (above), regarding the fact that Authority A normally reserved 3 large residential establishments for accommodating delinquent type youngsters (i.e. where such youngsters were not placed in CHE'S outside the Authority's area).

27. Youngsters at CH2 were regarded as being relatively unproblematic to manage. The aim of the Home was purported to be that of preparing adolescents for independent living. Hence, residents took turns at cooking the evening meal and did their own laundry. CH3 also accommodated adolescents (including a handicapped teenage girl), but also a few younger children, one of whom - a boy - was a Down's syndrome child; again, the children at CH3 were considered to present no serious handling difficulties. The same point applies equally to the children at CH4, who included youngsters under 10 years of age. A fair proportion of CH4 children were awaiting foster placement. As noted in the previous chapter, there was a fifth Authority B Children's Home that was not studied. This was because during the course of fieldwork the Home was in the process of being closed in order to later re-open at a site some distance from its original location in the heart of a deprived inner-city area, which was believed to be the main cause of the controversy and problems associated with the Home's operation. For example, a local press report implied that adolescent girls from the Home were engaging in prostitution, a member of staff had been physically assaulted by local youths, and staff morale was rather low. However that may be, the important point about this fifth Home is that prior to its closure it had accommodated what were said to be the Authority's most difficult to manage adolescents. Some of these youngsters were temporarily placed at CH1. However, none were included in the study because they did not arrive at CH1 until after the completion of research at the Home.

28. Unfortunately, it was impossible to measure truancy rates with a greater degree of precision, owing to the lack of detailed information in children's files.

29. Data concerning school behaviour problems prior to children's present placements produced a chi-square of 4.39426 and significance of 0.2219 (cells with E.F. < 5 = 4 of 8). Hence, differences between the two groups were not statistically significant at 0.05 level.

30. Data on the educational performance of children prior to their present placements had a chi-square of 1.00398 and significance of 0.8003 (cells with E.F. < 5 = 4 of 8). Thus, differences between the two groups were not significant at the 0.05 level.

31. The data on handicap - physical or mental - produced a chi-square of 3.91354 and significance of 0.2710 (cells with E.F. < 5 = 6 of 8). Therefore, differences observed between the two groups were not statistically significant at the 0.05 level.

32. Differences between the two groups regarding traumatic illness were not statistically significant at the 0.05 level (chi-square = 4.42076; significance = 0.1097; cells with E.F. < 5 = 4 of 6).

33. However, it was not possible to interview one of the male foster parents, who was working away from home at the time of fieldwork. A questionnaire was left for him to self-administer but was not returned.

34. The crosstabulation of data concerning the marital status of foster parents had an associated chi-square of 14.82290 and significance of 0.0051 (cells with E.F. < 5 = 6 of 10). Thus, observed differences between foster parents and residential staff were statistically significant at the 0.01 level.

35. Differences between the ages of the foster parent and staff groups were statistically significant at the 0.01 level (chi-square = 14.26718; significance = 0.0026; cells with E.F. < 5 = 2 of 8).

36. The crosstabulation of original data on total numbers of natural children of caretakers showed that differences between foster parents and staff were statistically significant at the 0.01 level (chi-square = 21.20131; significance = 0.0035; cells with E.F. < 5 = 6 of 12). Certain categories were collapsed for the table presented in the main text.

    The original data on numbers of natural children of caretakers under 16 years of age had a chi-square of 8.89646 and significance of 0.0637 (cells with E.F. < 5 = 4 of 10). Thus, differences between the two groups were very close to being significant at the 0.05 level (certain categories were collapsed for the table in the main text).

    Original data on numbers of natural children of caretakers 16 years of age and over had a chi-square of 13.66521 and significance of 0.0336 (cells with E.F. < 5 = 10 of 12). Hence, differences between the two groups of caretakers were statistically significant at the 0.05 level. Again, certain categories were collapsed for the table in the main body of the text.

37. See: *Office of Population, Censuses and Surveys (1980): Classification of Occupations and Coding Index.*

38. One foster family was placed in Social Class 2. because the male foster parent was employed on a full-time basis as a *professional* foster parent. By contrast with the other special foster parents, the individual concerned received a salary rather than a fee. Prior to becoming a professional foster

parent he (and hence his family) would have been placed in Social Class 5 in view of his unskilled occupation.

Another foster family that was placed in Social Class 2 involved a family where the wage-earner was the female foster parent. The male foster parent was registered as unemployed and carried out most of the domestic chores in the home.

Finally, 12 female foster parents referred to themselves by the term housewife when asked about their employment status.

39. That relatively few Children's Homes staff hold professional qualifications is well known. See, for example, Berridge, 1985; and, Social Services Inspectorate of the Department of Health and Social Security, Inspection of Community Homes, 1985.

40. That is, the CQSW (Certificate of Qualification in Social Work), CSS (Certificate in Social Service) or CRCCYP (Certificate in Residential Care of Children and Young Persons). In fact, no staff member held the CQSW; one senior staff member held the CSS and another held the CRCCYP (i.e. the Head and Deputy-Head of CH1, respectively). Nearly half of those who held any kind of qualification in child care had obtained the PCSC (Preliminary Certificate in Social Care), whilst 5 per cent of staff had completed an NNEB (Nursery Nursing) course, and a further 5 per cent had been awarded in-service training certificates of attendance. Some 63 per cent of staff with any kind of child care qualification were employed in CH1. One senior staff member at this Home was undertaking the CSS (which is a part-time course) at the time of research, as were the the Head and a second senior member of staff at CH4 and a further senior staff member at CH3. None of the staff at CH2 held any sort of qualification in child care. The dearth of qualifications among a group of people with relatively high occupational status is reflected in the fact that differences between residential staff and foster parents with respect to the variable in question were not found to be statistically significant at the 0.05 level (chi-square = 6.65316; significance = 0.4659; cells with E.F. $< 5 = 12$ of 14). The only caretaker who did possess the CQSW was a female foster parent; an experienced social worker, who left social work in order to have children. Moreover, all the foster parents had undertaken an introductory course on the fostering of *hard to place* youngsters prior to having foster children placed with them. Staff had also typically received assorted bits of in-service training, but few appeared to have been afforded the opportunity to undertake anything approximating a coherent and substantial course of training.

41. Table 2.22 has an associated chi-square of 7.42682 and significance of 0.1150 (cells with E.F. $< 5 = 4$ of 10), indicating that differences between the two groups of caretakers were close to statistical significance at the 0.05 level.

42. The crosstabulation for original data regarding the duration of caretakers' previous experience showed that differences between foster parents and residential staff were statistically significant at the 0.01 level (chi-square = 16.3203; significance = 0.0060 (cells with E.F. $< 5 = 8$ of 12).

43. Original data on the nature of caretakers' previous experience revealed that differences between the two groups were significant at the 0.01 level (chi-square = 11.27999; significance = 0.0103 (cells with E.F. $< 5 = 2$ of 8).

3 Four dimensions of care

Introduction

Now that we have learnt something about the characteristics of the children accommodated in the foster homes and Children's Homes visited, we may begin to examine the nature of the care experienced by such children. This chapter compares the foster homes and Children's Homes in terms of four dimensions of care - the management of recurrent (mainly daily) social events, children's community contacts, the provision of physical amenities, and the controls and sanctions employed by foster parents and residential staff in relation to children's behaviour. Each of these aspects of care practice occupy a separate section of this chapter, and are examined in the order in which they are listed here.

1. The Management of Recurrent - Mainly Daily - Social Events.

As noted in Chapter 1, when studying the daily lives of mentally retarded children in residential institutions, King *et al* (1971) operationalised four attributes described by Goffman (1961) as characteristic of staff-inmate interaction in total institutions: namely, rigidity of routine, *block treatment*, depersonalisation, and social distance between staff and inmates [1]. King *et al* (1971) argued that care can be conceived as a continuum along which practices may be seen to vary. They labelled the two ends of this continuum *child-oriented* and *institutionally-oriented*, and constructed an index in order to measure the management of recurrent - mainly daily - social events in the institutions concerned. The four concepts drawn from the work of Goffman

(1961) were used to guide the formulation of the 30 items which comprise King *et al's* (1971) scale.

However, although extremely useful, the instrument was not sufficiently sensitive to discriminate between care practice in different substitute child care settings which (as was shown in the preceding chapter) almost exclusively accommodate non-handicapped children. Accordingly, I used the four concepts provided by Goffman (1961) to generate additional items, discarding or modifying those original scale items which my earlier studies (unpublished) had revealed to have low discriminating potential, in order to facilitate the level of sensitivity required. Ideas for the new items were obtained from the following sources: my experiences as a member of staff in residential child care settings, and previous researches in this field; a Charter of Rights for Children in Institutions formulated by Taylor *et al* (1979, pp.88-89) [2]; and, Sinclair's (1975) Scale of Restrictiveness, which the author deployed in his study on probation hostels for young offenders.

The *Index of Child-Management* (ICM) (so-called to distinguish it from King et al's (1971) index, which the authors named the *Revised Child Management Scale* following modification of an earlier scale), along with the other three instruments discussed in this chapter, was applied at the twelve special foster homes comprising the original pool of Authority A foster homes (FH1 to FH12), the four Children's Homes administered by Authority B (CH1 to CH4) and the eight Authority A Children's Homes (CH5 to CH12). The technique of data collection associated with the application of the ICM involved interviews with foster parents and senior residential staff and observation [3], and was based on King *et al's* (1971) approach. The ICM also retains the original scoring procedure devised by the authors [4]: a score of 0 for individual items indicates child-oriented care practice, a score of 2 reflects institutionally-oriented care practice, and a score of 1 denotes a mixed pattern (i.e. care practice which lies somewhere between child-oriented and institutionally-oriented) - see Appendix (c). Hence, the closer to zero the total ICM score obtained, the more child-oriented care practices were considered to be [5].

Table 3.1 shows the total scores assigned to the foster homes and Children's Homes, and the overall rank order of settings in terms of the degree to which the management of recurrent - mainly daily - social events at each was child-oriented. It can be seen that the foster homes were generally found to be considerably more child-oriented than the Children's Homes on the dimension of care concerned. All the foster homes achieved a higher rank than the Children's Homes with respect to degree of child-orientation, and statistical significance for the differences observed between foster homes and Children's Homes was obtained at the 0.0001 level (exact two-tailed probability) [6].

The reader may recall from Chapter 1 that the eight Authority A Children's Homes were recruited to the study in order to gain some idea as to whether care practice in the four Authority B Homes (i.e. where in-depth research was carried out) could be regarded as representative of that which generally prevails in Children's Homes. Therefore, it is of interest to note that statistical significance at the 0.05 level or less was not obtained for differences between the scores of the two sets of Children's Homes [7]. Moreover, an item analysis showed the ICM to be a highly reliable research instrument, producing

Table 3.1
Care practice scores for foster homes and Children's Homes

PLACEMENT	ICM SCORE		RICI SCORE	RIPE SCORE		ICS SCORE		N CHILD	N ADULTS
F. Homes									
FH1	17	(1)	1000 (12)	2100	(1)	2	(5)	1	1
FH2	14	(8)	1200 (6)	1782	(3)	0	(1)	1	2
FH3	16	(12)	1400 (2)	1715	(5)	5	(12)	4	2
FH4	15	(10)	1050 (11)	1550	(10)	3	(7)	4	2
FH5	9	(3)	1250 (4)	1723	(4)	3	(7)	2	2
FH6	13	(7)	1000 (12)	1650	(8)	1	(3)	1	2
FH7	14	(8)	1150 (9)	1524	(12)	7	(16)	6	1
FH8	8	(2)	1250 (4)	1550	(10)	4	(9)	6	2
FH9	15	(10)	1400 (2)	1882	(2)	4	(9)	1	2
FH10	10	(4)	1200 (6)	1675	(7)	0	(1)	2	2
FH11	10	(4)	1500 (1)	1684	(6)	2	(5)	4	2
FH12	11	(6)	1100 (10)	1440	(15)	1	(3)	8	2
MEAN	11.83		1208.33	1689.58		2.66		3.33	1.83
Ch. Homes									
CH1	49	(21)	835 (18)	1265	(20)	10	(21)	21	27
CH2	41	(17)	763 (21)	1542	(13)	10	(21)	10	8
CH3	40	(16)	928 (15)	1414	(16)	10	(21)	11	12
CH4	49	(21)	781 (20)	1355	(18)	6	(13)	26	22
CH5	41	(17)	665 (23)	1312	(19)	8	(17)	17	20
CH6	47	(20)	588 (24)	1229	(22)	12	(24)	13	16
CH7	38	(15)	903 (17)	1615	(9)	9	(19)	6	6
CH8	54	(24)	909 (16)	1244	(21)	8	(17)	9	8
CH9	20	(13)	1200 (6)	1099	(24)	4	(9)	7	5
CH10	46	(19)	760 (22)	1501	(14)	6	(13)	13	15
CH11	37	(14)	929 (14)	1384	(17)	9	(19)	6	7
CH12	51	(23)	810 (19)	1178	(23)	6	(13)	8	6
MEAN	42.75		839.25	1344.83		8.16		12.25	12.66

N.B. The rank order of each setting (from most favourable score - 1 - to least favourable score - 24) with respect to the ICM (Index of Child- Management), RICI (Revised Index of Community Involvement), RIPE (Revised Index of Physical Environment) and ICS (Index of Controls and Sanctions) are given in parentheses alongside the raw scores awarded to each setting.

N CHILD denotes total numbers of children accommodated at each setting (including natural children of foster parents living at foster homes).

N ADULTS refers to the total numbers of foster parents and staff at each setting (including domestic and ancillary staff employed at the Children's Homes).

an *unbiased estimate of reliability* of .95 [8]. The ICM was also found to be a very robust instrument [9].

Individual ICM items for which differences observed between the foster homes and Children's Homes were found to be statistically significant at the

0.05 level or less are listed below in Table 3.2 (Mann-Witney, exact two-tailed probabilities). It should be emphasised that statistical significance was only obtained for items where the management of recurrent - mainly daily - social events was discovered to be markedly more child-oriented in the foster homes than in the Children's Homes. Statistical significance for differences observed between foster homes and Children's Homes was not obtained at the 0.05 level or less in relation to the few items for which the Children's Homes achieved more favourable combined scores than the foster homes (i.e. items 1,19, 41, 42, and 43).

Table 3.2
ICM items in relation to which differences between foster homes and Children's Homes were found to be statistically significant

ITEMS	SIGNIFICANCE LEVEL
Rigidity of Routine	
2. Whether children always went to bed at the same time during the week.	0.05
5. Whether there were set times when visitors could come to see the children.	0.001
6. Whether tea was served at the same time each day.	0.001
7. Whether children had baths/showers at a set time each day.	0.01
Block Treatment	
14. Whether there were any routine/group shoe cleaning sessions.	0.001
Depersonalisation	
16. Whether there was a routine admission procedure.	0.0001
18. Whether children had participated in the decision about where they had been placed.	0.0001
20. What was done with children's possessions.	0.001
21. Whether children possessed all items on a list of basic clothing.	0.001
26. Whether children were able to switch on the TV, radio, record player, etc., without first seeking permission from caretakers.	0.05
27. Whether children were allowed some measure of choice as to the sorts of food they ate.	0.01

29. How children's birthdays were celebrated.	0.05
30. Whether children were able to send and receive sealed correspondence.	0.01
31. Whether children were able to make and receive confidential telephone calls.	0.001
32. Whether children had unrestricted access to whatever facilities were available for physical exercise and recreation.	0.05
34. Where children's pocket money was kept.	0.001
36. Whether young persons had access to contraception, etc., on the same basis as other young people in the community.	0.001
37. Whether children were permitted to style their hair according to their own tastes/wishes.	0.01

Social Distance

44. Whether children had access to the kitchen.	0.0001
48. Whether caretakers watched T.V. with children.	0.0001
49. Whether children, as well as caretakers, were permitted to make drinks and snacks, etc.	0.0001
50. Whether caretakers had a day room (e.g., a staff room) from which children were excluded.	0.01
51. Whether there was an office on the premises.	0.0001
52. Whether caretakers had accommodation on the premises from which children were excluded.	0.001

For reasons that will become clear in due course, it is important to note here that, irrespective of their size, all the Children's Homes visited had an office.

The following guides to daily routines prepared by the Heads of CH6, CH8 and CH9, respectively (though not for the purposes of this study), further highlight how the daily lives of children in residential care contrast with those of children living in family settings. The documents are reproduced in completely unabridged form, and complement the systematic nature of ICM data. Bearing in mind the ICM rankings awarded to the three Children's Homes involved, note how the CH9 (the most child-oriented Children's Home, according to the ICM) document differs in tone and content from the first two documents, thereby appearing to confirm the ICM results. The reader will see from Table 3.1 that the ICM results suggest that the three Homes selected are representative of the Children's Homes visited.

TIME 7.00 - 7.30 a.m. Staff on duty to make staff bed and tidy sleeping in room. Wake young persons as required.

7.30 a.m. All children remaining in bed to be woken. The two staff on duty should divide the tasks in the following manner:-

Staff Member 'A' to remain upstairs and supervise the children carrying out the following tasks:-

    (1) Wash/Clean teeth.
    (2) Make beds.
    (3) Dress for the days needs.
    (4) Tidy bedrooms.
    (5) Ensure that wash bags and towels are hung up.
    (6) When all tasks are completed the children are to gather in the T.V. room prior to breakfast.

Staff member 'B' is to come downstairs and supervise the following:-

    (1) Supervise and assist in the preparation and serving of breakfast.
    (2) Supervise children in the T.V. room prior to breakfast.
    (3) Supervise and assist where required and ensure the kitchen and dining room are left clean and tidy.
    (4) Supervise in conjunction with staff member 'A' the children during breakfast

8.15a.m Prior to children leaving the dining room the staff on duty are to allocate jobs ...[to children]... as per the job list.

When and not before all jobs are completed and checked children may smoke (T.V. and record Room only).

At the same time dinner moneys and bus fares are to be given out.

Note!

Staff should ensure children attending outside school are:-

    a) In possession of relevant equipment.
    b) Are aware of any appointments they may have.
    c) Are correctly dressed.
    d) Are not wearing jewellery or make up.
    c) Leave at the correct time.

The remaining children should be <u>supervised</u> until 9.15 a.m. when they are to assemble in the T.V. room prior to being escorted to Unit 1 School Unit.

The member of staff escorting the children to school is to <u>ensure</u> children are:-

 a) In possession of relevant equipment.
 b) Are aware of any appointments.
 c) Are correctly dressed.
 d) Are not wearing jewellery or make up

Having handed the children over to school staff:-

 a) Deliver outgoing mail to Unit 1 office.
 b) Collect incoming mail.
 c) Collect expenses/clothing money as required.

<u>Prior to 10.00</u>

 a) Inform cooks of numbers for lunch.
 b) Write up log.

<u>10.00 a.m. - 12.30 a.m.</u>

 a) Check attendance where appropriate at schools and places of work.
 b) Ensure appointments are kept and accompany children where needed.
 c) Arrange future appointments where required.
 d) General caseworking duties as per monthly plan of instructions of Unit Leader/Deputy.

<u>12.30 p.m.</u>   Collect children from school unit. Escort to unit 2 for lunch. Children are to:-

 a) Hang up coats in downstairs cloakroom.
 b) Wash hands.
 c) Assemble in Dining Room for lunch.

<u>Note</u>!

 a) One member of staff per table where possible.
 b) One child for each table to serve.
 c) No children to leave dining room until the meal is finished.

After lunch children are to be <u>supervised</u> until their return to the school unit at 1.30 p.m. escorted by staff.

1.30 - 3.00 p.m.	Write up log and prepare to handover to oncoming staff
3.00 p.m.	Handover.
3.30 p.m.	Collect children from school unit.
3.30 - 4.30 p.m.	The following tasks are to be completed prior to the evening meal and supervised by staff on duty.

a) Change out of school uniform.
b) Clean shoes.
c) Put clean laundry away.
d) Identify the following days needs.
e) Organise evening routine.

| 4.30 p.m. | Evening Meal. |

EVENING ROUTINE GENERAL

MONDAY	Group activity as arranged by children and staff in advance
TUESDAY	Boys domestic evening. Laundry. Ironing. Clean bedrooms. Any other tasks identified by Caseworker [staff]. Girls free.
WEDNESDAY	Free evening.
THURSDAY	Girls domestic evening. Boys free.
FRI) SAT) SUN)	As per individual arrangements.

BEDTIMES

| WEEKDAYS | 10.30 - 11.00 p.m. Any later at staff discretion. |
| WEEKENDS | At staff discretion. |

LAUNDRY

Collected and listed prior to children going to bed. Placed in laundry next morning.

CH8 RUNNING ROUTINE

<u>7.40 a.m.</u>	Children awakened - supervised washing Breakfast
<u>8.15 a.m.</u>	Jobs (...[children's]...Teams) Rest of boys supervised - cleaning teeth and tidying bedrooms
<u>8.25 a.m - 9.20 a.m.</u>	Supervised children leaving for schools on time
<u>3.30 p.m - 4.00 p.m</u>	Children supervised changing into play clothes
<u>4.25 p.m.</u>	Wash hands
<u>4.30 p.m - 5.00 p.m.</u>	Tea and jobs (teams)
<u>5.00 p.m.</u>	Evening activities discussed with children (arranged beforehand as much as possible)
<u>8.00 p.m.</u>	Commence suppers Younger group supervised Younger group clean kitchen (table and dishes) Older group supper Older group tidy kitchen table, dishes and floor
<u>8.45 p.m.</u>	Clean shoes
<u>9.00 p.m.</u> <u>9.30 p.m.</u> <u>10.00 p.m.</u> <u>10.30 p.m.</u>	Bedtime 10 - 13 years Bedtime 13 years Bedtime 14 & 15 years Bedtime 16 years

NO LATE NIGHTS UNLESS 'SPECIAL PRIVILEGE' GRANTED BY SENIOR OR STAFF ON DUTY.

1. Hands must be washed before every meal

2. Bedrooms will be left tidy, washing in basket, clothes folded in drawers, books and comics put away. <u>No</u> shoes or trainers in bedrooms.

3. School coats upstairs in wardrobe, others <u>on pegs</u> in cloakroom.

4. Clothes cannot be <u>swapped</u> or other boys clothes worn.

5. <u>Back garden only</u> to be played in.

77

CH9 ROUTINE AND PROCEDURE

Clients

Morning call 7 a.m.	After washing and dressing, down to the kitchen to prepare and eat breakfast.
School Children	- out to school 8.30 am.
Workers	- out various times.
Unemployed	- out to job centre, if possible, with a member of staff. This is not always possible with normal staffing levels.
Mother and Baby	- up when baby wakes, on average 6.30 am. Various visits during the day eg clinics, family centre, two afternoons home tuition, 1 day in college, plus school work between seeing to baby's needs. Lunch for unemployed and mother and baby.
Unemployed	- in the afternoons, interviews, outside visits or job around the house.

Individuals have one domestic evening a week when they clean the kitchen after tea,change their bedding and do all their personal washing and ironing.

Working on a weekly rota system each person makes out the week's menu, compiles a shopping list, then estimates the cost. This is then discussed with a member of staff looking at:

(a) Balanced meals.
(b) Presentation eg colour, textures.
(c) Financial budgetting.
(d) Time factor, eg what time they...[the youngster concerned]... arrive home, if they have time to prepare the meals or if any part can be prepared the evening before.

The individual then cooks the house evening meal for their week.

After tea when all chores are completed the people going out for the evening shower and change. Others do various activities, the main ones being T.V., records, reading, crafts and games. Quite often spontaneous group discussions develop, arising from the day's events or news items of interest.

Supper is at any time up to 10.00 p.m. depending on what activities are going on. People out for the evening return by 10.30pm unless a request is made to the member of staff on sleep-in duty for an extension. Normally all in bed between 11.00 - 11.30 pm, time given to read or chat quietly before settling down for the night. If something of real interest is on TV late, prepare for bed before settling down to watch it, to bed and settled immediately at the conclusion.

In addition to providing interesting and valuable insights about the daily lives of the residential children studied, the three documents also reveal much concerning the nature of staff roles - which, along with those of foster parents, forms part of the subject matter of the chapter which follows.

The documents pertaining to CH6 and CH8 clearly manifest elements of the four attributes said by Goffman (1961) to be characteristic of residential institutions (see note 1). It would appear that CH9 has gone much further than the other two Homes in attempting to provide child-oriented care. Yet, the fact that the person who wrote the CH9 document considers it noteworthy that..."quite often..., [in the evening], ...spontaneous group discussions develop arising from the day's events or news items of interest"....provides a fascinating illustration of the pervasiveness in the Children's Homes of the four attributes distinguished by Goffman (1961). For is it not the case that the latter would be expected to make spontaneity and a relaxed group climate - things that we take for granted in family living situations - novel ? To be fair, it seems likely that the writer of the CH9 document is probably aware of this, and perhaps her comments mirror efforts to normalise daily life at CH9.

Finally, it may be noted that staff at CH6 and, particularly, CH9 appear to be making some attempt to help youngsters develop domestic skills (e.g., learning to cook, clean, wash clothes, etc.). The same can be said of CH8 (as an inspection of ICM data concerning this Home confirmed), although the tone of the document may suggest that the children at this Home are merely routinely engaging in household chores. The issue of whether youngsters discharged from care at 18 years of age have received adequate preparation for independent living was addressed by item 40 of the ICM. The item was included because it is well known that young people are often discharged from care inadequately prepared to look after themselves (see, for example, Berridge, 1985). Whilst ICM data show that, in general, the preparation for independent living given to the foster children compared favourably with that provided for residential youngsters, the difference concerned was not statistically significant at the 0.05 level or less.

2. Children's Community Contacts

Capitalising on the work of King *et al* (1971), Raynes *et al* (1979) reasoned that the polarities child-oriented and institutionally-oriented could be used to measure other aspects of care practice in residential institutions [10]. Thus, the authors developed scales to measure residents' involvement in community

79

activities and the provision of physical amenities, and applied these in their study of three residential facilities for mentally retarded persons in the United States (the second scale will be discussed in the next section of this chapter). Raynes *et al's* (1979) 13 item *Index of Community Involvement* required modification, involving the construction of a number of additional scale items and revisions to original items, in order to produce an enlarged 16 item index that could be applied in both foster homes and Children's Homes [11].

My *Revised Index of Community Involvement* (RICI) - see Appendix (d) - measured the extent to which the foster and residential children's involvement in community activities was child-oriented. Data for the completion of the index was collected during interviews with foster parents and senior residential staff. Foster parents experienced no difficulty whatsoever in answering the questions put to them. However, because of factors such as the relatively large numbers of children accommodated at some of the Children's Homes, and the shift systems governing staff working hours, interviews with senior residential staff took considerably longer to complete; and, to ensure the accuracy of information collected, detailed scrutiny of the diaries and daily log books maintained at the Children's Homes was usually necessary.

The scoring procedure adopted by Raynes *et al* (1979) with respect to scale items involved collapsing raw percentages down to one of five possible scores (i.e. 80 - 100 % of children had participated in a given activity = 0; 60 - 79 % = 1; 40 - 59 % = 2; 20 - 39 % = 3; and, 0 - 19 % = 4). Whilst this method offered a means of standardising the RICI scoring procedure with that of the ICM (i.e. the closer to zero the score obtained, the more child-oriented care practice was deemed to be), it also seemed to entail the unnecessary loss of information. Accordingly, I elected to express scores for each item simply in terms of the percentage of children who had participated in associated activities (e.g., 100 % of children had participated = 100; 80 % = 80; 65 % = 65, and so on). Therefore, by contrast with the procedure adopted by Raynes *et al* (1979), the closer to zero the scores obtained, the less child-oriented management practices were considered to be.

The method of scoring adopted meant that foster homes could be awarded a score of 100 (the most favourable score for each item) by virtue of the fact that a lone foster child had participated in a given activity. However, it was also the case that foster homes could be (and were) given a score of zero (the least favourable score) where the lone foster child had not taken part in an activity. Moreover, had the Raynes *et al* (1979) scoring procedure been employed child-oriented scores would have been given where, in fact, relatively large numbers of children had not participated in activities; for example, a score of 0 for an item (as indicated above, the most favourable score in the Raynes *et al* (1979) method) might have meant that as many as 20 per cent of youngsters at a given Children's Home had not participated in the activity concerned. Hence, given that my concern centred on the welfare of the individual child, to have retained the scoring method devised by Raynes *et al* (1979) would have produced seriously misleading results.

Table 3.1 shows the total scores awarded to each research setting where the RICI was applied, and the rank order of settings in terms of degree of child-orientation. The total possible score per setting ranged between 0 (the least favourable total score) and 1600 (the most favourable total score). With the exception of CH9, the scores for the Children's Homes compare unfavourably with those obtained by the foster homes [12]. Statistical significance at the 0.001 level was obtained for the difference between the means of total scores assigned to the foster homes and Children's Homes [13].

With respect to individual RICI items, statistical significance at the 0.05 level or less was obtained for differences between the means of scores for foster homes and Children's Homes in relation to items listed in Table 3.3.

Table 3.3
RICI items in relation to which differences between the means of scores for foster homes and Children's Homes were statistically significant

ITEM	SIGNIFICANCE LEVEL
1. Whether children had participated in some kind of organised leisure activity in the community in the fortnight preceding data collection (e.g., youth clubs, disco's, scouts, guides, etc.).	0.05
6. Whether children had been to a restaurant or cafeteria in the month preceding data collection.	0.05
7. Whether children had visited a house other than that of their natural parents in the fortnight preceding data collection.	0.001
11. Whether children who required such services in the three months preceding data collection (and who had been fit to do so), had been to a doctor or dentist in the community.	0.05
15. Whether children had friends stay for tea in the month prior to data collection.	0.01
16. Whether children had played/associated informally with other children in the locality in the week preceding data collection.	0.01
18. Whether children had received letters or telephone calls in the fortnight preceding data collection.	0.01
19. Whether children had been visited by their field social workers in the month preceding data collection.	0.01

Statistical significance was not obtained for remaining RICI items. However, items 2 (whether children had been shopping for clothes in the month preceding data collection), 8 (whether children had been for a car ride in the fortnight preceding data collection) and 17 (whether children attended schools in the community) would have been statistically significant had the 0.10 level of significance been used instead of the more conservative 0.05 level [14].

Except for item 5 (whether children had travelled on a public bus, or on a train, in the fortnight preceding data collection) - which, as indicated, did not produce statistical significance at the 0.05 level or less - the foster homes achieved more child-oriented scores than the Children's Homes for each scale item. Hence, it is clear that care practice in relation to children's community contacts was, overall, considerably more child-oriented in the foster homes than in the Children's Homes visited. Perhaps the magnitude of the difference found between foster homes and Children's Homes was somewhat unexpected in view of the belief in some quarters that children in Children's Homes receive treats and enjoy outings at a rate in excess of that afforded the average child in the community [15]; although in attempting to measure children's involvement in community activities, the RICI goes beyond treats and outings.

As was also shown to be the case with respect to the ICM, the difference between the means of total scores awarded to the two groups of Children's Homes (i.e. Authority B and Authority A Homes) was not found to be statistically significant at the 0.05 level or less [16]. An item analysis produced an estimated reliability for the RICI of .71 (coefficient alpha) and an *unbiased estimate of reliability* of .73.

Also requiring mention is the point that the RICI originally comprised 19 items. However, three items concerning children's contacts with their natural families were excluded from the index owing to problems associated with standardising scores over cases. Scores for the three items were calculated as follows. During interviews, the number of children able to have contact with their natural families was established (e.g, natural families existed, their whereabouts was known, and contact with children was permitted). Then, the number of children who actually had the sorts of contacts involved (see below) was ascertained. The latter was subsequently expressed as a percentage of the former in order to arrive at the score awarded. This appeared a satisfactory means by which to avoid the danger of penalising foster homes and Children's Homes for matters beyond their control. However, it became clear that the majority of foster children were unable to have contact with their natural families, and this was also reported to be the case with respect to considerable numbers of residential youngsters. Thus, to have included the three family contact items in the scale would have sometimes entailed awarding favourable scores where no contacts of the kind specified had, in fact, occurred between children and their natural families.

The three items in question concerned: (1) whether children able to do so had been for overnight visits to their natural parents home within the fortnight preceding data collection; (2) whether children able to do so had been on holiday with their natural parents in the year preceding data collection; (3) whether children able to do so had received visits from members of their natural families within the month preceding data collection. The following tables show the percentages of foster and residential children able to have the three forms of contact involved and the percentages who actually did so.

Table 3.4
Overnight visits by children to their natural parents homes within the fortnight preceding data collection

	% able to visit	(N)	% who actually visited	(N)
Foster children	29.41	(5)	11.76	(2)
Authority B Homes children	92.42	(61)	33.33	(22)
Authority A Homes children	73.68	(56)	54.43	(43)

Table 3.5
Children's holidays with natural parents within the year preceding data collection

	% able to go on holiday	(N)	% who actually went on holiday	(N)
Foster children	29.41	(5)	11.76	(2)
Authority B Homes children	57.57	(38)	3.03	(2)
Authority A Homes children	69.62	(55)	7.59	(6)

Table 3.6
Visits by natural families to children's placements within the month preceding data collection

	% able to receive visitors	(N)	% who actually received visitors	(N)
Foster children	29.41	(5)	17.67	(3)
Authority B Homes children	100.00	(66)	34.84	(23)
Authority A Homes children	87.34	(69)	16.45	(13)

The above tables do not appear altogether consistent with the seemingly fairly widespread assumption that residential placements are necessarily more successful than foster placements with regard to maintaining relations between children and their natural families [17]; a point which seems to be supported by findings that 50 per cent of the total numbers of foster children able to have the first two forms of family contact did so, and 60 per cent of foster children able to have the third type of contact with their natural families had done so. However, only 36 per cent, 5.26 per cent and 34.84 per cent of the total numbers of Authority B Children's Homes youngsters able to experience the first, second and third forms of family contact, respectively, had actually done so. Although 76.78 per cent of Authority A Homes children able to have the first type of contact did so, as few as 10.90 per cent and 18.84 per cent able to do so actually experienced the second and third forms of family contact, respectively.

Whilst it is plain that no firm conclusions may be drawn from the data concerned, given that relatively few foster children were able to have contact with their natural families in the first place, it is perhaps worth mentioning that a number of the foster parents interviewed had clearly been instrumental in helping foster children to maintain relations with their natural families. It may also be said that if contacts between foster children and their natural families were more frequent than anticipated, contacts between residential children and their families occurred markedly less often than expected.

3. The Physical Environment

The third aspect of care practice examined in this chapter concerns the physical environments of the substitute care settings visited. Raynes *et al* (1979) not only argue that..."more involvement in the community is better...", but also cite evidence which demonstrates that improvements in the physical environment can result in..."appropriate and productive behaviour for institutionalised children"... (Raynes *et al*, 1979, p.83). As stated, the authors devised a scale to measure the provision of physical amenities in residential institutions for mentally retarded persons in the U.S.A.

Although it was possible to make use of the items comprising the data collection instrument - the *Physical Environment Inventory* - in more or less their original form, items constituting the scale itself were modified considerably. This was done with a view to producing a scale conditioned by a somewhat more generous notion of what constitutes a reasonable standard of physical living environment (see Appendix (e)), thereby enhancing the capability of the index to discriminate between different research settings.

The scoring procedure for the physical environment index designed by Raynes *et al* (1979) was also altered, and in a manner similar to that earlier reported in relation to the RICI. The original scoring system involved a combination ratio and percentage scales. These were subsequently converted to one of five possible scores ranging from 0 to 4 (0 being the most favourable score, indicating a high degree of resident-orientation, whilst 4 was the most unfavourable score and relected a high level of institutionally-oriented management practice). This scoring method was dispensed with because it appeared to entail the unnecessary loss of information, and I again elected to base scores for percentage scale items on raw percentages (e.g.100% = 100; 80 per cent = 80, and so on). In order to standardise the results for ratio and percentage scales, ratios were calculated and then expressed in percentage terms before the scores for the items in question (see Appendix (e)) were arrived at [18].

The RIPE initially comprised 23 items and, hence, was significantly larger than the 13 item Raynes *et al* (1979) index. However, item 15 of my revised index was excluded from statistical analysis comparing total scores of foster homes and Children's Homes because it was found to have zero variance (i.e. all bedrooms at the foster homes and Children's Homes visited had curtains). Thus, possible scores for each of the 24 settings with regard to the total scale ranged between 0 (the least favourable possible score) and 2,200 (the most favourable possible score). Scores for individual items ranged between 0 (least favourable possible score) and 100 (the most favourable score possible).

Table 3.1 displays the total scores awarded to each research setting and the rank order of settings in terms of the extent to which each was determined to be child-oriented in relation to the provision of physical amenities. It can be seen that the foster homes generally obtained more child-oriented total scores than the Children's Homes. That FH12 fell into the ranks of the Children's Homes is partly attributable to the fact that the family concerned lived in an overcrowded council house [19]. By contrast, youngsters at CH7 (the Children's Home which achieved the highest ranking) enjoyed comparatively spacious living accommodation. Statistical significance at the 0.001 level was obtained for the difference between the means of total scores for the foster homes (1689.58) and Children's Homes (1344.83) [20]. However, the difference between the means

of total scores awarded to Authority B Children's Homes (1394.00) and
Authority A Children's Homes (1320.25) did not produce statistical
significance at the 0.05 level or less [21]. The 22 item RIPE was also found to
have a reliability coefficient of .77 (unbiased estimate of reliabilty) [22].

Tests were also performed comparing the mean scores of foster homes and
Children's Homes for each individual scale item. Statistical significance at the
0.05 level or less was obtained in relation to the items presented in Table 3.7.
The means of foster homes scores compared favourably with those of the
Children's Homes for all nine items listed.

Table 3.7
RIPE items in relation to which statistical significance was obtained for differences between
the means of scores for foster homes and Children's Homes

ITEM	SIGNIFICANCE LEVEL
3. Ratio of bath tubs/showers to residential children/family members.	0.01
4. Percentage of bath tubs/showers in rooms with doors that could be locked.	0.01
9. Percentage of toilets with doors that could be locked.	0.05
12. Percentage of children with their own (as distinct from shared) wardrobes.	0.05
13. Percentage of children with different bedspreads (i.e. different in colour/pattern).	0.001
14. Percentage of children's bedrooms with posters, pictures, photos, etc.	0.01
17. Ratio of TV's and radios to residential children/family members.	0.001
19. Ratio of occasional tables to residential children/family members.	0.01
23. Ratio of dayrooms to residential children/family members.	0.05

Statistical significance was not obtained at the 0.05 level or less for
differences between the means of scores obtained by foster homes and
Children's Homes with respect to other RIPE items [23]. However, except for
items 2 (ratio of handbasins to residential children/family members), 5 (ratio of
mirrors to residential children/family members), 7 (ratio of toilets to residential
children/family members) and 18 (ratio of armchairs and settees to residential
children/family members), the scores awarded foster homes for remaining items
compared favourably with those obtained by the Children's Homes.

Accordingly, it seems reasonable to conclude from the results reported that,
overall, physical amenities in the foster homes compared well with those in the
Children's Homes. However, the RIPE findings perhaps fail to convey the true

extent of the differences observed between the foster homes and Children's Homes. This is partly due to the way in which I sought to standardise the scoring of items; for example, the reader may have observed that ratio items concerned only children from the Children's Homes - with staff excluded, while all household or family members were included for the foster homes. The decision to exclude residential staff was determined by the knowledge that none of the staff in the Children's Homes visited were resident (i.e. did not live at the Homes when off-duty). Given that staff clearly used facilities such as armchairs and handbasins, etc., it is obvious that the Children's Homes scores were somewhat inflated.

That the contrast between foster homes and Children's Homes was underestimated by the RIPE also owes much to the emphasis which the index placed on factors which could be easily and reliably measured. Thus, important matters were not addressed because they were less amenable to quantification. For example, the RIPE results do not reflect the institutionally-oriented character of the architectural exterior design of some of the Children's Homes visited (see below), or testify to other features observed inside certain Children's Homes but absent from foster homes such as: excessively high ceilings and large day rooms; dormitory type bedrooms; large laundries; sophisticated fire alarm system boxes, fire bells, large red fire extinquishers, fire hoses and EXIT signs fixed to walls (necessary, of course, but not found in ordinary households); observation windows designed to facilitate the supervision of children by staff; long corridors with linoleum tiled floors and pale walls; offices replete with the paraphenalia of small business concerns; and, furniture of a strictly functional and basic design [24]. It should be stressed that some of these features were not present in all the Children's Homes visited, and indubitable attempts had been made in some Homes to provide children with a physical environment of good quality.

However, a further feature which frequently distinguished the Children's Homes and foster homes, and which permits reliable comparison of settings, was type of kitchen. Three main sorts of kitchen were observed. First, those with exclusively domestic equipment and fittings (e.g., cookers, fridges, sink units, washing machines, storage cupboards, and so on). Second, those with mainly conventional domestic equipment, etc., but with some of the features characteristic of industrial or institutional type kitchens (see below). Third, kitchens which were mainly industrial or institutional in nature (i.e. characterised by, for example, their comparatively large size, high ceilings, tiled floors; their large tables, cookers, dishwashers, sink units, storage cupboards, and so on; by features such as large, automatic, potato pealers, deep friers, mixers; and, by equipment like giant mixing bowls, colanders, ladels, baking trays, etc.). These kitchens resembled those typically found in places such as schools and factories.

All the foster homes had kitchens of the first type, as did CH3 and CH9. The kitchens at the following Children's Homes were of the second kind: CH2, CH6, CH7, CH8, CH10, CH11 and CH12. Finally, the three largest Homes - CH1, CH4 and CH5 - had kitchens of the third, industrial/institutional, sort.

It was also possible to distinguish several major types of exterior of building or residence: first, conventional family houses (either terraced, semi- detached or detached), which blended in completely with surrounding houses); next, small scale conversions (e.g., two, originally separate, houses joined to make a

86

single residence) which blended reasonably well with surrounding houses; third, relatively large conversions with big gardens, and made conspicuous by attributes such as their ample tarmac car parking areas; and, fourth, purpose built (i.e. constructed to serve as Children's Homes) and distinguished from neighbouring houses by their design (see below), and also by features such as relatively large car parking facilities.

The foster families all lived in the first type of residence delineated. Their homes ranged from small council owned properties through to large, owner-occupier, family houses. CH7, CH8 and CH9 can also be placed in the first category identified. CH2, CH3 and CH12 belong to the second category, whilst CH1 and CH6 were representative of the third type of residence. The remaining Children's Homes - CH4, CH5, CH10 and CH11 - were all purpose built and, hence, may be placed in the fourth category outlined.

CH9 was the least conspicuous of the twelve Children's Homes and impossible to tell apart from adjoining houses. Incidentally, it is therefore interesting that CH9 obtained the poorest RIPE score; the more so because my subjective impression was that CH9 was the Children's Home which most resembled the high scoring foster homes. Other Homes perhaps gained more favourable RIPE scores than CH9 because they were better equipped. But, it will be appreciated that if, say, 20 children are accommodated in a single setting, in order to be adequately equipped, provisions assume an institutional appearance; for example, toilet areas are characterised by a relatively large number of cubicles, wash basins, etc., separate bedrooms for children necessitate long corridors, kitchens must be large, and so on.

However that may be, it was not necessary to know the relevant street numbers, etc., to locate the other Children's Homes. Whilst placed in the first of the four categories, CH7 and CH8 might very easily have been put in the second, because both residences had attributes which, although trivial in one sense, somehow set them apart from surrounding houses; for example, paint work on doors and window frames was rather drab and colours typical of local authority establishments were in evidence (e.g. dark greens) - giving the buildings an official appearance, gardens were tidy but relatively uncultivated with few flowers at a time when these were in abundance in neighbouring gardens. Similar observations were made in relation to the Homes grouped in the second category - CH2, CH3 and CH12, and these were of course further distinguishable from surrounding houses by the fact that all three were constituted by two joined, but originally separate, council houses. CH1 and CH6 were both very large, old, houses which had served as Children's Homes of one kind or another for many years. Both were set in extensive gardens and signs announcing their function were placed at the entrances to their driveways. Of the two, CH1 was the larger: originally the home of a wealthy Victorian jeweller and his family, a classroom block had more recently been built onto one of its wings and administrative offices were accommodated in an annexe (although the main building where the children lived also contained a well equipped office) which began life as a coach house and living quarters for servants. Both CH1 and CH6 were situated in affluent areas where houses of similar size were the norm.

The purpose built Homes - CH4, CH5, CH10 and CH11 - were least in harmony with nearby houses owing to their unmistakable institutionally-oriented architecture [25]. CH5, with its large, squat, chimney, asphalt play ground, spacious car park and lawn, resembled a small post-war, state, primary school. It was built of buff coloured brick and its paintwork was a distinctive shade of red. CH5 was older than the other three Homes comprising its category. CH4, CH10, and CH11 were recent constructions, and with their neatly trimmed lawns and rose beds, brown stained window frames and low wooden fences, gently sloping slated roofs, and contemporary dark brown brickwork, seemed to have much in common with small, modern, office accommodation. The interior of all three Homes appeared to have been designed in such a way that they could be readily converted to alternative uses should the need arise; for example, the living area of CH4 was of an open-plan design, which together with its floor to ceiling windows (and others that were presumably designed to facilitate the observation of children, for they served no other conceivable use), meant that children were living in a sort of Goldfish bowl (and hackneyed though the expression might be there is no better description for the curious design of CH4).

In ending this section, it is worth noting that during the course of the study evidence was collected indicating that some youngsters living at the Children's Homes experienced a sense of stigma as a consequence. For example, the senior member of staff interviewed at CH5 related that children at the Home elected to travel by bus to a Youth Club a considerable distance away from the locality in which CH5 is situated, rather than attend the Youth Club sited just a few hundred yards from the home. This was because they were ashamed to be known by local younsters as children from ..."that Home"... and because children living at CH5 had been bullied by local youths on several occasions [26]. Also meriting note at this juncture is the point that many of the residential settings visited were located in areas some distance away from the children's home localities, and often in predominantly middle-class neighbourhoods. This, together with the concept of stigma mentioned already, helps to condition the extent of residential children's involvement in community activities [27], and as such partly explains some of the findings reported in the previous section.

4. Controls and Sanctions

The final section of this chapter reports findings concerning a fourth aspect of care practice; namely, the controls and sanctions employed by foster parents and residential staff with respect to children's behaviour. This topic was addressed via a questionnaire - the CIQ (*Control Interview Questionnaire*) - which was applied during interviews with foster parents and a senior member of staff at each of the Children's Homes. The items included in the CIQ (see Appendix (f)) were mainly based on Millham *et al's* (1981) writings concerning control in residential child care settings which, in turn, were grounded in the authors empirical researches.

Millham *et al* (1981, pp.36-52) distinguish between what they regard as appropriate and effective controls and sanctions, on the one hand, and those which they believe to be inappropriate and ineffective, on the other [28]. Inappropriate/ineffective controls and sanctions include: corporal punishment, transferring or threatening to remove children to other residential settings, group punishments (e.g., punishing a group of children when, say, an individual culprit cannot be identified), limiting children's access to the outside world (i.e.

88

confining children to the Home and temporarily curtailing activities which they undertake outside - for example, preventing children from visiting their friends), public disapproval (e.g., admonishing children in the presence of others; sometimes done with the express purpose of shaming children in front of their peers, etc.), placing children in secure rooms, and the use of drugs. The authors question the efficacy of such measures and highlight their adverse implications.

In attempting to specify approaches to control which are both appropriate and effective, Millham *et al* (1981) begin by reporting their observation that effectively controlled residential child care settings are characterised by a sparing use of sanctions. According to the authors, it is the ethos of the residential setting which controls by fashioning a system of mutually held expectations, values and norms of conduct that exercise restraint on members. Where sanctions are required, Millham *et al* (1981) consider that children's short term ..."instrumental pre-occupations mean that they can be controlled by manipulation of rewards and sanctions which are immediate and tangible. Rules should be clear and self evident, reiterated by staff but open to discussion with children and holding the possibility of change... Manipulation of pocket money, access to treats and expeditions like cinema visits, late T.V. or staying up late should be sufficient for daily control. Sanctions can include ...chores... [such]... as mowing the lawn, ...washing the van ...[and so on]... Instrumental sanctions... have a moral justification, in that if unpleasant jobs are to be done, those who disrupt the community well-being should do them"...

Yet the authors acknowledge that it is more difficult to stipulate codes of conduct for staff in relation to the moral, social and sexual areas of children's behaviour. Here they argue that personal example is of great import because it confers moral authority on the adults reproaching youngsters for their errors. It is vital that the ethos of residential settings emphasise values that are generally accepted in the outside world, say the authors, and they assert that ..."control in sexual and moral areas can only be achieved by sensitive, tolerant and good-humoured counselling. There is no other way"...

Serious violations of expectations such as aggression, theft, and absconding should, in Millham *et al's* (1981) view, be .."met by... [the]... stricture and voiced disappointment of the adult closest to the child within the... home. Then censure may be supplemented... by... some instrumental sanction - if only as a token to the wider audience"... But, according to the authors, ..."reproach only works if the offender values the esteem and affection of the adults chosen to exercise such normative sanctions... It is important to stress that in order to maintain control, praise, reward and encouragement always need greatly to outweigh negative sanctions. The more rewarding the place, the more it can manipulate instrumental sanctioning"...

The CIQ can be seen as an attempt to test the extent to which the Children's Homes and foster homes studied conformed to the ideas set out by Millham *et al* (1981) with respect to appropriate/effective and inappropriate/ineffective controls. Items 3, 4 and 5 of the questionnaire were used to create a 22 item *Index of Controls and Sanctions* (ICS - see Appendix (f)), consisting of three subscales, each of which was related to one of the three behavioural areas discussed by Millham *et al* (1981) and reported above; viz., (a) relatively minor, day-to-day, infractions of rules, norms of conduct and expectations, by children; (b) serious violations of rules, etc., such as aggression and theft; and, (c) children's misdemeanours regarding moral, social and sexual matters.

Scale items were treated as dichotomous variables, with controls and sanctions judged to be appropriate/effective for each of the three areas of behaviour involved awarded scores of 0 when used by foster parents and staff. Those considered inappropriate/ineffective were assigned a score of 1 when utilised by caretakers. Controls and sanctions which, in themselves, do not appear to be inappropriate/ineffective, but which were not specifically recommended by Millham *et al* (1981) in relation to one or other of the three areas of children's behaviour defined, were excluded from the analysis of the subscales in question. This was to resolve confusion as to whether they should or should not be used in such instances (the items referred to can be distinguished on the CIQ presented in Appendix (f) by the continous rows of asterisks which are placed alongside them).

Given the possibility that caretakers may have used one or more of the methods excluded from the analysis of subscales 1 and 2, in preference to those included in the analysis of these subscales, item 3 (manipulation of rewards and sanctions) on subscale 1, and items 10 (voiced disappointment by adult closest to child), 11 (manipulation of rewards and sanctions) and 12 (individual stricture) on subscale 2 were awarded scores of 0 whether or not the methods concerned were used by caretakers. However, in accordance with Millham *et al's* (1981) recommendations, items 6 (praise, reward and encouragement) on subscale 1, and 18 (personal example) and 22 (counselling) on subscale 3 were not treated as interchangeable with excluded items. Hence, where these methods were not used, a score of 1 was awarded.

Two controls discussed by Millham *et al* (1981) and which featured in the CIQ - placing children in secure accommodation, and the use of drugs - were excluded from the ICS. None of the Children's Homes visited had secure provision (although it appeared that such provision had been used indirectly on rare occasions by a few of the Children's Homes; this practice is covered by the ICS items regarding the transfer of children to alternative placements). Equally, none of those interviewed reported the use of drugs for the purpose of exercising control over children. A third inappropriate/ineffective control referred to by Millham *et al* (1981) - corporal punishment - was re-termed physical chastisement and included in the ICS. Whilst there were no reports of corporal punishment being administered in terms of the use of implements such as canes or leather straps, several respondents, including a number of both residential staff and foster parents, confided that corporal punishment in the form of cuffing, slapping, smacking children, and so on, was used, albeit very rarely (and contrary to the formal policy of the local authority Social Services Departments concerned) - see below. Thus, whilst not strictly necessary, the term physical chastisement was substituted for that of corporal punishment in order to avoid possible ambiguity with respect to the items involved.

It should be noted that each of the three subscales comprising the ICS feature more or less the same methods of control. This reflects the notion that certain controls are inappropriate/ineffective *per se* (i.e. for any of the three broad areas of behaviour distinguished) - for example, transfer or threat of removal to another place - and, the idea that some controls may be appropriate/effective for more than one of the three behavioural areas (e.g., manipulation of rewards and sanctions can be used for relatively minor, day-to-day, infractions of rules, etc., by children and also for serious matters such as aggression and theft).

As was the case in relation to the ICM (but not the RICI and RIPE), the closer the total ICS score for each setting is to 0, the more child-oriented care practice is deemed to be. Table 3.1 shows that the total ICS scores attained by the foster homes generally compared favourably with those awarded to the Children's Homes (interestingly, FH7, which obtained a relatively poor score was headed by a widow who, prior to becoming a special foster parent, had for many years worked in residential child care settings). The reader will also observe that CH9 again succeeded in breaking into the ranks of the foster homes. Statistical significance for the difference between the means of scores for foster homes and Children's Homes was obtained at the 0.0001 level [29]. Only 16 of the 22 items initially constituting the ICS were included in this computation. Items which were found to have zero variance when an item analysis was performed on the ICS data were excluded (i.e. items 1, 3, 10, 11, 12 and 22). The 16 item ICS has an associated reliability coefficient of .84 (unbiased estimated reliability of the scale; coefficient alpha =.83).

Once again, data analysis of full scale scores revealed that, although care practice in the foster homes was significantly more child-oriented than that generally prevailing in the Children's Homes, care practice observed in Authority B Homes did not differ significantly from that found in Authority A Homes [30]. The same can be said about subscales 1 and 2 of the ICS; however, in relation to the third subscale, although the overall difference between foster homes and Authority B Children's Homes was statistically significant at the 0.05 level, statistical significance at the 0.05 level or less was not achieved for the overall difference between foster homes and Authority A Children's Homes [31].

With regard to results pertaining to the individual items comprising the ICS, items associated with subscale 1 will be considered first. At none of the substitute care settings visited did caretakers employ transfer or threat of removal when dealing with minor, day-to-day, misbehaviour by children. However, limiting children's access to the outside world was used at 10 of the 12 Children's Homes, compared to 3 of the foster homes. It will be recalled that both of the methods referred to are regarded as inappropriate/ineffective. Manipulation of rewards and sanctions - an appropriate/effective method - was employed at all 24 settings. Two of the senior residential staff interviewed reported that they had known physical chastisement to be used by staff at their Homes. By contrast, none of the foster parents interviewed reported the use of this method in relation to the everyday control of foster children. Half of the Children's Homes were said to make use of public disapproval (an inappropriate/ineffective method), compared to a single foster home. Caretakers at all settings, save one of the Children's Homes, were reported to employ the appropriate/effective method of praise, reward and encouragement. Finally, although the inappropriate/ineffective method of group punishment was used at only one of the foster homes, eight of the Children's Homes employed this method for controlling children on a day-to-day basis.

Turning to the second subscale - the methods used by caretakers in attempting to deal with serious violations of rules, norms of conduct and expectations by children, all 12 Children's Homes, against 5 of the foster homes, employed the inappropriate/ineffective method of transfer or threat of removal. Every

Children's Home visited also used the inappropriate/ineffective method of limiting children's access to the outside world, compared with 7 of the foster homes. Caretakers at all 24 substitute care settings were reported to use the appropriate/effective methods of voiced disappointment by the adult closest to the child, manipulation of rewards and sanctions and individual stricture. Caretakers at three of the foster homes and two Children's Homes had resorted to the use of physical chastisement. The also inappropriate/ineffective technique of public disapproval was practised at 8 Children's Homes, but only 2 foster homes. Finally, group punishment (an inappropriate/ineffective control) was used at 10 of the Children's Homes but its application restricted to a single foster home.

Results for items concerning the third subscale (moral, social and sexual matters) [32] were as follows: first, transfer or threat of removal was used at 5 of the Children's Homes but only one foster home. Limiting children's access to the outside world was employed at 10 Children's Homes and 5 foster homes. Except for one of the foster home respondents, all those interviewed reported the use of personal example (appropriate/effective method) with regard to influencing children's behaviour in relation to social, moral and sexual matters. The use of physical chastisement was restricted to two settings only - a foster home and one of the Children's Homes. The application of two other inappropriate/ineffective controls - public disapproval and group punishment - was also limited to a single foster home in each case, but the former method was used by staff at 6 Children's Homes with the latter technique practised at 5 of the Children's Homes. Counselling (appropriate/effective method) was used by caretakers at all the settings studied when attempting to influence children's behaviour in relation to moral, social and sexual matters.

What emerges from the findings associated with individual ICS items is that Children's Home staff made far greater use of inappropriate/ineffective techniques of control than did foster parents. Moreover, residential staff tended to employ such methods irrespective of the behavioural area concerned. Limiting children's access to the outside world, public disapproval and group punishment were used by residential staff for all three of the behavioural areas distinguished, whilst transfer or threat of removal to another place was used by staff for both serious forms of anti-social behaviour by children (e.g., aggression and theft) and for children's misdemeanours in relation to moral, social and sexual matters. By contrast, foster parents appeared to rely more on those methods defined as appropriate/effective by Millham *et al* (1981) in exercising control over foster children.

Although the CIQ did not attempt to collect data on the frequency with which the various techniques of control were used by caretakers it is, by definition, plain that methods reported with regard to day-to-day infractions of rules, and so on, by children must have been practised more often than methods used in relation to the other two behavioural areas. But, it is important to reiterate that the use of physical chastisement seemed rare; and, when resorted to, usually appeared to involve momentary loss of control on the part of adults - in response to difficult/testing behaviour by children - rather than premeditated acts. Certainly no instances of the sort concerned were observed during the course of the 12 months which I spent at the settings studied.

However, it was not unusual to observe male staff at CH1 physically restraining youngsters who had lost control during conflict situations with staff.

At times, it seemed that these situations might have been avoided had the staff concerned attempted to diffuse tensions rather than appearing to do the reverse. The confrontational approach sometimes adopted by certain staff at CH1 was probably made possible by the large number of male staff employed at the Home, since the sort of incidents reported were not observed at the other Children's Homes where male staff did not predominate. But it should be noted that the three remaining Authority B Homes were able to solve their control problems by having difficult youngsters transferred to CH1. The Authority A Homes could also transfer children who proved troublesome; and the same point, of course, applies to the foster homes. Hence, staff at CH1 were expected to control children who were regarded as being too difficult for staff at the other three Authority B Homes to manage.

Finally, further evidence that the control practices used by foster parents were generally more child-oriented than the methods characteristically employed by residential staff is provided by data pertaining to item 9 of the CIQ, which asked: "Are the rules open to discussion with the child(ren) and can they be changed as a result of such discussion"? All but one of the 12 foster home respondents answered this question in the affirmative; however, as many as 7 Children's Homes respondents did not. Thus, whilst it seemed that foster children typically participated in the rule making process, the same could not be said of residential children [33]. Yet the following comments by Millham et al (1981, p.50) underline the importance of participation by residential children in the process by which rules are made: "the aim of control should not be merely to maintain the power and authority of the adult world vis-a-vis the child. It should be to motivate the young person towards more active participation in the community home and to internalise its values"...

Notes

1.   King *et al* (1971, pp.207-211) provide the following definitions for the four concepts which they derived from Goffman (1961).

Rigidity of Routine

..."Management practices are institutionally-oriented when they are inflexible from one day to the next, and from one inmate to another: individuals in different situations are treated as though they were in the same situation and changes in circumstances are not taken into account. Management practices are child-oriented when they are flexible, being adapted to take into account individual differences among the children or different circumstances"...

'Block Treatment'

..."Child management practices are institutionally-oriented if the children are regimented - that is, all dealt with as a group - before, during or after any specific activity. These practices involve queuing and waiting around, with large groups of other children and with no mode of occupation during the waiting period. Management practices may be described as child-oriented where the organisation of activity is such that residents are allowed to participate or not as they please, and where they are allowed to do things at their own pace"...

Depersonalisation

..."Child management practices may be seen as institutionally-oriented when there are no opportunities for residents to have personal possessions or personal privacy. Depersonalisation is also shown where there is an absence of opportunities for self-expression, or of situations in which initiative on the part of the child may be shown. Where there are opportunities for residents to show initiative, to have personal possessions, to be alone if they so desire, the child management practices may be described as child-oriented"...

Social Distance

..."Management practices are institutionally-oriented when there is a sharp separation between the staff and inmate worlds. This may be because separate areas of accommodation are kept for the exclusive use of staff, or because interaction between staff and children is limited to formal, and functionally specific, activities. Child orientation involves the reduction of social distance by the sharing of living space, and allows staff and children to interact in functionally diffuse and informal situations"...

2.   Taylor *et al's* (1979) *Charter of Rights for Children in Institutions* draws on three principle sources: the Council of Europe's Resolution 77 (33) on the placement of children (adopted 3rd November 1977), a text preparted by MIND as a statute for formal admission to and discharge from a treatment facility, and a document *Declaration of the Rights of the Child* written by a *Voice of the Child in Care Working Party*.

3.   Interviews were carried out on an individual basis with senior residential staff, although in some foster homes both foster parents participated in the ICM interviews. The reader will see from Appendix (c) that questions are rather bluntly phrased. Thus, because certain ICM items address sensitive issues, considerable tact was exercised by the researcher during interviews, which meant that some questions were put to respondents indirectly. In order to ensure that the answers obtained were accurate, ICM interviews were fairly lengthy affairs. It was initially envisaged that answers to certain items would be confirmed by observation and that observation would be the sole means of data collection for other items (see Appendix (c)). However, owing to difficulties associated with travelling to and from some research venues, and the fact that the numbers of children in the Authority A Children's Homes were somewhat depleted at the time of fieldwork due to school holidays (i.e. some children at these establishments were on home leave), greater reliance was placed on collecting ICM data by interview than was originally anticipated.

Initially, the index consisted of a pool of 101 items. However, shortly before commencing the second phase of fieldwork, this number was reduced to 52 items. This involved the deletion of all early morning observational items (because of the difficulties entailed in travelling to most of the research settings in order to arrive prior to children being woken) and, items which were perhaps made redundant by other items, along with certain items which seemed to have low discriminating potential, so as to reduce the length of interviews.

4.   The original scoring procedure adopted by King *et al* (1971), though crude, was retained because it has a common-sense interpretation; something which could not be said about a more elaborate scoring

94

method, given that it was not possible to measure or determine the true distance between practices deemed to be child- oriented, on the one hand, and institutionally-oriented, on the other.

5. Although 52 items comprised the version of the ICM that was used during the major period of fieldwork, four items (i.e. items 8, 9, 12 and 25) were found to have zero variance (i.e. no discriminating power) when the index was tested for reliability (items comprising additive scales that have zero variance are excluded from the computation of reliability coefficients by the SPSSx statistical package used in data analysis; hence, items found to have zero variance, when reliability coefficients were computed for additive scales reported in this account, were subsequently also excluded from the scales concerned; however, very few items were shown to have no discriminating power). Accordingly, the total scores presented involve the sums of the 48 remaining items, only - which means that the least favourable possible total score was 96.

6. The mean ranks of foster homes and Children's Homes were compared via a Mann-Witney test (two-tailed test) with the following results:

	CASES	MEAN RANK
Foster homes	12	6.50
Children's Homes	12	18.50
TOTAL	24	

			CORRECTED FOR TIES	
U	W	EXACT 2-PROB	Z	2-TAIL PROB
0.0	78.8	0.0000	-4.1614	0.0000

Because the sample size was <30 the exact probability is used. A T-test was also performed on the means of scores obtained by foster homes and Children's Homes and the results were as follows:

	N CASES	MEAN	SD	SE	F VALUE	2-TAIL P
Foster homes	12	11.8333	3.040	0.878		
					8.74	0.001
Children's Homes	12	42.7500	8.986	2.594		

SEPARATE VARIANCE ESTIMATE

T VALUE	DF	2 TAIL PROB
-11.29	13.49	0.000

The two tailed probability associated with the T value confirms the results obtained by the non-parametric Mann-Witney test. However, given that the ICM does not strictly speaking involve interval level measurement, perhaps the latter (used for ordinal level measurement) is the more appropriate test.

7. The results produced by the application of the Kruskal-Wallis, non-parametric, one-way analysis of variance test were as follows:

	CASES	MEAN RANK
Foster homes	12	6.50
Authority B Children's Homes	4	19.13
Authority A Children's Homes	8	18.19
TOTAL	24	

CASES	CHI-SQ.	SIG.	CORRECTED FOR TIES	
24	17.3269	0.0002	CHI-SQ.	SIG.
			17.3646	0.0002

It can be seen that the mean ranks awarded to the two groups of Children's Homes were very similar. This view was confirmed by the results of the Scheffe multiple comparison procedure (see Norusis, 1983, pp.111-112) that was applied in conjunction with the parametric one-way analysis of variance test. The former revealed that whilst the mean of scores of foster homes differed significantly from those of both groups of Children's Homes, the means of scores for each set of Children's Homes were not significantly different at the 0.05 level. The means of scores on which the scheffe test was based were as follows:

	MEAN
Foster homes	11.8333
Authority B Children's Homes	41.7500
Authority A Children's Homes	44.7500

8.   Smith (1975, pp.58-61) relates that there are several ways to test measurement reliability, one of which is to correlate (associate) each item in a scale against every other item and obtain the average intercorrelation for the entire set of correlations or associations. This procedure produces the most stable index of reliability. Cronbach (1951) has provided a fairly efficient estimate of this average intercorrelation, coefficient alpha. The coefficient presented in the main body of the text, however, involves a correction for the bias of alpha based on the correction proposed by Kristof (1963) - see also, for example, SPSS Inc (1983, pp.717-718), and coefficient alpha for the ICM was .94.

Some idea as to the satisfactory nature of the reliability coefficients obtained for the ICM can be gained from the fact that Nunnally (1967, p.226) considers that..."in the early stages of research on predictor tests or hypothesised measures of a construct, one saves time and energy by working with instruments that have only modest reliability, for which purposes reliabilities of .60 or .50 will suffice... For basic research it can be argued that increasing reliabilities beyond .80 is often wasteful. At that level correlations are attenuated very little by measurement error"...

9.   During the course of my research the ICM and the other research instrumemts employed were shown to a number of academic sociologists, social psychologists, social work academics and researchers specialising in the child care field. With a single exception, those concerned felt that the items comprising the instruments were satisfactory. However, items

16, 17, 18, 40 and 43 of the ICM were, quite reasonably, questioned by one of my associates on the grounds that they appeared to be inconsistent with other items constituting the scale (i.e. they appeared to address a dimension other than recurrent - mainly daily - social events; although my associate was unable to specify the dimension concerned). My associate also thought that item 51 may have been biased against the larger Children's Homes, because these could be expected to have offices. Hence, re-analysis of the ICM was undertaken, with the items referred to excluded from the index. Also omitted from this exercise was item 36, which as the reader will see in Appendix (c) concerns the issue of whether young people in care have access to contraception, etc., on the same basis as other youngsters living in the community. This item, the results of which indicated that the foster children enjoyed better access to contraception than their residential counterparts, was excluded because of the controversy surrounding the question of contraception for young people at the time of writing.

Re-analysis of the ICM entailed the re-computation of all the tests previously performed for the 48 item index, with the following results. Differences observed between foster homes and Children's Homes were statistically significant at the 0.0001 and 0.001 levels for the Mann-Witney and T-test, respectively. The oneway anova and Kruskal-Wallis oneway anova both produced significance levels of 0.001, and the Scheffe multiple comparison procedure confirmed that the foster homes were significantly different from both sets of Children's Homes (i.e. Authority B Homes and Authority A Homes), but that the two groups of Children's Homes did not differ significantly in statistical terms. The unbiased estimate of reliability obtained for the depleted ICM was .94 (coefficient alpha = .93). Hence, the results of the re-analysis were identical with the findings associated with the analysis of the full scale (i.e. 48 items with items with zero variance excluded).

Also entirely consistent with the results pertaining to the 48 item index were the findings obtained from the analysis of a much reduced 26 item version of the ICM. The 26 items (i.e. items 2, 3, 5, 6, 7, 14, 15, 16, 18, 20, 26, 27, 29, 31, 32, 33, 35, 36, 37, 44, 45, 48, 49, 50, 51 and 52) were selected through the application of a very strict item analysis suggested by Maxwell, 1961) and used by King *et al* (1971) when analysing their original child-management index. Items excluded were those which failed either a test of discrimination or a test of linearity (see Maxwell (1961, pp.154-157). A Mann-Witney test on the difference between the mean ranks awarded the foster homes and the Children's Homes showed this to be statistically significant at the 0.0001 level - thus confirming the results obtained for the larger 48 item index, and the unbiased estimate of reliability for the 26 item index was .96 (coefficient alpha = .96).

10. Raynes was, in fact, a member of the King et al (1971) team.
11. As is the case with respect to the ICM (and the research instrument which was used to measure the provision of physical amenities in the foster homes and Children's Homes - see the next section of this chapter), the RICI represents a stricter test of care practice than the original version of the instrument.

97

12. That CH9 was able to enter the ranks of the foster homes suggests that the RICI was not biased against producing favourable scores for the Children's Homes.

13. The results of a T-test were as follows:

	N CASES	MEAN	SD	SE
Foster homes	12	1208.3333	162.135	46.804
Children's Homes	12	839.2500	155.169	44.793

F VALUE	2 TAIL P	POOLED VARIANCE ESTIMATE		
1.09	0.887	T VALUE	DF	2-TAIL P
		5.70	22	0.000

14. Mann-Witney tests were also computed for the mean ranks achieved by the foster homes and the Children's Homes in relation to both the full RICI and individual items. The results obtained were very similar to those produced by the T-tests.

15. For example, some foster parents said that they could not afford to provide treats and outings for their foster children to the extent that Children's Homes can for residential children.

16. This was established through the use of the Scheffe multiple comparison procedure, performed together with the one-way analysis of variance test. The mean of total RICI scores for Authority B Children's Homes was 826.7500, whilst that of Authority A Children's Homes was 849.3750. As reported above and also in the main text (see Table 3:1), the mean of total RICI scores awarded to the foster homes was 1208.3333.

17. See Fuller and Stevenson (1983, p.114).

18. When calculating ratios, decimals were rounded to the nearest whole number (as were percentages). It is important to note, therefore, that the percentages associated with ratio items were obtained from previously rounded numbers. Hence, the percentages in question are not true percentages. However, the procedure was adopted in order to save time, and all cases were treated alike.

19. At the time of fieldwork the FH12 family had just received notice that they were soon to be re-accommodated in a substantially larger council house.

20. The results of a T-test were as follows:

	N CASES	MEAN	SD	SE	F VALUE	2-TAIL P
Foster homes	12	1689.5833	177.420	51.217		
					1.32	0.652
Children's Homes	12	1344.8333	154.325	44.550		

POOLED VARIANCE ESTIMATE		
T VALUE	DF	2 TAIL P
5.08	22	0.000

A Mann-Witney test performed on the mean ranks awarded foster homes and Children's Homes produced an identical significance level (exact 2-tailed probability = 0.000).

21. This was established via the application of the Scheffe multiple comparison procedure which demonstrated that whilst the foster home group was significantly different from both groups of Children's Homes, the two Children's Homes groups were not significantly different at the 0.05 level.
22. Coefficient alpha = .75.
23. The means of scores for foster homes and Children's Homes with respect to individual RIPE items were compared via T-tests. Similar results were obtained from the use of the Mann-Witney test on the mean ranks awarded foster homes and Children's Homes for individual scale items.
24. A recently published inspection of Children's Homes by the DHSS is critical of the quality of the physical environment associated with such provisions. See *Social Services Inspectorate of the Department of Health and Social Security Inspection of Community Homes September 1985*.
25. Interesting accounts of the nature and function of the architecture of residential institutions are provided by Foucault (1975) and Rothman (1971).
26. That children in residential care may experience a sense of stigma was reported in Chapter 1 in the section concerning types of provision for children in care.
27. Also see Berridge (1985) for a discussion of these issues.
28. For a theoretical discussion of the concept of control in residential institutions see Millham *et al* (1972) and Millham *et al* (1975).
29. A T-test comparing the means of total scores obtained by foster homes and Children's Homes for the ICS produced the following results:

	N CASES	MEAN	SD	SE	F VALUE	2-TAIL P
Foster homes	12	2.6667	2.103	0.607		
					1.18	0.783
Children's Homes	12	8.1667	2.290	0.661		

POOLED VARIANCE ESTIMATE

T VALUE	DF	2 TAIL P
-6.13	22	0.000

A Mann-Witney test was also calculated comparing the mean ranks obtained by foster homes and Children's Homes, the results of which were as follows:

	MEAN RANK	CASES
Foster Homes	7.00	12
Children's Homes	18.00	12
TOTAL		24

U	W	EXACT 2-TAIL P	CORRECTED FOR TIES	
6.0	84.0	0.0000	Z	2 TAIL P
			-3.8255	0.0001

Initially, a chi-square test was performed comparing the total ICS scores obtained by the foster homes and Children's Homes. This demonstrated that observed differences between foster homes and Children's Homes were significant at the 0.0001 level. However, the T-test and Mann-Witney test reported were later carried out because, although ICS data involves the nominal level of measurement, the chi-square test entailed more than one contribution per cell by each case. Hence, the T-test and Mann-Witney test were computed in order to ensure against the possibility that the chi-square test had produced a distorted significance statistic and were, therefore, intended to reflect a conservative approach to the analysis of the data concerned.

30. This was established by way of the Scheffe multiple comparison procedure which demonstrated that the mean of total ICS scores for Authority B Children's Homes did not differ significantly from that of Authority A Children's Homes. The former of the two means was 9.0000 whilst the latter was 7.7500. As noted in the main body of the text, these compared with the 2.6667 obtained for the foster home scores.

31. Again these results were gained through the use of the Scheffe test. Means of scores for each of the three subscales were as follows:

Subscale 1:
Foster homes   = .4167
Authority B Children's Homes   = 2.0000
Authority A Children's Homes   = 2.7500

Subscale 2:
Foster homes   = 1.5000
Authority B Children's Homes   = 3.5000
Authority A Children's Homes   = 3.7000

Subscale 3
Foster homes   = .7500
Authority B Children's Homes   = 2.0000
Authority A Children's Homes   = 2.7500

32. Respondents in settings accommodating adolescent girls characteristically talked about sexual matters when answering questions pertaining to the third ICS subscale. This was especially true of the Children's Home respondents. It would appear that alleged promiscuity by adolescent girls was a source of strain for the caretakers involved.

33. The results of items 6, 7 and 8 of the CIQ were also interesting. Only 2 foster homes had a clear tariff or scale of sanctions, against 7 of the Children's Homes (item 6), and in only a single Children's Home, and none of the foster homes, were sanctions fixed by rule (item 7). Except for one of the Children's Home respondents, all those interviewed reported that the rules of the establishment/household were clear and understood by children. With respect to items 6 and 7, it would appear that Millham *et al's* (1981) recommendations (i.e. regarding the need for a clear tariff of sanctions, and for sanctions to be fixed by rule rather than varied at the discretion of caretakers) have more relevance for Children's

Homes than for foster homes, because inconsistency or lack of fairness in relation to the application of sanctions is perhaps more likely to occur in the former than in the latter. This seems to follow from the fact that relatively large numbers of caretakers are employed in the Children's Homes.

4 Caretakers' roles, and behaviour and attitudes towards children

Introduction

The previous chapter compared the foster homes and Children's Homes in terms of four aspects of care practice. This chapter is exclusively concerned with the adults who were directly responsible for the daily care of the children studied - foster parents and residential staff. The opening section examines the role activities of foster parents and staff (as recorded during structured observation), and their perceptions of the roles which they perform. The second section compares the observed behaviour, both verbal and non-verbal, manifested by foster parents and staff towards children; it also reports findings concerning the relative frequencies by which foster parents and children, and their residential counterparts, initiate caretaker-child interaction. The final section of this chapter explores the attitudes of foster parents and residential staff towards the children concerned.

1. The Roles of Foster Parents and Residential Staff

Observed role activities of caretakers

In order to delineate and compare the role activities of foster parents and residential staff, two contrasting, but complementary, approaches were adopted. One involved structured observation; the other method will be reported in detail in the second part of this section. However, in addition to collecting data on caretaker role activities, the observations referred to were also used to gather information on the behaviour of caretakers towards children (i.e.

what caretakers said to, and did with children, etc.) and on the responses manifested by children. Details concerning the design and application of the observational technique used, which supplement those about to be given, are presented in Appendix (i). Accordingly, the reader is invited to refer to these when reading the first two sections of this chapter, and the opening section of Chapter 5 where findings concerning children's responses are related. It can be seen from Appendix (i) that the recording sheet used during structured observation - the *Narrative Recording Schedule* (NRS) - has several rows and columns. Each row (seven per record sheet) represents a 30-second period and recordings were made whilst observing. The 30-second interval is one that was adopted by both King *et al* (1971) and Bartak and Rutter (1975) for similar undertakings. The decision to observe and record simultaneously issued from the realisation that not to have done so would have resulted in the loss of interesting data. Trials had shown that the observer needed to be clear about what would be observed/recorded and what would be ignored; otherwise, the material collected would have lacked the detail necessary for the application of the codes used during data analysis (see Appendix (i)). Thus, I elected to observe and record only the following during each 30-second interval:

(a)   the identity of the caretaker being observed;
(b)   the location of observation;
(c)   the activity of the caretaker being observed;
(d)   whether interaction between the target caretaker and child(ren) occurred, and if so, whether interaction was initiated by the caretaker or the child(ren);
(e)   the speech used by the caretaker (i.e. what the caretaker said to the child(ren));
(f)   the tone of voice used by the caretaker when speaking to the child(ren)
(g)   the physical gestures involving bodily contact used by the caretaker in relation to the child(ren);
(h)   the bodily expressions, such as facial expression and gesture, used by the caretaker *vis a vis* the child(ren);
(i)   the child(ren)'s behaviour (i.e. general activity, affect, and language - see Chapter 5 and Appendix (i)).

The observations involved the 12 Authority A foster homes (FH1 to FH12) and the 4 Authority B Children's Homes (CH1 - CH4), in relation to which the local authorities concerned had consented to in-depth research being carried out. It was not possible to carry out observations at two of the twelve foster homes: FH10 and FH12 - in the case of FH10 because the foster placement was on the point of breakdown at the time of fieldwork, whilst the youngster (a youth aged 17 years) at FH12 spent a good deal of his time outside the foster home; therefore, to have requested his presence for the specific purpose of observing his interactions with the foster parents would have resulted in artificially contrived findings.

One hour of observation was completed at each of the remaining ten foster homes. Periods of two-and-a-half hours of observation were carried out at each of the four Authority B Children's Homes. Hence 10 hours of observation was undertaken for both the foster homes and Children's Homes. Where possible, observation commenced on the children's return from school and continued until the observation period was complete (i.e. one hour in the foster homes and two-and-a-half hours in the Children's Homes) in an attempt to observe the same functional period at each setting. In the foster homes, whenever possible, husbands and wives were observed for periods of 30 minutes each. Lone foster parents, and female foster parents whose husbands were out at work during the functional period concerned, were observed for the full hour. Given the numbers of staff employed at the four Children's Homes and the limited time at my disposal, I was unable to observe all staff. Thus, those on-duty at the times arranged for the exercise were observed. At CH1 five different staff were observed, each for a period of 30 minutes. Certain staff were observed for more than one 30 minute period at CH2, CH3 and CH4. This was because fewer numbers of staff than at CH1 were on-duty at any given time at these Homes; hence, less staff were available for observation at CH2, CH3 and CH4 than was the case at CH1. A summary of who was observed, when, and for how long is given in Appendix (i).

Where required, short breaks were taken by the observer after each 30 minute period of observation. When there was no possibility of caretaker-child interaction occurring (e.g., all the residential children in a given Children's Home were out at play, etc., whilst the member of staff being observed remained indoors; or, the foster child left the house to run an errand for the foster parent) observations were discontinued until such interaction could occur (e.g., residential children returned indoors from play, and so on).

Findings concerning the role activities of caretakers can now be reported, beginning with results obtained from the application of five coding categories

Table 4.1
Observed role activities of caretakers - King *et al* (1971) categories

	Foster Parents	Residential Staff
Domestic	28.39 (462)	5.52 (88)
Functional Child Care	2.70 (44)	3.51 (56)
Social Child Care	46.71 (760)	17.83 (284)
Administration	1.72 (28)	33.60 (535)
Supervisory	2.76 (45)	30.21 (481)
Miscellaneous	17.63 (287)	9.29 (149)
TOTALS	100.00 (1627)	100.00 (1592)

N.B.*The raw frequency counts for each activity category are given in parentheses below the percentages listed for each category* [1].

derived from King *et al* (1971): Domestic (D), Functional Child Care (CF), Social Child Care (CS), Administration (A), Supervisory (S), and Miscellaneous (M). Definitions of these categories are given in Appendix (i). Table 4.1 reveals that foster parents engaged in Social Child Care activities with significantly greater frequency than did residential staff. Foster parents also undertook Domestic activities markedly more often than residential staff. The major activity categories of staff were Administration and Supervisory. Foster parents, on the other hand, seldom carried out these forms of activity. Results associated with the role activities of residential staff appear to be consistent with the impression of staff roles conveyed by the guides to daily routines at three of the Children's Homes - particularly that of CH6 - presented towards the end of the first section of the preceding chapter. The documents concerned pertained to three Authority A Homes, while the results in Table 4.1 relate to Authority B Children's Homes. Thus, it seems likely that staff role activities at Authority A Homes were similar to those observed in relation to Authority B staff.

The findings listed in Table 4.1 are confirmed by Table 4.2, which reports results from the application of a more elaborate set of caretaker activity categories drawn from the work of Cawson (1978), namely: Domestic (D), Administration (A), Education (E), Work Training (WT), Keeping Order and General Supervision (KOGS), Protecting Society (PS), Care Planning (CP), Contact with Children's Natural Families (CCNF), Showing Concern for Children (SCC), and Social Training (ST). The Miscellaneous category was added in order to account for activities not embraced by Cawson's (1978) categories. Table 4.2 indicates that Showing Concern for Children was the activity category engaged in with greatest frequency by foster parents, followed by Domestic. By contrast, the activity categories most used when coding the activities of residential staff were Administration and Keeping Order and General Supervision. The Showing Concern for Children and Domestic categories accounted for comparatively few of the observed role activities of staff.

The relatively high frequency with which foster parents carried out domestic tasks is attributable to the fact that several female foster parents were engaged in the preparation of the evening meal for the households concerned when observed. As previously stated, where possible, observations were conducted from the children's return from school; hence, as anticipated, some female foster parents were observed cooking, etc. Domestic staff usually carried out such tasks in the Children's Homes, which explains why residential staff activities were not assigned the Domestic code - D - with the same relatively high frequency as their foster home counterparts. The comparatively heavy use that was made of the M (Miscellaneous) category when coding the observed activities of foster parents reflects the fact that both sets of coding categories were originally formulated for application in residential settings, and are therefore better suited to the analysis of staff activities than to those of foster parents; however, the use of the M category in relation to foster parent activities was not so great as to threaten the validity of the results. Most staff activities coded M involved conversations between staff members which were unrelated to their work. Conversations between foster parents unrelated to the foster children were also coded M, as was talk between foster parents and their natural children. Thus, it is not surprising that the M category was employed with greater frequency in relation to foster parent activities than for those of staff.

Table 4.2
Observed role activities of caretakers - Cawson (1978) categories

	Foster Parents	Residential Staff
Domestic	28.71 (495)	8.51 (136)
Administration	0.00 -	31.41 (502)
Education	8.64 (149)	6.88 (110)
Work Training	0.00 -	0.00 -
Keeping Order, etc	2.32 (40)	30.22 (483)
Protecting Society	0.00 -	0.00 -
Care Planning	1.62 (28)	2.37 (38)
Contact with Children's Natural Families	0.00 -	0.00 -
Showing Concern for Children	38.34 (661)	10.76 (172)
Social Training	1.16 (20)	0.05 (8)
Miscellaneous	19.19 (331)	9.32 (149)
TOTALS	100.00 (1724)	100.00 (1598)

N.B.The raw frequency count for each activity category is given in parentheses below the percentages listed for categories[2].

The total numbers of recorded caretaker role activities given in Table 4.1 and Table 4.2 differ because the Cawson (1978) categories allowed a greater number of distinctions to be made between caretaker activities than did the less numerous King *et al* (1971) categories. Thus the total numbers of recordings for categories listed in Table 4.2 exceed those of Table 4.1; although the difference associated with residential staff activities is negligible, which owes much to the fact that staff did not combine activities to the extent that foster parents did.

The essentially supervisory and administrative nature of the residential staff role by contrast with the tending character of the foster parent role is further evidenced in Table 4.3, which presents findings concerning the location of the observations undertaken. The data reveal that the living room and kitchen were the focal points of daily life in the foster homes. Conversely, the centre of staff activities was the office, where staff were observed to spend over a third of their time, irrespective of the facts that (a) children were always present in the Homes when observations were conducted and that (b) children were generally not permitted access to office areas. The sight, therefore, of youngsters congregating outside offices seeking the attention of staff was not an unfamiliar one in the Children's Homes.

Whilst some 45 per cent of observations on foster parents took place in kitchens, this should not necessarily be regarded as a reflection of the extent to which foster parents were observed engaging in the preparation of food. Although, as reported, some of the female foster parents were observed cooking, etc., others were simply sitting around the kitchen table talking and relaxing with other household members, or eating their evening meal. Equally, the frequency of observations at various locations in the Children's Homes should not be assumed to mirror staff engagement in activities normally associated with the locations concerned. For example, staff were not necessarily observed eating in dining rooms, cooking, etc., in kitchens, washing clothes, and so on, in the laundry, or carrying out administrative tasks in the office.

The location of observations data indicate that residential staff were more active than foster parents. Staff moved from one location to another relatively frequently. Foster parents, on the other hand, more or less confined their activities to the living room and the kitchen, and were consequently far easier to observe than the residential staff. Again, the difference reflects the primarily supervisory nature of the staff role.

Residential staff were often observed to position themselves at locations which facilitated the supervision of children. Certain locations appeared strategic to this end, in the sense that they made possible the surveillance of the largest number of children at any given moment. Staff at CH1, for example, would typically seat themselves on, or stand beside, a radiator just inside the door of the large living room (or lounge, as it was referred to) where the majority of children were usually to be found. Or, they would sit or stand in the hallway. This enabled them to monitor the movement of children between all the downstairs rooms and also informed them whether children went upstairs. Positioning themselves on the upstairs landing allowed staff to supervise children's baths and showers and/or monitor the activities of children in any of the bedrooms.

The open-plan design of the downstairs living area at CH4, mentioned in the previous chapter, made the surveillance of children a particularly simple matter. A seat in virtually any position allowed individual staff to observe large numbers of children. On the children's return from school, a member of staff would position him/herself in one of the living areas and coordinate the movement of children as they entered the building through the laundry door

107

(children at CH4 and, indeed, at a number of the other Children's Homes visited were not permitted to enter the building via the front door). As the

Table 4.3
Location of observations

	Foster Parents	Residential Staff
Living Room (or Lounge)	53.09 (738)	13.72 (200)
Dining Room (separate)	0.00 -	15.78 (230)
Kitchen	45.32 (630)	10.29 (150)
Office	0.00 -	36.99 (539)
Halls and Passageways (downstairs)	0.57 (8)	5.35 (78)
Laundry (separate)	0.00 -	1.02 (15)
Garden	0.00 -	4.94 (72)
Caretaker Toilet (only)	0.00 -	1.23 (18)
Children's Toilet	0.00 -	0.68 (10)
Landing/Passageways (upstairs)	0.21 (3)	4.46 (65)
Child(ren)'s Bedroom(s)	0.00 -	2.60 (38)
Recreation/Games Room	0.00 -	2.19 (32)
Other Locations	0.79 (11)	0.67 (10)
TOTALS	100.00 (1390)	100.00 (1457)

N.B. *The raw frequency count for each location is given in parentheses below the percentages listed for locations* [3].

children arrived at intervals, the staff member checked that youngsters removed their shoes, put on their slippers and collected any freshly washed clothes from their pigeon holes in the laundry. Children were then instructed to go to their bedrooms and change out of their school clothes, after which they would clean their school shoes before returning to the lounge area.

By contrast with staff, many foster parents remained seated during much of the time that they were being observed and seldom appeared to engage in purely supervisory activities. Moreover, foster children's return from school was a comparatively relaxed affair, and foster parents were able to spend time talking at some length with children about the affairs of the day. Conversely, residential children's return from school seemed to signal "action stations" for staff. In addition to the relatively high frequency of movement by both staff and children, as the sorts of routines just described in relation to CH4 were operationalised, the group climates in the Children's Homes were noticeably more tense than was the case in the foster homes. Staff appeared to have less time to give to discussing the day's events with individual children.

The summary of who was observed, when, and for how long presented in Appendix (i) shows that it was not possible to commence observations from the children's return from school at CH1 and CH3 (although I was able to carry out a portion of the observations at both homes around tea-time - the period observed at the foster homes and the other two Children's Homes). This was because children at both Homes had school holidays on the days when observations were undertaken. Consequently, observations had to be conducted at times when the children concerned were present in the Homes.

However, if observations not carried out after school hours in CH1 and CH3 are excluded from analysis, the effect on the Domestic (D), Functional Child Care (CF), Social Child Care (CS) and Miscellaneous (M) categories derived from King et al (1971) is negligible, and involves a very slight increase in the percentages of total observed staff activities for each category (i.e. little more than 1 percentage point for any of the categories). The Supervisory (S) category increases somewhat from 30.21 per cent to 34.37 per cent of total recorded staff activities. However, the Administration (A) category decreases from 33.60 per cent of total recorded staff activities to 25.97 per cent; hence, it falls from first to second place in terms of rankings for percentage shares of total recordings obtained by each activity category. But the percentage share of the A category still far outstrips those of the D, CF, CS and M categories.

A similar pattern emerges when the observations not undertaken after school hours at CH1 and CH3 are removed from the Cawson (1978) activity categories. Keeping Order and General Supervision (KOGS) increases from 30.22 per cent of total recordings to 34.50 per cent, with Administration (A) slipping from 31.41 per cent of total observed staff activities to 23.83 per cent. Four of the remaining categories - Domestic (D), Education (E), Social Training (ST) and Miscellaneous (M) - increase their percentage share slightly (i.e. by no more than 2 percentage points). Three categories, Work Training (WT), Protecting Society (PS) and Contact with Children's Natural Families (CCNF), obviously show no change since there were zero recordings for these categories. However, the percentage shares of the Care Planning (CP) and Showing Concern for Children (SCC) categories actually decline; albeit by less than one percentage point in both cases.

Thus although removing observations not undertaken outside school hours at CH1 and CH3 reduces the percentage share of the administrative categories and increases the share of the supervisory categories, other categories remain unaffected. Moreover, the share of the administrative categories is still high. This assertion is supported by data concerning the location of observations. When observations not carried out after school hours at CH1 and CH3 are excluded from analysis, the effect on the percentage shares of the various locations involved is very small and, except for the Office category, entails changes - mainly increases in percentage shares - of no more than 2 percentage points. The percentage share of the Office category diminishes from 36.99 per cent to 30.04 per cent, which does not appear to be a significant change considering that the location with the second largest percentage share - the Dining Room category - accounts for only 18.72 per cent of total recordings.

Caretaker perceptions of their roles

In order to gain further insights about the nature of caretaker roles, I employed a role definition questionnaire devised by Cawson (1978) for use in her study of residential staff in CHE's. The application of the categories comprising the questionnaire for analysing NRS data on caretaker activities was reported in the first part of this section. Cawson's (1978) role definition questionnaire helped constitute the ST/FPIQ - referred to in Chapter 2 (see Appendix (g)). The reader may recall that the application of the ST/FPIQ involved interviews with 33 foster parents (all save three of whom cared for children from Authority A) and 40 staff (i.e. from the four Authority B Children's Homes). Although the ST/FPIQ collected a large amount of detailed material on caretaker roles, the limits of space mean that I must be selective in discussing associated results.

Appendix (g) reveals that individual caretakers were asked to rank 10 activity categories (i.e. the categories derived from Cawson (1978), excluding the Miscellaneous (M) category) in the order of importance which these had for their role as it actually was. Senior residential staff were asked to rank the categories in the order of priority which they felt their establishment gave to them, in recognition of the fact that their roles sometimes entailed less direct contact with children and, more duties of an admininstrative nature, than those of junior staff. This involved three senior staff at CH1, one at CH2, one at CH3 and three at CH4. Caretakers were then asked to re-rank the categories in terms of the order of importance which they thought they ought to have. Hence, respondents were first asked to state their perceptions of their actual roles and then asked to specify their conceptions of what their roles would ideally entail. Thus the data collected were of a different order to data gathered by the NRS in that they concerned caretaker perceptions of their roles; perceptions, moreover, about the relative import of each of the 10 role aspects in question. This does not neccesarily mean that foster parents and staff took into account the relative frequency with which they engaged in the activities embraced by each category - despite being urged to do so when interviewed.

The Kendall Coefficient of Concordance was employed for the analysis of caretaker perceptions of both their *actual* and *ideal* roles [4]. Table 4.4 compares the mean ranks assigned to each variable or role aspect by foster parents and residential staff with respect to their actual roles [5].

Table 4.4
Caretaker perceptions of their actual roles

MEAN RANKS

	Foster Parents	Residential Staff
Domestic	4.55	6.22
Administration	7.64	6.15
Education	4.70	6.42
Work Training	7.00	7.77
Keeping Order and General Supervision	2.58	2.25
Protecting Society	6.58	7.70
Care Planning	8.06	4.27
Contact with Children's Natural Families	6.94	6.90
Showing Concern for Children	2.61	2.97
Social Training	4.36	4.32

It is clear from Table 4.4 that both groups assigned the Keeping Order, etc. and Showing Concern for Children categories first and second highest ranks, respectively. But in order to gain a better idea of the import of differences between the mean ranks awarded to each role aspect by the two groups of caretakers, Mann-Witney tests were performed (i.e. two tailed tests). These tests demonstrated that differences between the mean ranks assigned by each group were not statistically significant at the 0.05 level or less in relation to the following categories: Keeping Order, etc., Protecting Society, Contact with Children's Natural Families, Showing Concern for Children and Social Training. Differences for the remaining categories were, however, statistically significant [6]. Before discussing caretakers' ideal conceptions of what their roles ought to entail, I want to comment very briefly on these findings and relate them to the NRS data previously reported.

Results concerning the Domestic category are consistent with NRS data in that both sets of findings show that foster parents devote more time than staff to the tasks involved. Table 4.4 and the relevant Mann-Witney test also confirm that the roles of staff entail more administrative duties than those of foster parents - though it would appear that staff grossly underestimate the degree to which they actually engage in such activities.

Table 4.4 and Mann-Witney data regarding the Education and Work Training categories are interesting. It seems that staff may devote less attention to residential children's education than foster parents give to that of foster children [7]. The same might be said about the Work Training category. But caution must be exercised here because the mean ranks presented in Table 4.4 are very similar.

Of perhaps even greater interest is the Table 4.4 and Mann-Witney data concerning the categories Keeping Order, etc. and Protecting Society. The mean ranks assigned to the Keeping Order, etc. category by foster parents and staff are very similar. The staff mean rank is consistent with NRS findings showing that the control and supervision of children is central to the staff role. However, the foster parent mean rank suggests that foster parents vastly overestimate the degree to which they engage in purely supervisory activities. Equally surprising is the fact that the foster parents awarded a higher mean rank to the Protecting Society category than staff did; a finding which contradicts my impressions of foster parent and staff roles (i.e. impressions gained indepedently of NRS observations).

The mean ranks awarded to the Care Planning category, however, do conform well to my impressions. Residential staff awarded this category a far higher mean rank than foster parents. This may reflect the fact that the duration of many residential children's placements are relatively short, and staff are expected to play a part in their admission and discharge (which includes writing reports and attending planning meetings or reviews on children); and, also, the drive to improve the professional standing of residential staff relative to that of field social workers, which recent years have witnessed. Until fairly recently, writing reports on children and attending reviews were the preserve of field social workers and senior residential staff. Self-interest on the part of residential staff may have contributed to this movement as well as concern about standards of child care. A similar point could be made about the Administrative category with respect to staff, for paper work is one means by which professional self- conceptions may be sustained; especially, when the objective grounds for such conceptions are thin - see, for example, Chapter 2 where the lack of professional training on the part of the great majority of staff is noted.

No NRS observations involving caretakers in the Contact with Children's Natural Families aspect of their roles were made. However, the Table 4.4 results concerning this category appear to support the tentative suggestion of the previous chapter that residential placements may not necessarily be more conducive to the maintenance of links between children and their natural parents than foster placements. Certainly the mean ranks awarded by the two groups for the category in question are very similar.

Both groups of caretakers assigned Showing Concern for Children second highest mean rank. However, although foster parents were observed to engage in this aspect of their role with great frequency, residential staff did not. Also requiring explanation is the fact that foster parents placed the category concerned below Keeping Order, etc. It could be argued that this was because the latter is a fundamental aspect of child care. This is unquestionable, but it does not account for the marked incongruence between NRS data and foster parents' perceptions of their roles. Little explanation, however, is required with respect to the Social Training category which both groups assigned a very similar, and reasonably high, rank. This finding can perhaps be understood simply in terms of an integral component of child care.

So much for caretakers' perceptions of their actual roles. Table 4.5 displays the results from the Kendall Coefficient of Concordance test computed with respect to caretaker views about the order of importance which the ten role aspects or categories would ideally have [8]. By contrast with Table 4.4 both groups assigned the highest mean rank to Showing Concern for Children, and would reduce the degree of emphasis placed on Keeping Order, etc., Protecting Society and Social Training. Both groups would also attach less import to the Domestic and Administration categories, but give greater priority to Education, Work Training, Care Planning and Contact with Children's Natural Families. The mean ranks awarded by the two groups for each category are, with important exceptions, perhaps not too dissimilar. The major differences concern the Domestic and Care Planning categories. Residential staff seem to regard the domestic aspects of their role as relatively unimportant, but would like to increase the emphasis given to Care Planning, which can be explained in terms of my previous comments in relation to the Care Planning category when discussing caretakers' perceptions of their actual roles. Also consistent with earlier remarks is the very low rank given to Protecting Society by residential staff.

Table 4.5
Caretaker perceptions of their ideal roles

MEAN RANKS

	Foster Parents	Residential Staff
Domestic	5.10	8.00
Administration	8.13	7.94
Education	4.68	5.60
Work Training	6.74	6.30
Keeping Order and General Supervision	4.23	3.97
Protecting Society	7.35	8.70
Care Planning	7.06	3.31
Contact with Children's Natural Families	5.54	4.32
Showing Concern for Children	1.87	1.92
Social Training	4.39	4.92

However, interesting though such matters may be, they must take second place to the main question raised by the data presented in Tables 4.4 and 4.5, which is: to what extent do caretaker perceptions of their *actual* roles correspond to their conceptions of their *ideal* roles?

Accordingly, Kendall's tau was computed for each individual case, comparing rankings for *actual* roles with those for *ideal* roles. The rank correlation method provides a score on a scale from +1 to -1. A higher level of agreement or congruence between actual and ideal roles results in a score closer to +1. Conversely, the stronger the incongruence between actual and ideal roles, the closer to -1 the score obtained. A score of 0 indicates no relationship between the two sets of rankings. A Mann-Witney test was subsequently performed in order to compare the coefficients obtained for the foster parents and residential staff. The foster parents were found to have a mean rank of 41.12, whilst that obtained for staff was 33.60. Hence, the overall degree of congruence between the actual and ideal roles of foster parents was greater than that for the actual and ideal roles of staff. The difference concerned just failed to achieve statistical significance at the 0.05 level, but was significant at the less conservative 0.10 level [9].

Evidence suggesting that, overall, foster parents derived greater satisfaction from their roles than staff was provided by data collected via item 12 of the ST/FPIQ - see Appendix (g). This revealed that 81.8 per cent of foster parents, compared with 64.9 per cent of staff, felt that their roles were, on the whole, as they should be. Some 35.1 per cent of staff, against 18.2 per cent of foster parents, reported that their roles were not how they ought to be. Once again, however, the differences referred to were not significant at the 0.05 level. But they did achieve statistical significance at the less strict 0.10 level [10].

The fact that foster parents enjoyed considerably more autonomy than residential staff may help to explain why their roles more closely corresponded to their ideas about what they ought to be doing. In response to item 14 of the ST/FPIQ, 72.7 per cent of foster parents, compared with only 24.3 per cent of staff, reported that they were afforded a very free hand (i.e. a high degree of autonomy) in the way they carried out their roles. An estimated 62.2 per cent of staff and 24.2 per cent of foster parents said that they were given a fairly or moderately free hand. Last, 13.5 per cent of staff, against 3.0 per cent (N=1) of foster parents claimed that they were permitted little autonomy [11]. It should be mentioned that those staff who reported that they were given a very free hand in the way that they performed their roles were mainly senior staff.

However, if foster parents seem to enjoy more autonomy than staff, they appear correspondingly more isolated in carrying out their roles. The main source of support for most foster parents is their spouse with whom they, of course, have daily contact. Residential staff, on the other hand, receive support and have daily contact with other staff at their establishments (including senior and junior colleagues and colleagues of the same status - depending on the grade of the individual staff member concerned).

Staff also seemed to have more frequent contact with children's social workers than did foster parents. Over half (53.9 per cent) of the staff interviewed reported that they had at least weekly contact with children's social workers, compared with less than 10 per cent of foster parents. However the majority of staff - 70.3 per cent - did not describe their field work colleagues as helpful and there seemed to be a degree of rivalry between the two groups of workers. Foster parents, on the other hand, did not appear to regard field social workers as rivals and over half (54.5 per cent) reported that social workers were helpful. Indeed, some 21.2 per cent of foster parents, against only 2.7 per cent of staff described social workers as very helpful. It is also worth pointing out that whilst staff appeared to have more frequent contact with children's social workers than foster parents, residential children appeared to see their social workers less often than did the foster children (see RICI findings reported in Chapter 3). This seeming contradiction may be explained by the possibility that at any given time staff had frequent contact with only some of the residential children's social workers and/or the possiblity that more contacts involving staff and social workers occurred via telephone than was the case between foster parents and social workers.

Foster parent contacts with other potential sources of support also seemed less frequent than those of staff. An estimated 65 per cent of staff, compared with as few as 21.3 per cent of foster parents, related that they discussed children's problems, progress, etc. with professionals other than social workers (e.g., G.P.'s, School teachers) about once a month. Contact between staff and children's natural parents was also more frequent than was the case for foster parents and natural parents of foster children. Some 37.5 per cent of staff, compared with only 12.1 per cent of foster parents reported at least weekly contact with children's natural parents. Given that far fewer foster than residential children were able to have contact with their natural parents this finding was not unexpected. Moreover, it may be that, at any given time, staff only had contact with some of the residential children's natural parents.

In addition to the sorts of contacts mentioned, staff attended regular meetings with colleagues at their establishments. Staff meetings were held on a weekly basis at CH1, CH2 and CH4 and fortnightly at CH3. Something approaching half - 45.5 per cent - of foster parents from Authority A attended Foster Parent Support Group meetings run by the Authority's Fostering Officers on a monthly basis. A further 42.4 per cent of Authority A foster parents attended such meetings, occasionally. Staff had also been provided with written job descriptions, and had usually received written rules about their work. Few foster parents reported having been given written job descriptions or rules about their roles.

But differences other than levels of support are indicated here with respect to foster parent and staff roles. Clearly, the roles of staff were subject to greater differentiation and formalisation than those of foster parents, reflecting the division of labour within Children's Homes and, the fact that Children's Homes are part of a larger formal organisation - the local authority Social Services Department (SSD). Where foster parent roles were differentiated, this was often in accordance with so-called traditional male and female roles. Female foster parents were mainly responsible for undertaking domestic chores and functional child care, whilst male foster parents were usually regarded as the major breadwinners; a division of labour within the households concerned which was unrelated to the goals of the SSD (although it should be said that certain female staff complained that they were expected to perform more domestic and functional child care duties than their male counterparts).

This is not to suggest that foster parents were completely autonomous from the SSD. Taking on their roles had meant a significant (and usually unexpected) intrusion on the privacy of foster parents' family lives by the SSD (i.e. via associated monitoring/support services such as fostering officers and social workers). Foster parents appeared to be partly employees of the SSD and partly clients. As such, they were simultaneously subject to control by superiors in the organisation and, the surveillance and scrutiny normally reserved for clients. A few of the male foster parents resented the encroachment into their family life by the agencies involved, which had brought a diminution in their power within the household. This may have been partly because foster parents did not enjoy full parental rights *vis a vis* foster children. But also, perhaps, because the intrusion by social work agencies seemed to have reduced the control which foster parents had, prior to receiving the foster children, exercised over their family lives.

Whilst in one sense it can, as I have indicated, be argued that formal sources of support (i.e. from the SSD) involve control as well as help, it was also the case that certain caretakers definitely required support in coping with children. Approximately the same proportions of respondents from both groups (48.5 per cent of foster parents and 51.3 per cent of staff) reported that they had regular supervision sessions with a superior, etc. - in the case of foster parents, fostering officers - which enabled them to discuss their work; and, 82.1 per cent of staff, against 72.7 per cent of foster parents, felt the supervision they received was adequate.

The areas of strain associated with foster parent and staff roles seem to correspond well to what was said earlier about the role activities of caretakers. Nearly half - 47.5 per cent - of the staff, compared with less than a quarter - 24.2 per cent - of the foster parents, selected the Keeping Order and General Supervision category as the aspect of their role which involved most strain. The same proportion of foster parents chose the Showing Concern for Children category, against 10 per cent of staff. Moreover, although 18.2 per cent of foster parents viewed the Domestic category as the major source of strain only 2.5 per cent of staff did. None of the foster parents chose the Administration category but 10 per cent of staff saw this as the major source of strain associated with their roles - and, 15.8 per cent of staff said Administration was the second most stressful aspect of their role. Similarly, although 10 per cent of staff selected the Care Planning category (and 23.7 per cent of staff chose this option as the second biggest area of strain), only 3 per cent of foster parents selected this option.

The above findings appear to lend yet more support to the point that the staff role is characterised by supervisory activities in relation to children and by the performance of administrative type activities (including both the Administration and Care Planning categories here). Also further reinforced is the claim that the foster parent role is distinguished from the staff role by the emphasis which the former gives to social child care and (albeit to a much lesser degree, and with particular reference to female foster parents) to domestic activities. It may also be noted that 15.2 per cent of foster parents compared with as few as 2.5 per cent of staff selected the Social Training category as the source of most strain, and 25 per cent of foster parents selected the category concerned as the second major area of strain.

2. Caretaker Behaviour Toward Children Observed

The coding categories employed in the analysis of caretaker behaviour toward children are presented in Appendix (i). Categories used for analysing the verbal behaviour of caretakers towards children fall under two headings: (a) Type of Speech; and, (b) Tone of Voice. The categories comprising the former were as follows: Informative Speech Value Neutral (ISVN), Informative Speech Approving (ISA), Informative Speech Disapproving (ISD), Controlling Speech (CS), Perfunctory Comment (PC), and Other Talk (OT). These categories were based on Raynes *et al's* (1979) *Informative Speech Index*, which I elaborated by distinguishing three types of informative speech; essentially, informative speech with either a positive, negative or neutral value content. The remaining categories were taken directly from the authors.

Raynes *et al* (1979) applied their index in a study, referred to in the previous chapter, of 3 residential facilities for mentally retarded persons in the USA. They argue that some types of interaction are likely to promote learning, and cite the work of Tizard (1972) which indicates that what Raynes *et al* (1979) term informative speech may foster development in the language comprehension and expression of persons in residential settings. Tizard (1972), for example, found that children's verbal skills were greater in residential nurseries where staff used more informative language. The author was able to assess the verbal skills of the children concerned by careful testing. Raynes *et al* (1979) were not able to do this with respect to the residents they studied, but nontheless did collect evidence suggesting that in the context in which they carried out their research informative speech also promotes language development. Raynes *et al* (1979) acknowledge that only carefully designed longitudinal studies of a kind they were unable to undertake can properly assess the effects of varying care practices on residents' development. However, they are convinced that their claims would be supported by the outcome of such a study.

Table 4.6 compares the results obtained in relation to the type of speech used by caretakers for the foster homes and Children's Homes where the NRS was applied (see previous section). It can be seen that the total number of recordings for residential staff exceed those for foster parents. This is because more children were accommodated in the Children's Homes than was the case at the foster homes, which meant that staff could interact with significantly greater numbers of individual children than foster parents. It should also be mentioned that interactions between foster parents and their natural children were excluded from analysis. Table 4.6 reveals that foster parents used proportionately more informative speech than residential staff. Moreover, the former utilised proportionately more informative speech of both an approving and value neutral type than the latter. Residential staff employed proportionately more informative speech of a disapproving nature than foster parents and also made greater use of controlling speech and perfunctory comment. With the exception of the last category referred to, it is evident that important differences were found between the type of speech used by foster parents, on the one hand, and residential staff, on the other.

The data presented in Table 4.6 appear to be consistent with results reported in the previous section concerning the nature of caretaker role activities. For example, the comparatively heavy use of controlling speech by staff and, the finding that staff employed considerably more informative speech of a disapproving nature, correspond well with the assertion that the staff role in relation to children is distinguished by activities of a purely supervisory nature. Equally, the proportionately greater use made by foster parents of informative speech - particularly informative speech of an approving kind - seems to bolster the view that the foster parent role is oriented towards social child care activities. The characterisation of the foster parent role as one that is essentially child-oriented is also consistent with the results reported in the previous chapter.

Table 4.6
Type of speech used by caretakers towards children

	Foster Parents	Residential Staff
Informative Speech Approving	22.82 (97)	8.86 (67)
Informative Speech Value Neutral	65.17 (277)	39.81 (301)
Informative Speech Disapproving	0.47 (2)	14.41 (109)
Controlling Speech	4.00 (17)	24.07 (182)
Perfunctory Comment	6.82 (29)	11.37 (86)
Other Talk	0.70 (3)	1.45 (11)
TOTALS	100.00 (425)	100.00 (756)

N.B. Raw frequency counts for each category are given in parentheses below the percentages listed for categories [12].

Table 4.7 compares the tone of voice used by foster parents and staff when speaking to children, and these results also appear consistent with previously reported findings about care practice. The tone of voice categories used were those adopted by Bartak and Rutter (1975) - Warm (TOVW), Neutral (TOVN) and Critical (TOVC) [13]. The majority of recordings for tone of voice used by

Table 4.7
Tone of voice used by caretakers towards children

	Warm	Neutral	Critical	TOTALS
Foster Parents	63.46 (231)	34.34 (125)	2.19 (8)	100.00 (364)
Residential staff	29.07 (166)	58.49 (334)	12.43 (71)	100.00 (571)

N.B. The raw frequency counts for each category are given in paretheses below the percentages for each category [14].

foster parents involved a warm tone, and the degree to which foster parents employed this tone far surpassed the extent to which residential staff made use of it. By contrast, residential staff made most use of a neutral tone of voice; they also used a critical tone of voice with proportionately greater frequency than foster parents. Thus, as was the case in relation to the type of speech used by caretakers, the differences observed between the tone of voice used by foster parents and staff are very marked.

The coding categories employed for analysing the non-verbal behaviour manifested by caretakers *vis a vis* children also owed much to earlier work by Bartak and Rutter (1975). Use was made of Bartak and Rutter's (1975) distinction between physical gestures involving bodily contact, on the one hand, and bodily expressions such as facial expression and gesture, on the other. I sub-divided the former into the following three categories: Approving Physical Gestures (APG), Disapproving Physical Gestures (DPG), and Value Neutral Physical Gestures (VNPG). Likewise, bodily expressions were also separated into three categories: Approving Bodily Expressions (ABE), Disapproving Bodily Expressions (DBE), and Value Neutral Bodily Expressions (VNBE).

Table 4.8
Bodily expressions used by caretakers towards children

	Approving	Value Neutral	Disapproving	TOTALS
Foster parents	84.14	13.41	2.43	100.00
	(138)	(22)	(4)	(164)
Residential staff	45.42	36.99	17.58	100.00
	(124)	(101)	(48)	(273)

N.B. The raw frequency counts for categories are given in parentheses below the percentages for categories [15].

Table 4.8 displays the results obtained with respect to the bodily expressions used by foster parents and residential staff. An overwhelming number of the bodily expressions used by foster parents were approving in nature (smiles accounted for much of this). Although something approaching half of the bodily expressions manifested by staff were also approving in kind, the proportion involved is very much smaller than that observed for foster parents. Moreover, the Disapproving Bodily Expressions code accounted for a far greater share of the bodily expressions of staff than of foster parents. It seems reasonable to conclude, therefore, that the data on bodily expressions conforms well with the pattern of research findings previously related.

However, as the reader can discern from Table 4.9, data regarding physical gestures involving bodily contact appear discrepant with results so far reported in that the proportion of approving physical gestures involving bodily contact with children for the staff group easily exceeds the figure for foster parents. But, 21 of the 34 APG's recorded for staff were manifested by staff at CH3 [16]. Of these, 10 APG's were recorded whilst observing "rough play" between a male member of staff and boy at CH3. A further 9 APG's were manifested by a female member of staff when comforting a distressed adolescent girl. The remaining APG'S recorded for staff mainly involved male staff at the other

Children's Homes engaging in rough play with youngsters. Interestingly, a fair amount of rough play was observed between certain male staff and children in the four Authority B Children's Homes during the course of fieldwork. This was typically initiated by the staff, brief in duration, and often set within a context of their characteristically fleeting interactions with relatively large numbers of individual children. Rough play seemed to be an important means by which some male staff expressed affection towards children.

Table 4.9
Physical gestures by caretakers involving bodily contact with children

	Approving	Value Neutral	Disapproving	TOTALS
Foster parents	21.42	78.57	-	100.00
	(6)	(22)	(0)	(28)
Residential staff	58.62	29.31	12.06	100.00
	(34)	(17)	(7)	(58)

N.B. The raw frequency counts for categories are given in paretheses below the percentages for categories.

Over three-quarters of the physical contacts observed in relation to foster parents were assigned the value neutral code. By contrast, just under a third of staff physical gestures towards children were accounted for by the VNPG code. Yet no physical gestures recorded for foster parents were disapproving in character, whilst 12.06 per cent of such contacts involving staff were. However, it is important to emphasise that none of these entailed the physical chastisement of youngsters by staff, but rather actions such as restraining children or pulling them away by the hand. All but one of the instances concerned were observed at CH4, and in every case they involved staff attempts to control truculent younger children (i.e. children under 10 years of age) [17].

I commented above that interactions between staff and residential children were characteristically fleeting in duration. Interaction between caretakers and children was assumed to be continuous when, despite breaks in speech, children and caretakers were clearly engaged in a joint activity (e.g., washing dishes, playing a game, or caretakers helping children with homework from school, etc.); and, when caretakers and children remained in close proximity whilst sharing an activity (for example, children and caretakers sitting down to watch T.V. together), but where conversation was intermittent only. Far more of these types of situation were observed for foster parents and foster children than for staff and residential children. Further, interactions involving foster parents and children were considerably longer in duration than those between their residential counterparts. These last two points can be discerned from the data on caretaker activities showing that foster parents engaged in social child care with considerably greater frequency than staff. They are also supported by data presented in Table 4.10 which reveals that, regardless of the fact that observations were conducted for the same number of hours in the foster homes and Children's Homes, residential staff participated in significantly more interactions with children than foster parents. This does not, however, mean that foster parents were observed to spend less time with children than staff did (the total numbers of responses for caretakers' verbal and non-verbal behaviour, which are reasonably similar for both groups of caretakers, rules out this possibility). On the contrary, it appears to suggest that individual foster children enjoyed much more uninterrupted adult attention than residential children, and that individual residential children shared the attention of their

Table 4.10
Initiation of interaction

	Children	Caretakers	TOTALS
Foster homes	45.12	54.87	100.00
	(37)	(45)	(82)
Children's Homes	26.89	73.10	100.00
	(103)	(280)	(383)

N.B. Raw frequency counts are given in parentheses below the percentages listed for each cell [18].

caretakers with relatively large numbers of other youngsters.

Table 4.10 also, of course, shows that nearly three-quarters of observed interactions between staff and residential children were initiated by staff. Conversely, the proportion of interactions initiated by foster parents, on the one hand, and foster children, on the other, were more or less even. This, along with all that has been said already, may reflect a familiarity and reciprocity between foster parents and children that did not exist between residential children and their caretakers. Significantly, perhaps, interactions initiated by residential children often involved children seeking permission from staff before engaging in an activity; or, children requesting information about various matters ranging from issues associated with their general situation (i.e. children in care) - for example, matters pertaining to a forthcoming case conference or arrangements regarding children's weekend leave home - to everyday matters such as the time of a meal or the nature of a group activity organised by staff (e.g., a visit to the local swimming baths); or, children requesting access to things. The prime examples here were things that were kept locked away in the office such as pocket money or cigarettes. A distinguishing characteristic of life at CH1 was the constant requests by youngsters for ... "five minutes"... This was the codename which children used when they wanted cigarettes from the office. These were smoked at the back of the house, out of sight of visitors. The term "five minutes" was coined by staff who were apprehensive about the possibility of censure should the fact that older youngsters were permitted to smoke become known to some unsympathetic but influential member of the public.

3. Caretaker Attitudes Toward Children

In the preceding section of this chapter I compared the behaviour manifested by staff and foster parents towards children. However, little explicit has so far been said about caretaker perceptions of, or attitudes toward, children. Heal *et al* (1973, p.223) assert that ..."behaviour is linked with perceptions in a peculiarly intimate way. A gesture may be neutral in itself, but we react to it according to whether we see it as hostile or friendly. Thus all actions are related to the actor's definition of the situation "... Heal *et al* (1973) would, therefore, argue that we can only begin to understand the variation observed in the behaviour of caretakers towards children if we can relate this to caretakers' perceptions of children. How then do foster parent perceptions of the foster children compare with staff perceptions of the residential children? In an attempt to answer this question use was made of an attitude scale devised by Cawson and Perry (1977) for measuring staff attitudes to youngsters in CHE's. Ideas for the scale were drawn, in part, from previous research in related fields, and also from the Home Office Advisory Council on Child Care publication, *Care and Treatment in a Planned Environment* (Home Office, 1970).

Cawson and Perry (1977) claim that the scale measures an underlying dimension which they call *traditionalism*, because they believe it reflects the extent to which adults accept ..."traditional values of orderly behaviour, outward expression of respect and firm discipline".... The scale comprises six subscales, three of which were intended to measure staff attitudes towards the control of children and three which attempted to assess staff perceptions of their relationships with children. The subscales (and their definitions) formulated to address the former were: Traditional Control - "the emphasis placed on maintaining a high level of control by traditional methods such as restrictions on freedom and contact with relatives, constant supervision and similar custodial techniques"; Work - "the belief that delinquents can be redeemed by being made to work hard"; Passivity -"the wish to avoid any open confrontation or emotional outbursts, resulting in a *laissez-faire* approach to children". The three subscales designed to measure staff attitudes towards their relationships with children were the following: Staff Status - "the belief that staff should maintain a front of adult superiority to children, rather than accepting a relationship of equality with them"; Distance - "a perception of the children as a hostile and abnormal group whose approaches to staff should be regarded with suspicion"; and, Suppression of Problems - "a wish to avoid a counselling relationship, and unwillingness to encourage discussion of personal problems".

In preparing the scale for use in both foster homes and Children's Homes the Work subscale was discarded because it was designed for use in residential settings - CHE'S - where a high proportion of the youngsters accommodated had committed offences. Further, remaining items were rephrased so that they would have meaning for foster parents as well as for residential staff. In this respect, care was taken to obtain equivalence without distorting the meaning of items. I named the modified version of the scale the *Staff/Foster Parent Attitude Scale* (ST/FPAS) - see Appendix (h) - in order to distinguish it from the original index.

The ST/FPAS was applied during the same interviews at which the ST/FPIQ was used and involved the 73 caretakers referred to in Chapter 2. In accordance with the scoring procedure devised by Cawson and Perry (1977), caretakers were simply asked to state their agreement or disagreement with the items in the scale along a six-point continuum from *strongly disagree* (1) to *strongly agree* (6). There was no mid-point score (which would have been 3.5); hence respondents were not allowed to give non-committal answers.

When analysing the data, I reversed the scoring procedure for item 25. Thus, the strongly disagree answer was awarded a score of 6 and the strongly agree

122

response a score of 1, and so on. The reader will see from Appendix (h) that this made the results for item 25 consistent with that of other items forming the Caretaker Status subscale. That the scoring procedure for item 25 was incongruent with that of the remaining Caretaker Status items during the interviews was intended to ensure that respondents would consider statements with care before giving their answers. It also permitted me to check that subjects were not simply agreeing with items because they may have felt that this was expected. Here, it should be added that I did emphasise at the outset of each interview that the statements did not reflect the opinions of the researcher, but rather were intended to ascertain the views of caretakers on the matters concerned.

Reliability coefficients were computed for the five subscales and for the total scale. Those obtained with respect to the former are given in Table 4.11. The

Table 4.11
Reliability coefficients for ST/FPAS sub scales

	Unbiased Estimate	Coefficient Alpha
Traditional Control	.71	.70
Passivity	.71	.70
Caretaker Status	.79	.78
Distance	.85	.84
Suppression of Problems	.53	.51

reliability coefficient computed for the full scale was: unbiased estimate of reliability = .90 (Coefficient Alpha = .89). Thus, the results of the exercise concerned were very satisfactory. None of the 44 individual items comprising the full scale were shown to have zero variance.

The scores of foster parents were then compared with those of residential staff for each of the five subscales, and for the total scale, using the Mann-Witney test. The mean ranks associated with foster parent scores exceeded those for residential staff in relation to the Traditional Control, Passivity, Distance and Suppression of Problems subscales. But the pattern was reversed for the Caretaker Status subscale (i.e. the mean rank of staff was greater than that of foster parents). However, the difference between the two groups for the latter subscale was very small and far from being statistically significant at the 0.05 level or less. Yet this was not the case for the other four subscales. Differences between foster parent and staff scores were statistically significant at the .001 level for the Traditional Control and Passivity subscales, and at the 0.05 level for the Distance and Suppression of problems subscales [19].

The mean rank pertaining to foster parent scores with respect to the full scale was also greater than that associated with the scores of residential staff and the difference between the two groups of caretakers proved to be statistically significant at the 0.01 level [20]. If we take Cawson and Perry's (1977) claim that the scale measures the extent to which caretakers accept traditional values of orderly behaviour, outward expression of respect and firm discipline, seriously, then it is obvious that these findings are grossly inconsistent with the findings reported in the previous chapter and those related in the preceding sections of this chapter. Moreover, if we except Heal et al's (1973) assertions about the relationship between behaviour and perception (see above), the discrepancy in question is puzzling.

Before examining factors which might account for the disparity in question, the findings associated with ST/FPAS items will be noted and variations between the foster homes and individual Children's Homes discussed. With respect to the first of these tasks, Table 4.12 lists the items for which differences between foster parents and staff scores were found to be statistically significant at the 0.05 level or less. All the items referred to entailed higher mean ranks for foster parents than for staff [21].

The next step in the analysis of ST/FPAS data was to compare the scores obtained for staff at each of the four Children's Homes. The purpose of this to establish whether the favourable overall scores obtained by residential staff were due to the responses of staff at a single Children's Home. This exercise involved both the full scale and the five subscales. The Oneway Analysis of Variance test was used, coupled with the Scheffe Multiple Comparison procedure. With respect to the full scale, the Scheffe test showed that no two groups were significantly different at the 0.05 level or less. The same result was obtained for the Traditional Control, Passivity, Caretaker Status and Distance subscales; and, only the scores of CH1 and CH2 staff were significantly different at the 0.05 level in relation to the Suppression of Problems subscale. These findings show that the differences between foster parent and staff scores reported above cannot be attributed to highly favourable scores on the part of a single Children's Home staff group.

However, still unaccounted for is the fact that in view of the findings reported in the previous chapter and preceding sections of this chapter, one might have expected the combined scores of residential staff to compare unfavourably with those of foster parents and not - as was found - the reverse. In seeking to explain this incongruence, I recollected that at the outset of interviews, having perused the ST/FPAS, certain junior residential staff asked something like: "Do you want me to answer this in terms of the way that I actually work, or in terms of my personal views on these matters"? My reply was always that the latter should be expressed. However, the point here is that a number of staff implied that a discrepancy existed between how they actually behaved towards children and their personal attitudes. Whilst, of course, how caretakers actually perform their roles is ultimately more important than any beliefs which they may profess to hold about children, work by Asch (1951) on conformity and Milgram (1974) on obedience to authority, for example, shows how individuals may abdicate initiative to an external source. Accordingly, I attempted to ascertain whether the attitudes of senior residential staff at the four Children's Homes differed from those of junior staff to see if pressures existed within the Homes whereby junior staff felt obliged to act towards children in ways that contradicted their beliefs.

At CH1 differences between junior and senior staff scores were not found to be statistically significant at the 0.05 level or less for any of the 5 subscales; and, except for the Suppression of Problems subscale, the means of scores of junior staff exceeded those of senior staff. Thus, it is plain that junior staff at

Table 4.12

ST/FPAS items in relation to which differences between the scores of foster parents and
residential staff were found to be statistically significant

ITEMS		SIGNIFICANCE LEVEL

Traditional Control

1.	Staff/foster parents should maintain order at all times, otherwise the sort of child you deal with would tend to get out of control.	0.05
3.	Modern practice in substitute child care is tending to become too permissive.	0.01
4.	If the sort of child you deal with is left to his/her own devices in recreation time he/she is likely to get into mischief.	0.01
5.	In general, the sort of child you deal with needs fairly close supervision to keep him/her from getting into trouble.	0.05
7.	The sort of child you deal with is too immature to be allowed much say in how the Home/home is run.	0.01
9.	Practical experience is more important for staff/foster parents than theoretical knowledge.	0.0001

Passivity

11.	Places such as this, where children in care live, should be organised so that children feel as much as possible as if they were living at home (i.e. with their natural parents).	0.05
12.	Children in care who cause the least trouble are the ones most likely to get on well after discharge.	0.01
16.	One of the main aims of a Home/foster home like this is to keep the emotional temperature down.	0.01

Distance

32.	The trouble with giving too much attention to the kind of children you look after is that they usually want to take advantage of you.	0.01

Suppression of Problems

38.	One of the main advantages of sending a child to a place like this is that s/he can forget about past troubles.	0.001
39.	It's best for children with a problem or worry not to think about it, but to keep busy with more pleasant things.	0.05

CH1 were not under pressure from their superiors to behave in ways contrary to their beliefs.

However, there was some evidence to suggest that senior staff at the other three Children's Homes were more inclined towards what Cawson and Perry (1977) term ..."traditional values of orderly behaviour, outward expression of respect and firm discipline" than their subordinates. Senior staff at CH2 had higher means of scores than their junior colleagues for the Traditional Control, Passivity, Caretaker Status and Distance subscales. But the pattern was reversed for the Suppression of Problems subscale. Moreover, statistical significance was obtained at the 0.05 level for the Distance subscale alone. Likewise, although the means of scores for senior staff at CH3 were higher than those of junior staff for all save the Passivity subscale, statistical significance was not obtained for any of the observed differences between junior and senior staff. Finally, whilst the means of scores for senior staff at CH4 exceeded those of junior staff on all five sub-scales, statistical significance was obtained at the 0.05 level for the Suppression of Problems subscale only. These results provide insufficient grounds for asserting that junior staff were generally subject to pressure from their superiors to behave towards children in ways that contradicted their beliefs.

Yet perhaps concepts such as conformity and obedience are more promising with respect to accounting for the shaping of foster parent attitudes towards foster children. In attempting to prepare fledgling foster parents for their roles, the fostering officers from Authority A, and those in similar positions at Authority B, strongly emphasised the problems sometimes experienced by those who foster *hard to place* children (in recognition, for example, that placement breakdowns can result from unrealistic expectations on the part of foster parents). This was done during the course of a series of group training sessions attended by all newly recruited foster parents. Furthermore, special foster parents of Authority A - from which, of course, all but a few of the foster homes studied were drawn - were subsequently encouraged to discuss any problems which they were experiencing in relation to their foster child(ren) at the monthly Foster Parent Support Group meetings attended by fostering officers and special foster parents. I sat in on several of these meetings during the course of fieldwork and was much struck by the fact that in relating problems, etc., certain dominant group members appeared to be competing in terms of attempting to establish that the children they had fostered were the most difficult to manage out of the pool of children concerned. The point being made here is that there may have been pressure on foster parents to conceive their foster children in ways that might account for the results obtained via the application of the ST/FPAS. This explanation is made more attractive by the knowledge that most foster parents' experience of hard to place children was limited to the particular children they had agreed to provide a home for (a number of foster parents pointed this out when interviewed). The ST/FPAS statements, however, involved generalisations about such children. Thus, in responding to statements, foster parents had been obliged to draw on impressions gained via their group encounters with fostering officers and other foster parents in which the negative aspects of their task were accentuated. However, a serious weakness with this notion is quite simply that it appears to assume too high a degree of influence on the part of the fostering officers responsible for the Authority A special fostering scheme.

Alternative explanations of the disparity between ST/FPAS results and findings previously reported include the possibility that age differences between the two groups of caretakers may account for the ST/FPAS results. As shown in Chapter 2, foster parents were generally older than staff. Hence, it could be argued that it is not surprising that foster parents scores indicated a greater acceptance of so-called traditional values of orderly behaviour, outward expression of respect and firm discipline, than did the scores of staff. However, this would be to forget that the actual behaviour of foster parents and staff towards children was very different from that which their respective performance on the attitude scale might lead one to expect.

A further possible explanation may be that, whereas foster parents' preparation for their roles had stressed the difficulties sometimes encountered by foster parents of hard to place children, the "in service" training given to staff might have stressed the unacceptability of authoritarian attitudes on the part of staff. Hence, if one possibility is that foster parents were socialised into producing unfavourable ST/FPAS scores, staff may have been conditioned to produce the reverse. The difficulty with this, however, is that the in service training afforded staff appeared, as noted earlier, to be very patchy, consisting mainly of *ad hoc* day seminars on various topics relating to residential child care. Furthermore, the values, etc., communicated to staff during such exercises are unknown.

The intriguing discrepancy between ST/FPAS results and previously reported findings concerning care practice at the foster homes and Children's Homes visited will be returned to in the final chapter of this account.

Notes

1. The percentages listed for both foster parents and staff, with respect to the role activity categories (King *et al*, 1971, categories), have not been rounded to sum to 100 exactly.

   The totals for raw frequency counts of role activities recorded for foster parents and staff do not tally because more than one activity could be recorded per each 30-second interval. Hence, the fact that the foster parent total exceeds that of staff simply reflects the fact that the former engaged in a slightly greater number of different activities than the latter.

   The raw frequency counts recorded with respect to the King *et al* (1971) categories for each of the four Children's Homes were as follows:

	D	CF	CS	A	S	M
CH1	7	15	44	173	140	51
CH2	18	11	41	136	156	45
CH3	5	12	87	184	65	5
CH4	58	18	112	42	120	47

2. The percentages listed for both staff and foster parents with respect to the role activity categories (Cawson, 1978, categories) have not been rounded to sum to 100 exactly.

   The raw frequency counts recorded with respect to the Cawson (1978) categories for each of the four Children's Homes were as follows:

	D	A	E	WT	KOGS	PS	CP	CCNF	SCC	ST	M
CH1	23	163	5	0	141	0	10	0	37	0	51
CH2	23	136	7	0	155	0	0	0	35	3	46
CH3	18	178	0	0	65	0	12	0	86	5	5
CH4	72	25	98	0	122	0	16	0	14	0	47

3. The percentages listed for locations of observations with respect to both staff and foster parents have not been rounded to sum to 100 precisely.

   The raw frequency counts for locations of observations do not correspond with the raw frequency counts for observed caretaker activities because caretakers could engage in more than one activity at a given location and at a given time.

4. In SPSSx, Kendall's Coefficient of Concordance ranks the k variables from 1 to k for each case, calculates the mean rank for each variable over all the cases, and calculates Kendall's W and a corresponding chi-square statistic, correcting for ties. W ranges between 0 and 1, with 0 signifying no agreement and 1 denoting complete agreement. The test assumes that each case is a judge or rater. A small probability indicates a high degree of concordance (see SPSSx User's Guide, 1983, p. 684)

5. The statistics associated with the Kendall test for data on foster parent perceptions of their actual roles were as follows: W = .4409; Chi-square = 130.9437; DF = 9; Significance = .0000 . The statistics for the Kendall test used in relation to the actual roles of residential staff were: W = .4073; Chi- square = 146.6127; DF = 9; Significance = .0000 .

6. The significance levels (two-tailed probabilities) obtained from the computation of Mann-Witney tests comparing the ranks assigned to the ten role aspects by foster parents and staff were: Domestic = 0.0106; Administration = 0.0257; Education = 0.0022; Work Training = 0.0409; Keeping Order and General Supervision = 0.2304; Protecting Society = 0.1198; Care Planning = 0.0000; Contact with Natural Families = 0.7328; Showing Concern for Children = 0.3634; and, Social Training = 0.8573.

7. Berridge (1985) rightly argues that insufficient attention is paid to the education of youngsters in Children's Homes.

8. The statistics associated with the Kendall test for foster parent rankings with respect to their ideal roles were as follows: W = .3784; Chi-square = 105.5665; DF = 9; Significance = .0000. The results of the Kendall

procedure with respect to staff rankings were: W = .5418; Chi-square = 195.0439; DF = 9; Significance = 0.0.

9. The Mann-Witney test associated with the attempt to compare the degree of congruence between staff and foster parent actual and ideal roles produced the following statistics :

	Mean Rank	U	W	CORRECTED FOR TIES	
Foster parents	41.12	524.0	1357.0	Z	2-TAILED P
				-1.5126	0.1304
Residential staff	33.60				

10. The Chi-square and corresponding significance level associated with the crosstabulation of foster parent and staff responses to the question concerning whether their roles are as they ought to be, were: Chi-square = 1.75031; DF = 1; Significance = 0.1858 (after Yates Correction).

11. The Chi-square and corresponding significance level regarding the crosstabulation of foster parent and staff responses to the question concerning the level of autonomy associated with their roles, were: Chi-square = 16.56844; DF = 2; Significance = 0.0003 (cells with E.F.< 5 = 2 of 6).

12. The percentages listed for each category with respect to foster parent and staff speech have not been rounded to sum to 100 exactly.
The raw frequency counts for type of speech categories with respect to each of the four Children's Homes were:

	ISVN	ISA	ISD	CS	PC	OT
CH1	79	20	11	47	28	4
CH2	65	9	40	19	16	4
CH3	83	23	13	43	15	2
CH4	74	15	45	73	27	1

13. The totals for tone of voice in Table 4.7 do not correspond with the totals given for type of caretaker speech listed in table 4.6. This is because it was not always possible to record the tone of voice used by caretakers owing to the attention given to the completion of the narrative record. However, the totals referred to are not so dissimilar and the errors were random, which means that the omissions do not invalidate the findings concerned.

14. The percentages for each tone of voice category with respect to both groups of caretakers have not been rounded to sum to 100 exactly.
The raw frequency counts for tone of voice categories with respect to each of the four Children's Homes were:

	W	N	C
CH1	23	102	27
CH2	26	70	20
CH3	65	61	6
CH4	52	101	18

15. The percentages for the various types of bodily expression concerning both foster parent and staff data have not been rounded to sum to 100 exactly.
The raw frequency counts for bodily expression categories with respect to each of the four Children's Homes were:

	ABE	DBE	VNBE
CH1	29	8	21
CH2	22	12	13
CH3	42	3	17
CH4	31	25	50

16. The percentages for physical gestures regarding foster parent and staff findings have not been rounded to sum to 100 precisely.
The raw frequency counts for physical gesture categories with respect to the four Children's Homes were:

	APG	DPG	VNPG
CH1	5	0	3
CH2	3	0	1
CH3	21	1	10
CH4	5	6	3

17. Three further coding categories used for the analysis of non-verbal behaviour manifested by caretakers towards children were: Attention (AT), Ignores- Tolerates (IGNT) and Ignores-Rejects (IGNR). These coding categories are defined in Appendix (i). AT accounted for 14.28 per cent of foster parent total non-verbal responses, against 11.31 per cent of total non-verbal behaviours recorded for staff. No IGNT or IGNR responses were recorded in relation to foster parents, but the IGNT code accounted for 0.52 per cent of the total non-verbal responses recorded for

staff and IGNR 1.05 per cent of such responses. This appears consistent with other data concerning caretakers non-verbal responses.

18. The percentages given for foster parents and Children's Homes with respect to the initiation of interactions between caretakers and children have not been rounded to sum to 100 exactly.
The raw frequency counts for the initiation of staff-child interaction at each of the four Children's Homes were:

	Initiated by children	Initiated by staff
CH1	31	73
CH2	17	64
CH3	31	61
CH4	24	82

19. The results of the Mann-Witney tests (two-tailed probabilities) comparing the scores of foster parents and staff in relation to the five ST/FPAS subscales were: Traditional Control - mean rank: foster parents = 45.97; staff = 29.60; $P = 0.0010$; Passivity - mean rank: foster parents = 45.50; staff = 29.99; $P = 0.0018$; Caretaker Status - mean rank: foster parents = 36.44; staff = 37.46; $P = 0.8371$; Distance - mean rank: foster parents = 41.94; staff = 32.15; $P = 0.0483$; Suppression of Problems - mean rank: foster parents = 42.61; staff = 32.38; $P = 0.0397$.

20. The results for the Mann-Witney test (two-tailed probability) computed in order to compare the scores of foster parents and staff for the full ST/FPAS were as follows: Mean rank - foster parents = 44.02; staff = 30.49; $P = 0.0064$.

21. The mean ranks for staff exceeded those of foster parents for only two items on the Traditional Control subscale - items 6 and 10. Neither item produced statistical significance with respect to observed differences between the two caretaker groups.
Quite how item 11 measures passivity is far from clear. Presumably Cawson and Perry (1977) felt that caretakers who strongly agree with the statement would be inclined to, as it were, let youngsters "have it too cushy", for the sake of a "quiet life" - or something like this. My view is that strong agreement with the statement concerned might have a positive connotation rather than the negative one which Cawson and Perry (1977) attach to it. However, the remaining items of the Passivity subscale are perhaps less equivocal and, item 19 apart, the mean ranks of foster parents exceeded those of staff for the items concerned.
Whilst statistical significance was not obtained for any of the Caretaker Status items, it is worth reporting that the mean ranks for foster parent scores exceeded those of staff with respect to items 21, 22, 23, 24 and 27. The opposite was true for items 25, 26 and 28.

The mean ranks for foster parents were greater than those of staff for all the items associated with the Distance subscale; although, as indicated in Table 4.12, only the scores for item 32 produced statistical significance.

With respect to items associated with the Suppression of Problems subscale, except for items 40 and 43 (in relation to which staff mean ranks were higher than those of foster parents) the mean ranks for foster parent scores outstripped those of staff. However, as shown in Table 4.12, the differences between the two groups of caretakers produced statistical significance for just two items - 38 and 39.

5 Children's perceptions and behaviours

Introduction

The two preceding chapters revealed that care practice in the foster homes was found to be more child-oriented than in the Children's Homes. This chapter attempts to examine the impact of the care practices concerned on foster and residential children. Of course the question of outcome can only be adequately addressed through carefully controlled longitudinal studies of a kind quite beyond the scope of the scant resources at my disposal. However, it was possible to collect some data which bears on the issue.

The chapter opens with a comparison of the directly observed behaviour of foster and residential children towards their caretakers. This involves data that were collected via the method described in the first part of the previous chapter. The second section of Chapter 5 compares foster and residential children's perceptions of their social environments. Also reported in this section will be an attempt to ascertain the views of foster and residential children's natural parents towards the placements visited. The final section begins by examining the performance of foster and residential children during the course of their placements. The progress (or otherwise) of foster and residential is then examined by comparing the current performance of children with their behaviour prior to their placements.

1. Children's Behaviour Towards Caretakers Observed

For reasons explained in Appendix (i), NRS observations were necessarily focused on caretakers and the only viable means of documenting children's directly observable behaviour was to record their responses during interactions with target caretakers. The coding categories used for analysing data on children's behaviour were derived from Bartak and Rutter's (1975) study of autistic children. The authors distinguish three major types of behaviour - *General Activity*, *Affect* and *Language*, each of which is sub-divided into *socially acceptable* responses, on the one hand and *deviant* behaviours on the other (see Appendix (i)). This dichotomy seemed useful in view of the claim by some of those responsible that children in care are increasingly exhibiting seriously anti-social behaviour [1].

With respect to the General Activity category, the socially acceptable code was assigned whenever children observed interacting with target caretakers had engaged in activities which were permitted and appropriate to the time and place, or where children had engaged in activities intended for them. By contrast, the deviant code was applied where youngsters had engaged in activities which were prohibited or inappropriate to the time and place, or which were not intended for them. Table 5.1 compares the results obtained for foster and residential children. It can be seen that a higher proportion of foster than residential children's general activities were considered socially acceptable.

Table 5.1
General activities of foster and residenial children compared

	Socially Acceptable	Deviant	TOTALS
Foster Children	99.73	0.27	100.00
	(1113)	(3)	(1116)
Residential Children	95.37	4.63	100.00
	(886)	(43)	(929)

N.B. The raw frequency counts for categories are listed in parentheses below the percentages for each category [2].

However, the difference between the two groups does not appear large.

The majority of the activities labelled deviant in relation to residential subjects involved younger children (i.e. children between 7 and 10 years of age) accommodated at CH3 and CH4. Adolescents at the Children's Homes were observed to engage in comparatively few general activities that could be described as deviant. Behaviour interpreted as deviant with respect to younger residential children varied greatly and, hence, is difficult to summarise. It ranged from one CH4 boy refusing to participate in a game of rounders after being "caught out" - instead he walked off the pitch angrily - to a boy at CH3 mischievously opening the dining room door at tea so that the sound of the record player in the adjoining living room made it difficult for other children and staff to hear themselves speak.

The three instances where the deviant code was applied in the analysis of data on foster children involved trivial departures from the activities intended for the youngsters concerned. Moreover, at least one such instance may have simply been a question of misunderstanding - for example, a female foster parent called to one of her two foster children to come downstairs, but the boy did not do so until called twice more. The foster mother scolded the boy (albeit mildly), but there appeared to be no reason not to accept the youngster's explanation that he had not heard his foster mother call.

The second behavioural area distinguished - Affect - consists of the following coding categories: Physical Gestures Involving Bodily Contact with caretakers; and, Bodily Expressions (such as facial expression and gesture). The reader will have noted that these categories were also used for analysing caretaker behaviour. Table 5.2 displays the results obtained for the physical gestures manifested by foster and residential children, and which involved bodily contact with caretakers. That the number of socially acceptable physical gestures recorded for residential children exceeded the total for foster children is not unexpected, given that some of the residential children's physical gestures were associated with the rough play referred to in the previous chapter. More important are the percentages listed. These reveal that the physical contacts of foster children with their caretakers were exclusively assessed as socially

Table 5.2
Physical gestures used by foster and residential children, involving bodily contact with caretakers

	Socially Acceptable	Deviant	TOTALS
Foster Children	100.00	-	100.00
	(13)	(0)	(13)
Residential Children	86.49	13.51	100.00
	(32)	(5)	(37)

N.B. The raw frequency counts for categories are given in parentheses below the percentages listed for each category [3].

acceptable. By contrast, 13.51 per cent of residential youngsters physical contacts with staff were assigned the deviant label. Again, the children responsible were between 7 and 10 years of age, and each recording was made at CH4. Examples of the sort of behaviour involved include one boy aggressively pushing a female member of staff from behind (although it should be said that immediately prior to this the staff member involved had teased the boy concerned for "sulking" following admonishment by her). However, no serious assaults on staff were observed during the application of the NRS.

The proportion of residential children's bodily expressions categorised as deviant also exceeds the share of foster children's bodily expressions given this label, as Table 5.3 reveals. Indeed, only a single facial expression was assessed as deviant with respect to the responses of foster children. Unlike the physical gesture category, deviant bodily expressions were exhibited by youngsters at all four Children's Homes visited; however, younger children at CH4 again contributed a larger share of the responses concerned than children at the other three Homes. It should be emphasised here that bodily expressions such as scowls, and so on, were not treated as deviant *per se*, but only where they were considered inappropriate to the situation observed. For example, if a caretaker gave a child an instruction and the child scowled in response (i.e. because s/he did not like the instruction), this was assigned the deviant code. With respect to the third major behavioural category listed earlier - Language - proportionately more deviant behaviours were again recorded for residential

135

Table 5.3
Bodily expressions manifested by foster and residential children

	Socially Acceptable	Deviant	TOTALS
Foster Children	99.56	0.44	100.00
	(225)	(1)	(226)
Residential Children	83.74	16.26	100.00
	(273)	(53)	(326)

N.B. The raw frequency counts for categories are listed in parentheses below the percentages for each category [4].

children than for foster children, as Table 5.4 demonstrates. Youngsters from all four Children's Homes contributed to the residential children's total of deviant responses [5]. Moreover, unlike the categories of behaviour previously discussed, the proportion of deviant responses recorded for residential children

Table 5.4
Language used by foster and residential children

	Socially Acceptable	Deviant	TOTALS
Foster Children	98.94	1.06	100.00
	(375)	(4)	(379)
Residential Children	90.84	9.16	100.00
	(466)	(47)	(513)

N.B. The raw frequency counts for categories are listed in parentheses below the percentages given for each category.

cannot be accounted for in terms of the actions of younger children at CH3 and CH4 (although this is not to suggest that younger children at CH3 and CH4 did not contribute to the total of deviant responses recorded for residential children).

As was also perhaps the case for the General Activity category, the very small proportion of foster children's verbal behaviour assessed as deviant is possibly indicative of over anxiety on the researcher's part to be scrupulously fair in analysing the data. Each of the four instances concerned entailed rather trivial matters, classified as deviant because they involved comments inappropriate to the situations under observation. For example, experiencing difficulty finding a telephone number in the directory, one foster child expressed frustration by angrily stating..."If I don't find it soon, I'm going to kill myself". The boy concerned was 15 years of age and the fact that his remark reflected a degree of immaturity also influenced my decision to treat the behaviour as deviant. Clearly, however, this sort of behaviour is of a different order to, say, displays of open hostily towards caretakers, and the analysis of residential children's language was not so refined. Instead, less ambiguous forms of deviant behaviour were recorded in relation to residential children, such as verbal abuse, cheek, and so on (i.e. behaviours which were plainly not condoned or tolerated by staff). However, it must be said that the use of foul language by residential youngsters - at least in the presence of staff - was very far from commonplace.

Also worth highlighting is the observation that the verbal behaviour of foster children in relation to their caretakers was manifest in conversational contexts. That is to say, foster children and parents were engaged in conversation which was typically longer in duration than the brief nature of the persistent requests made of staff by different residential children - referred to in the previous chapter, and the sometimes monosyllabic speech used by residential children when responding to staff; a point exemplified by the response, "Ysir", characteristically delivered by CH1 children when given instructions by staff, and frequently accompanied by an impassive facial expression and straightening of the upper body. This military type dressage and language on the part of children was, though less pronounced, also sometimes observed at the other three Children's Homes.

Whilst it has been shown that, overall, the directly observed behaviour of foster children compared favourably with that of residential children, the data concerning residential children's behaviour is somewhat misleading in that target residential staff were observed interacting with larger numbers of children than the foster parents. This means that the deviant behaviours recorded in relation to residential youngsters were manifested by relatively large numbers of different children. At any one time during the observation periods, most residential children were behaving in socially acceptable ways. This assertion is supported by observations made independently of the NRS.

Furthermore, a proportion of the responses coded deviant for residential children might be regarded as *adaptive*. The deviant behaviours exhibited by younger residential children (i.e.those under 10 years of age) at CH3 and CH4, for example, sometimes appeared to be the product of frustration associated with the patterns of daily life at the two Homes. The boy at CH3 who opened the living room door during tea - see above - did so whilst waiting for other children to finish their first course before the second course could be served. On being told to stop by a member of staff in attendance, the boy asked to be excused from the table..."What, don't you want any sweet, Anthony?".. responded the member of staff..."Yes, but it takes ages"...groaned the boy, despairingly.

Attention seeking by children also helps to account for the deviant behaviours recorded with respect to residential youngsters. All the examples cited in relation to such children can be interpreted, at least to some degree, in this way. Individual residential children must compete with relatively large numbers of other children for the attention of caretakers. Whilst staff-children ratios were found to be reasonable, it seems that a large part of staff time is taken up by administrative type duties. Multiple caretakers and the shift systems operated by staff also serve to negate continuity in the care provided for residential children.

It should be pointed out that NRS observations failed to capture an instance where staff at CH1 resorted to the use of physical restraint in order to control children. This is not to imply that I expected to document such practice via the NRS, since the physical restraint of children was not a daily occurrence at CH1. Rather, the point is made in acknowledgement of the fact that staff at CH1 were sometimes subject to difficult and testing behaviour of a degree not witnessed at the remaining three Authority B Homes. Interestingly, as far as the four

Authority B Children's Homes are concerned, the deviant category was used least of all in relation to CH1 youngsters. This appears to be because although the supervision of children was no less close at CH1 than at the other three Homes, the expectations of staff at CH1 were perhaps not as high as those of staff at CH2, CH3 and CH4. Staff at CH1 were happy to settle for reasonable standards of conduct by youngsters who may well have rebelled against the expectations held by staff at the other three Homes - particularly those of CH2 and CH4 staff.

Turning to the data on foster children, the NRS observations (and, indeed, observations made independently of the NRS) appear to contrast sharply with the complaints made by some foster parents regarding foster children's behaviour when the ST/FPIQ was completed (and, for that matter, the comparatively negative overall view expressed about foster children by their caretakers via the ST/FPAS). This might be because the foster children were, so to speak, on their best behaviour when observed. However, the perceptions of foster parents referred to were typically not based on the sort of behaviours I observed. Rather, they concerned behaviours not so amenable to relatively brief periods of direct observation by an outsider, and usually centred on foster children's capacity for integration into the foster family and the ability of foster children to meet foster parent's aspirations regarding the parent-child relationship. The seeming refusal or incapacity of some foster children to make an emotional investment *vis a vis* their foster parents, thus denying foster parents satisfactions that they hoped to gain prior to such children's placement, was frequently mentioned with respect to the latter. Factors associated with the former were more varied and problems cited by foster parents included difficulties between foster children and the natural children of foster parents (though this was not mentioned often); and the failure of foster children to adapt to the expectations of foster parents with respect to, for example, table manners, personal hygiene, etc. Promiscuity on the part of adolescent girls was also a cause for concern for some foster parents, as was the lack of progress made educationally by some foster children. One foster parent told me that she had not expected the contrast between her own values and those of the foster child - an adolescent girl - to be so great.

The points rehearsed here perhaps help to explain why *Showing Concern for Children and Social Training* - see previous chapter - were regarded as two of the major sources of strain associated with foster parent roles. By contrast, it will be recalled that the largest proportion of residential staff selected *Keeping Order and General Supervision* as the biggest area of strain pertaining to their roles. What follows from this is that the expectations of foster parents with respect to foster children seem to be of a very different order to those held by staff in relation to residential children. Irrespective of the ST/FPAS results, staff appear to settle for outward expressions of conformity by children. Because the control aspect of the staff role tends to take precedence over the care element, and because relationships between staff and children have more in common with relations between residents and staff in institutions or pupil-teacher relationships than they do with conventional parent-child relationships, residential children are not usually subject to the expectation that they will make an emotional investment in their caretakers [6]. Moreover, residential children are not required to adjust to the values and lifestyle of a family in the way that foster children are; and, residential staff are more easily able to dissociate themselves from children's perceived shortcomings - uncouth manners, promiscuity, lack of adequate training with respect to personal hygiene, poor educational attainment, and so on - than foster parents (although this distancing is not achieved by staff, but rather it is inherent in the nature of the staff-resident or pupil-teacher relationship).

Ironically, in the face of the sorts of flouted aspirations referred to, a few of the foster parents studied confided that they had fallen back on the fostering fee as a rationalisation for continuing to provide their foster children with a home..."It's only a job"...is, of course, a statement which one might expect to hear from staff, but not foster parents [7]. Perhaps the stance concerned is understandable for, in addition to the sorts of problems described already, a number of foster children had taken money and valued items (in one case the wedding ring of the foster mother) from the foster homes. These sorts of responses by foster children seemed especially difficult for foster parents to cope with because, as one foster parent put it, ..."It's a kick in the teeth, and really hurts"... However, such instances were not the norm. Nor should it be thought that the behaviour of residential children was any less problematic than that of foster children and issues such as delinquency will be returned to in the final section of this chapter. That said, it may be noted that troublesome behaviour by children in care seems to be far more difficult for adults to cope with in family settings than in residential living situations. Unlike foster parents, staff are supported by a group of colleagues who share responsibility for the control of children and they are protected from the implications of problem behaviour by children (e.g., feelings of rejection, guilt, bitterness, and so on) not only by the distance inherent in the staff-resident or teacher-pupil relationship, but also by the separation between their work and home lives. As one member of staff said when discussing the control of children..."It's alright for us, we can go off-duty at the end of the day. Foster parents can't "...

2. Children's Perceptions of their Social Environments

In closing my report on the direct observations of children's behaviour, I returned once more to the views of caretakers. This section, however, compares foster and residential children's perceptions of their social environments or placements and owes much to the work of Heal *et al* (1973) - referred to in the preceding chapter. Heal *et al* (1973) devised a scale - the *Social Climate Scale* - for use in assessing how boys in CHE's perceived their social environments. The scale involves very simple statements about the social environment in CHE's which are checked as either true or false by children, and consists of the following six subscales: *Staff Support* (the degree to which staff are perceived as interested, warm and supportive); *Strictness* (children's perceptions of the authority relationship between themselves and staff); *Satisfaction* (the degree to which children express favourable attitudes towards their placements); *Boy Friendliness* (the degree to which the boys perceive each other as friendly); *Behaviour* (the amount of aggressive and dishonest behaviour which children observe); *Work* (the emphasis which the establishment is perceived to place on hard work).

139

Cawson (1978) claims that the Social Climate Scale is conceptually related to the staff attitude scale which she helped to develop (Cawson and Perry, 1977), because the two scales are constituted by similar dimensions or subscales. Heal *et al* (1973) assert that empirical evidence suggests that favourable scores for each subscale on the Social Climate Scale are associated with successful CHE placements in terms of low rates of absconding (during placements) and re-offending (on discarge) by children.

However, as was the case with respect to the scale used to measure caretaker attitudes towards children, the terminology and phrasing of items comprising the Social Climate Scale required modification so that it could be applied in small scale residential and foster settings. Again, the Work subscale was discarded. This was because, unlike youngsters accommodated in CHE's, most of the children in my study attended school in the community and some of the items constituting the subscale concerned necessitated that children attend school on site.

I augmented my revised version of the Social Climate Scale with an additional question based on work by Cawson (1978). This was intended to probe children's levels of involvement with their placements. The main attraction of the Social Climate Scale and the extra item was that they provided a means of examining the views of foster and residential children towards their placements in a way that facilitated reliable comparison (a similar point can be made about the ST/FPAS). Moreover, items were readily comprehensible to most older children and adolescents. The Revised Social Climate Scale (RSCS) and the additional item are presented in Appendix (j) and were applied during individual interviews with 60 children - 26 foster children (two of which were in the care of Authority B, whilst the remaining children were from Authority A) and 34 residential children (11 from CH1, 6 from CH2, 6 from CH3 and 11 from CH4). These were all children on which data were collected via the application of the CCQ - see Chapter 2. Three foster children on which CCQ data were collected were not, however, interviewed owing to the breakdown of two of the placements concerned (see below), and the fact that a visit to the remaining foster home could not be arranged within the period allocated to data collection (this placement was among the additional foster homes recruited from Authority A, and which were visited towards the end of fieldwork).

Each interview took between 25 and 45 minutes to complete, and the exercise was perhaps the most enjoyable aspect of the study. At the outset of interviews the purpose of the questions was explained in terms of an attempt to ascertain children's views about their placements and considerable care was taken to reassure children of the strict confidentiality of the information which they provided. In addition to the intrinsic interest of the data being collected, what made the interviews particularly pleasurable was the enthusiasm and frankness which the children brought to the task and the enjoyment which, without exception, they seemed to derive from it. I was also much impressed by the very sensible and responsible attitude adopted by children.

As already mentioned, the scale consisted of statements which children were asked to rate as true or false. To simplify this requirement, I substituted the term Yes for true and No for false. In order to ensure that children understood the statements, I read these aloud and worked through the questionnaire with children. During data analysis, responses to items were scored dichotomously - 0 or 1. Hence, the higher the score for a given subscale the higher the individual child had rated his placement on the dimension concerned. Cases with missing values for any of the five subscales were excluded from the analysis of the subscale(s) in question and from the analysis of the full scale (separate analyses were carried out for each subscale - see below). All such cases involved foster children. Youngsters from foster homes where there were no other children had to be excluded from the analysis of the Child friendliness and Behaviour subscales, which entailed statements about other children living with subject children. Five cases fell into this category. One of these was also excluded from the analysis of the Strictness subscale because the child concerned - a mentally retarded boy - was unable to comprehend the meaning of several items on this subscale. The sibling group mentioned in Chapter 2 was totally excluded from the analysis of the RSCS. As noted, the children involved were below the age of 10 years and all experienced difficulty understanding quite a few of the items. However, it was possible to include two of these children in the analysis of the additional item, but the youngest child had to be excluded from this exercise also. No children under 10 years were interviewed at the Children's Homes.

One item on the Strictness subscale (The staff/foster parents here take fighting by the kids (children) seriously) was discarded because to have retained it would have meant excluding foster children living at placements where there were no other children from the analysis of the Strictness subscale. When computing scores for the full scale, the whole of the Strictness subscale was excluded owing to misgivings about the way that the concept of strictness is operationalised by the subscale in question. It seemed that affirmative answers to some of the items comprising the Strictness subscale might well be indicative of an authoritarian approach to children rather than sound care practice [8]. Whilst it may be that strictness on the part of caretakers has been found to be associated with successful placement outcomes, the empirical research (Sinclair, 1975) on which the Strictness subscale is based was carried out in Probation Hostels accommodating young offenders. As the evidence produced by the application of the CCQ indicates (see Chapter 2), relatively few of the children included in my study could be described as delinquent.

Reliability coefficients were computed for the full RSCS (i.e. with the Strictness subscale excluded). The *unbiased estimate of reliability* was .86 and Coefficient Alpha = .85. Table 5.5 lists the reliability coefficients obtained for each of the five subscales. Given that relatively few items comprise each

Table 5.5
Reliability coefficients for RSCS subscales

	Unbiased Estimate	Coefficient Alpha
Strictness	.59	.57
Child Friendliness	.66	.64
Caretaker Support	.65	.64
Satisfaction	.69	.68
Behaviour	.76	.75

subscale, and in view of the exploratory nature of my work, the coefficients concerned are satisfactory (see Chapter 3, note 8).

One of the items on the Behaviour subscale - item 35 (There's a fight here almost every day) - was found to have zero variance (i.e. all children interviewed said that the statement was false). Hence, item 35 was excluded when the scores obtained by foster and residential children were compared. This task first involved comparing the scores of foster and residential children for each of the five subscales. Residential children rated their caretakers stricter than the foster children considered theirs; a difference which just failed to obtain statistical significance at the 0.05 level or less. Statistical significance was, however, obtained at the 0.001 level in relation to differences between the two groups for the Child Friendliness subscale. Foster children rated other children who they lived with friendlier than residential children perceived their peers to be. Foster children also rated their foster parents as more supportive than residential children rated staff. This difference also just failed to reach statistical significance at the 0.05 level. With regard to the Satisfaction and Behaviour subscales, differences between foster and residential children's responses were found to be statistically significant at the 0.0001 level in both cases. Foster children not only generally rated their satisfaction with their placements higher than residential children, but also witnessed less anti-social behaviour at their placements than did their residential counterparts [9]. That foster children's perceptions of their placements on the whole compared very favourably with those of residential children is confirmed by the results obtained for the full scale. Differences between the two groups of children were statistically significant at the 0.0001 level [10].

Individual RSCS items which produced statistical significance at the 0.05 level or less for observed differences between foster and residential children's responses are listed in Table 5.6, together with the significance levels obtained [11]. Setting aside, for a moment, the Strictness subscale item - item 1, foster children's responses compared favourably with those of residential children for all items listed. Worth highlighting is the finding that two of the Satisfaction subscale items appear to support the point made in Chapters 1 and 3 that some children placed in residential settings feel stigmatised as a consequence. With respect to the Strictness sub-scale item, 97.1 per cent of residential youngsters against 72.7 per cent of foster children felt that the statement concerned was true. As may be deduced from what was said previously, the view taken here is that the foster children's overall response to item 1 compares favourably with that of the residential children's (an opinion which seems to run contrary to the claims of the researchers who designed the Social Climate Scale). At least there appears to be some room for doubt amongst foster children as to whether arguing with foster parents leads to censure or punishment, etc. By contrast, almost all residential children believed that the latter would result from an argument with staff.

The additional question put to foster and residential children, and referred to earlier, was: "If you had a personal problem on your mind, who would you discuss it with"? Children were then asked to rank five categories in order of preference. The Kendall Coefficient of Concordance was computed in order to obtain the mean rankings assigned by the two groups for each category [12], which are compared in Table 5.7. Foster children awarded the highest mean rank to foster parents, followed by a member of their natural family. By

Table 5.6
RSCS items for which differences between foster and residential children's scores were found to be statistically significant

STRICTNESS	SIGNIFICANCE LEVEL
1. If you argue with the staff/foster parents here, you get into trouble	0.05 *
CHILD FRIENDLINESS	
10. The kids here laugh if you talk about your feelings	0.01
12. Kids rarely help each other	0.05
CARETAKER SUPPORT	
18. The staff/foster parents here know what kids want	0.05
SATISFACTION	
29. You're proud of this Home/home	0.01
31. You'd be ashamed to tell your mates outside that you're here	0.01
32. The first you hear about things here is when they happen to you	0.001
BEHAVIOUR	
34. Kids here get away with a lot without getting caught	0.01
36. Kids here often boast about breaking the law	0.01
38. Weak kids are sometimes forced to give things to stronger kids	0.05
39. Kids here often lose their tempers with one another	0.001 *
40. If you leave things lying around here they will get stolen	0.0001
41. There's very little swearing here	0.001

*N.B. * denotes crosstabulations which have cells with expected frequencies < 5.*

contrast residential children gave the highest mean rank to a member of their natural family, with staff placed second overall. Interestingly, however, the foster children gave a slightly higher mean rank to members of their natural families than did residential youngsters. This suggests that foster children's natural families remained important to them. But the reader should not assume that foster children were necessarily referring to their natural parents. In certain cases foster children stated that they had siblings in mind, which sometimes meant the brother or sister with whom they were placed.

Table 5.7
Mean ranks awarded by foster and residential children when asked to state who they would most prefer to consult over a personal problem

	Foster Children	Residential Children
A friend outside	3.55	3.76
Your social worker	3.14	2.81
One of the staff/foster parents	1.91	2.57
A friend here	4.05	3.46
A member of your natural family	2.36	2.40

In order to gain some idea about the import of the differences between the two groups, Mann-Witney tests were carried out on the raw data collected. Statistical significance at the 0.05 level was obtained for the *staff/foster parent* and *friend here* options, but not for the other categories [13]. That residential children appear more dependent for support on the peers they live with than the foster children is not surprising given that the residential children lived with relatively large groups of other youngsters: foster children usually did not (and, of course, in some cases, there were no other children living with foster children). However, both groups assigned the lowest ranks to other children. The significance level associated with the staff/foster parent category seems to be consistent with RSCS data and may suggest that, in general, foster children's level of involvement and identification with their placements is greater than the corresponding levels for residential children. However, the high mean rank given by foster children to their natural families indicates that foster children maintained a strong commitment to their families of origin. The mean rank assigned to staff by residential children was also high, perhaps suggesting that the importance of staff in the lives of residential children should not be underestimated either. It might well be that the differences in the mean ranks awarded by the two groups of children to their caretakers (i.e. foster parents and staff), on the one hand, and their natural families, on the other, owes something to the fact that fewer foster than residential children were able to have contact with their natural parents. Thus, foster children were somewhat more dependent on foster parents for support and guidance, etc., than residential children were on staff.

I will come back to children's natural parents shortly. At this juncture it can be said that the recipients - foster children - of the care assessed as the more child-oriented of the two forms studied appeared to express greater overall levels of satisfaction than the consumers - residential children - of the type of care evaluated as being the less child-oriented of the two forms. Children's satisfaction with and commitment toward their placements are perhaps among the keys to the successful placement of children in care. Thus, despite the problems which can be associated with family placements for older children, the results reported so far in this section seem to show that the problems experienced by some foster parents interviewed may be far from insurmountable. As such the findings concerned appear to offer encouragement to foster parents of *hard to place* children.

In order to complement the highly structured nature of the RSCS and the additional item reported, and to allow the more articulate youngsters to express their views about their placements in their own words, children were asked what they enjoyed and did not enjoy about their placement (see Appendix (j)). The data collected were entirely consistent with that so far reported on children's views and care practice. Many foster children felt that their foster placements compared favourably with their previous residential placement(s), and drew on their residential experiences in order to highlight the positive features of their foster placements. For example (and these were factors recurrently mentioned), foster children spoke enthusiastically about the freedom they enjoy to associate with friends in the locality and to bring friends home, about the privacy occasioned by having a bedroom to themselves, about the sense of security and belonging derived from being part of a family, about the support provided by foster parents, and about the relaxed atmosphere (or social climates) prevalent in their foster homes. Such factors were typically contrasted with the restrictions on access to the outside world, lack of privacy and rigidity of routines (e.g., many foster children cited bedtimes as inflexible) within Children's Homes. Despite considerable and subtle probing, very few foster children articulated negative opinions about their foster placements. Indeed, the page on the questionnaire intended for the recording of such reponses was characteristically left completely blank.

Several foster children, however, acknowledged that they had experienced some difficulty adjusting to their new homes when first placed. One youngster (a boy aged 15 years) said that he initially experienced a conflict of loyalty with regard to his natural and foster parents which would not have occurred had he remained in a residential placement. He felt that this was because children in residential settings receive far less by way of individual attention from adults than foster children do, owing, in his view, to the relatively large numbers of children accommodated in Children's Homes and the operation of shift systems which govern staff working hours. Hence, relations between residential children and staff tend to be somewhat superficial by comparison with those which exist between foster parents and children. In retrospect, the boy was glad that he had been placed with his foster parents who were able to help him resolve his conflicting loyalties (the boy enjoyed regular contact with his natural parents) and had also provided him with a stable home life and continuity of care that would not have been available in a Children's Home. A second foster child (again a boy aged 15) was somewhat unsettled in his placement due to difficulties in his relationship with the male foster parent. However, he was adamant in not wanting to return to a Children's Home, and expressed a wish to be placed with an alternative family should relations with his foster father deteriorate further. He believed that social work agencies too readily assume that residential placement is the only option for youngsters whose foster placements breakdown. In his view, several foster placements failures should have occurred before such conculsions are reached with respect to individual children.

The shortcomings associated with residential life reflected on by foster children were accentuated and elaborated by the youngsters living in the

Children's Homes. These children sometimes spoke bitterly about factors such as lack of privacy, inflexible daily routines (again bedtimes, which were regarded as... "too early"..., were a frequently mentioned source of discontent), the unfairness of group punishments, bullying by other children, insufficient adult attention due to the relatively large numbers of children accommodated in the Homes visited and the shift systems worked by staff, inconsistencies between staff in their approach to children, the sense of stigma experienced as a consequence of being placed in a Children's Home (..."People think we've done wrong, that we're 'bad' because were here"...), restrictions on access to the world outside, and so on; in short, precisely the sorts of issues examined in Chapters 3 and 4. A good number of residential children expressed a strong desire to live with a family. For some children this meant their natural family, whilst others hoped to be placed with a surrogate family.

This is not to suggest that residential children did not articulate positive views about their placements. Some children spoke very warmly of staff and said that they were grateful for efforts made by staff on their behalf. It is worth reporting that whilst residential children generally seemed to believe that they were deprived of experiences taken for granted by children living in family settings, the majority did not feel antagonistic towards staff or blame staff. Criticisms made about the latter were usually noticeably restrained. Whilst there seems to be evidence which suggests that some older children in care express a clear preference for a residential placement because they do not wish to identify with a new family unit (see, for example, Fuller and Stevenson, 1984; Berridge, 1985), none of the residential children interviewed articulated such a view; although it must be stressed that this issue was not addressed systematically during the course of the study.

However, two points emerged quite plainly from the information provided by residential children. First, the more deprived the previous homelife of the residential children, the more likely they were to appreciate the material benefits resulting from their placements: activities, outings and holidays organised by staff (children at CH1 typically mentioned such things), and regular pocket money, were frequently cited in this respect; moreover, such children also appreciated the improved diet and clothing which their placement in a Children's Home had brought. Second, those residential children who appeared to derive most satisfaction from their placements were usually older youngsters who consistently cited the enjoyment of things that were not generally afforded children younger than themselves in the Homes visited. I refer here to things that were regarded as "privileges" by the youngsters concerned. Being allowed to come in and go to bed later than younger children was often mentioned in this respect.

There appear to be some uncomfortable similarities between findings associated with the Children's Homes so far reported and, the experiences recounted by one of the groups of adults interviewed as part of the recent retrospective study on the outcome of adoption and residential care undertaken by Triseliotis and Russell (1984). All those comprising the group concerned had spent considerable periods of their childhoods in residential care (see Triseliotis and Russell, 1984, p.19). The authors report that ..."though most residential people had few very good words to say about their experience in residential care, they also avoided being extravagent in their criticisms or of appearing vindictive. Many felt, however, that the experience had spoiled their whole childhood and was affecting them in their current lives. They generally saw it as a 'waste' of their childhood. Most of the criticism had to do with the lack of individualised care, the absence of opportunities for close relationships, with being treated as a group, the absence of privacy, the lack of explanation and discussion about the circumstances of being in care or in the establishment, the rigidity of rules, the harshness of punishments and the endless routine. The feelings of being isolated from the 'real world' came in for particular criticism, as well as their perception of being stigmatised by the wider community. It was their firm belief that the community equated being 'in care' with...being bad. In fact some came to refer to themselves as not normal. The frequent staff changes also instilled in them a feeling of mistrust towards adults and particularly towards new staff trying to get close to them. Interaction between staff and children at a personal level was at a premium and was mostly confined to situations when orders were being given or discipline enforced"...(Triseliotis and Russell, 1984, pp.182-183)

In concluding this consumer view of foster and residential care, I want to comment on the views of foster and residential children's natural parents with respect to the placements of the two groups of children. Tables 5.8 and 5.9 compare the views of foster and residential children's natural mothers and natural fathers, respectively. The data concerned were collected via the application of the CCQ (see Chapter 2 and Appendix (b)) from children's field social workers. This represented the only viable means of obtaining such data.

Table 5.8
Natural mothers' views of children's placements [14]

	Foster Children's		Residential Children's		ROW TOTAL	
	%	(N)	%	(N)	%	(N)
Positive	46.7	(7)	33.3	(9)	38.1	(16)
Ambivalent	6.7	(1)	18.5	(5)	14.3	(6)
Indifferent	13.3	(2)	33.3	(9)	26.2	(11)
Negative	33.3	(5)	14.8	(4)	21.4	(9)
COLUMN TOTAL	35.7	(15)	64.3	(27)	100.0	(42)

Table 5.9
Natural fathers' views of children's placements [15]

	Foster Children's		Residential Children's		ROW TOTAL	
	%	(N)	%	(N)	%	(N)
Positive	33.3	(4)	26.1	(6)	28.6	(10)
Ambivalent	8.3	(1)	39.1	(9)	28.6	(10)
Indifferent	50.0	(6)	17.4	(4)	28.6	(10)
Negative	8.3	(1)	17.4	(4)	14.2	(5)
COLUMN TOTAL	34.3	(12)	65.7	(23)	100.0	(35)

means of obtaining such data. Interviews with natural parents were impossible given the limited time and money at my disposal. No reports were available for natural parents of large numbers of children from both groups, with the foster children group particularly affected by this problem (see chapter notes 14 and 15). Accordingly, parents for whom no reports were available were excluded from the analysis. It can be seen from Tables 5.8 and 5.9 that the proportions of foster children's natural mothers and fathers who held positive views about their children's placements exceeded the proportions of residential children's natural mothers and fathers holding such views. Although the proportion of foster children's natural mothers who held negative views about their children's placements exceeded that for natural mothers of residential children, proportionately more natural fathers of residential children than natural fathers of foster children held negative views about their children's placements. More natural parents of residential children than natural parents of foster children were ambivalent towards their children's placements. Whilst proportionately more natural mothers of residential children than natural mothers of foster children were indifferent towards their children's placements, this pattern was reversed with respect to the natural fathers of foster and residential children. Hence, it is difficult to draw conclusions from the data concerned. However, although extreme caution is appropriate in view of the large numbers of cases for which no reports were available and the second hand nature of the data collected, perhaps the inconclusive nature of the data presented in Tables 5.8 and 5.9 supports the point made earlier that residential placement need not be more conducive than fostering to the maintenance of relations between children and their natural parents [16].

3. Children's Progress During their Placements

Having related children's views about their placements in the previous section, I will now report findings concerning my attempt to gain an impression of the respective overall progress, or otherwise, made by foster and residential children during the course of their placements. Data were collected through the application of the CCQ at interview with children's social workers (see Chapter 2 and Appendix (b)).

The reader will recognise the kinds of behaviours examined as being identical or similar to those discussed in relation to children's background characteristics in Chapter 2. Previously we looked at the issues concerned in terms of children's behaviour prior to their placements, and I will return to this later. As a first step in data analysis, the overall performance of foster ($N = 29$) and residential ($N = 34$) children throughout their placements was compared. However, despite efforts to "force a result" out of the data in question [17], statistical significance was not obtained for differences between foster and residential children for any of the areas examined. This is not to suggest that differences of interest were not found. Foster children's performance appeared to compare somewhat favourably with that of residential children in relation to 7 of the 12 areas of behaviour explored, whilst the pattern was reversed for a further 2 areas. Differences between the two groups were negligable with respect to the remaining three aspects of behaviour.

Some 38.2 per cent of residential, against 20.7 per cent of foster, children had absconded one or more times during their placement (Chi-square = 1.53028;

Significance = 0.2161 - after Yates correction). The 79.3 per cent of foster children who had not absconded compared with proportions of non-absconders for the four Children's Homes of 45.5 per cent (CH1), 66.7 per cent (CH2), 66.7 per cent (CH3) and 72.7 per cent (CH4). Thus, although the CH1 absconding rate was higher than that of the other three Homes, the rates for all four homes compared unfavourably with that obtained for the foster children.

Moreover, 14.7 per cent of residential (N = 5), compared with 3.4 per cent of foster (N = 1), children had committed offences whilst absconding (Chi-square = 1.18079; Significance = 0.2772 - after Yates correction). But all save one of the residential youngsters concerned were accomodated at CH1 - the Home in which Authority B typically placed children who had engaged in delinquent type activities; the remaining residential child was from CH3.

An estimated 11.8 per cent of residential (N = 4) and 3.4 per cent of foster (N = 1) children had been physically violent at some stage in their placements (Chi-square = 0.56189; Significance = 0.4535 - after Yates correction; cells with E.F.<5 = 2 of 4). The 96.6 per cent of foster children with no record of physical violence during their placement was slightly less impressive than the CH3 and CH4 figures of 100 per cent in each case, but compared favourably with the 81.8 per cent and 66.7 per cent for CH1 and CH2, respectively. The assault by the foster child was on a member of the public. One of the two attacks by CH1 youngsters involved a member of staff at the Home and the other a domestic pet. The two violent episodes at CH2 concerned an assault on another child and an attack on a pet.

There was no evidence to suggest that 86.2 per cent of foster, and 85.3 per cent of residential, children were otherwise generally aggressive (Chi-square = 0.00000; Significance = 1.0000 - after Yates correction; cells with E.F. <5 = 2 of 4). No indication of aggressiveness was found with respect to 63.6 per cent and 81.8 per cent of children from CH1 and CH4, respectivly; and no evidence of aggressive behaviour existed in relation to 83.3 per cent of children at each of the other two Homes. Hence, the performance of CH1 youngsters was least impressive. The results for foster children were slightly better than those for children at the remaining three Homes. Most of the children described as aggressive were reported to be this way inclined towards people rather than property.

The proportions of foster and residential children who were said to exert a negative influence on other children living at their placements was very similar - 17.2 per cent and 17.6 per cent, respectively (Chi- square = 0.00000; Significance = 1.0000 - after Yates correction). The percentage of foster children who were not described as a bad influence on other youngsters living with them (82.8 per cent) was roughly equal to that for CH3 (83.3 per cent) and CH4 (81.8 per cent) children, but larger than the proportions obtained for CH1 and CH2 children (72.7 and 66.7, respectively). Seven children (including three foster children) were said to deliberately cause trouble, whilst two (one of whom was a foster child) children were purported to set a bad example to other children. No details were forthcoming in relation to a further three youngsters (one foster child and two residential children) who were alleged to be a bad influence on other children.

Evidence of difficulties in relations between children and their caretakers was found with respect to 34.5 per cent of foster, and 29.4 per cent of residential, children (Chi-square = 0.02543; Significance = 0.8733 - after Yates correction). As indicated, statistical significance was not obtained for differences between the two groups. But the proportions of children in both groups who were experiencing difficulties in the area concerned are perhaps larger than one might expect. As few as 48.3 per cent of foster children were said to be positively well liked (as distinct from there merely being no evidence of difficulties - see Appendix (b)) by their foster parents. The proportions of residential children said to be positively well liked by staff were as follows: CH1 = 45.5 per cent; CH2 = 66.7 per cent; CH3 = 66.7 per cent; and, CH4 = 45.5 per cent. However, where evidence of difficulties in relations between caretakers and children existed, this was usually set within a context of contradictory reports (i.e. either written reports contained in children's social work files were contradictory, or the view of the social worker interviewed contradicted reports kept in children's files - this occurred, for example, where the social workers interviewed had taken over children's cases only a short time prior to data collection, or a residential child was said to get on well with some staff but not others, or a foster child was said to get on well with one foster parent but not the other).

Table 5.10 compares the proportions of foster and residential children in relation to whom evidence existed indicating that they were cheeky, abusive or disobedient towards their caretakers. The differences between the two groups just fail to attain statistical significance at the 0.05 level (Chi-square = 3.28813; Significance = 0.0698 - after Yates correction). Despite this, it is clear that the results pertaining to foster children compare unfavourably with those for residential children. The proportions of children not said to be cheeky, etc., towards their caretakers at each of the four Authority B Children's Homes exceed that for foster children in each case, and were as follows: CH1 = 63.6 per cent, CH2 = 83.6 per cent, CH3 = 66.7 per cent and CH4 = 72.7 per cent.

Table 5.10
Proportions of foster and residential children reported as cheeky, abusive or disobedient towards their caretakers

	Foster Children		Residential Children		ROW TOTALS	
	%	(N)	%	(N)	%	(N)
No evidence	44.8	(13)	70.6	(24)	58.7	(37)
Evidence	55.2	(16)	29.4	(10)	41.3	(26)
COLUMN TOTAL	46.0	(29)	54.0	(34)	100.0	(63)

However, that residential children were found to be generally less cheeky, etc., than foster children is not surprising in view of, for example, the emphasis placed on control with respect to staff roles *vis a vis* children; this will be returned to later.

Interviews with children's social workers revealed that 10.3 per cent of foster (N = 3), against 20.6 per cent of residential (N = 7), children had made one or more court appearances as alleged offenders during their placements (Chi-square = 0.58231; Significance = 0.4454 - after Yates correction; cells with E.F. <5 = 1 of 4). All court appearances made by residential children were by youngsters at CH1, where as few as 36.4 per cent of children had not been

150

required to appear in court during their stay at the Home. Six of the children (one foster and five youngsters from CH1) who appeared in court made only one such appearance. Two foster and two CH1 youngsters made more than one court appearance.

Some 17.2 per cent of foster (N = 5), compared with 14.7 per cent of residential   (N = 5), children were reported to have been found guilty of offences whilst at their placements (Chi-square = 0.00000; Significance = 1.0000 - after Yates correction; cells with E.F <5 = 1 of 4). All except one of the residential children were from CH1, with the remaining residential youngster placed at CH2. The types of offences committed by children mainly involved petty theft (e.g., shoplifting), with a few instances of more serious offences such as burglary. Only three youngsters (two foster and one child from CH1) were found guilty of more than one offence. Interestingly, fewer residential children than foster children had been found guilty of offences during their placements. But it is important to emphasise that the differences between the two groups were negligible and also that no evidence of delinquent type activity was found with respect to most of the foster and residential children studied.

The seeming discrepancy between the proportions of children who made court appearances and the proportions of children actually found guilty is accounted for by: (a) the fact that not all children who made court appearances were found guilty; and, less obviously, (b) the fact that a number of youngsters received a Police Caution or warning and did not appear in court. It may also be that certain residential children's cases were adjourned and that they were required to appear before the court a second time in relation to the same offences, and these were mistakenly construed as court appearances for different offences.

Each of the final three areas of behaviour were associated with children's schooling. Evidence of school truancy was found with respect to 24.1 per cent of foster (N=7), and 32.4 per cent of residential (N = 11), children (Chi-square = 0.19328; Significance = 0.6602 - after Yates correction). Evidence of truancy was reported for 36.4 per cent of CH1 children, 16.7 per cent of children at CH3 and 18.2 per cent of CH4 children. As many as 66.7 per cent of CH2 youngsters had a record of school truancy during the course of their placements. All but three children (one foster and two from CH1) had truanted only occasionally, with the remaining children said to have truanted very frequently.

Evidence of behaviour problems at school was uncovered in relation to 20.7 per cent (N = 6) of foster and 26.5 per cent (N = 9) of residential youngsters (Chi-square = 0.05770; Significance = 0.8102 - after Yates correction). There were reports that children's behaviour was less than satisfactory with respect to 16.7 per cent of CH2 children and 18.2 per cent of children at CH4. The school behaviour of all CH3 children was said to be satisfactory. But the school behaviour of 54.5 per cent of CH1 children was not.

The educational performance of 24.1 per cent (N = 7) of the foster children and 26.5 per cent (N = 9) of residential children was claimed to be less than satisfactory (Chi-square = 0.00000; significance = 1.0000 - after Yates correction). Some 16.7 per cent of CH2 children were said to be performing less than satisfactorily at school, as were 27.3 per cent of children accommodated at CH4. As many as 45.4 per cent of CH1 youngsters were not performing to a satisfactory standard in relation to their school work. However, all children at CH3 were performing satisfactorily.

Negative findings regarding the residential settings owe much to the influence of CH1 youngsters. However, the results discussed so far in this section have concerned children's performance during the course of their present placements (i.e. the placement at which they were studied). The problem with this approach is that it takes no account of how children were performing prior to being placed at the settings where they were studied. Hence, I compared foster and residential children's performance during their present placements with their behaviour prior to these with respect to five of the twelve areas discussed above.

Table 5.11 compares the proportions of foster and residential children reported as manifesting physical violence prior to and during their present placements. It would appear that both groups show an overall improvement in

Table 5.11
Proportions of foster and residential children reported as having manifested physical violence prior to and during their present placements

| | Prior to Placement | | During Placement | |
	%	(N)	%	(N)
Foster Children	20.6	(6)	3.4	(1)
Residential Children	21.0	(7)	12.0	(4)

the area concerned, with the progress made by foster children somewhat more impressive than that of their residential counterparts. Whilst some 79.3 per cent of foster children had not been physically violent prior to their present placement, the same was true of 96.55 per cent of such children during their present placement. The Children's Home improvement was shared by CH1, CH3 and CH4 children, but not by youngsters accommodated at CH2. The performance of CH1 and CH4 youngsters improved by roughly 10 per cent in each case (i.e. the proportion of youngsters at CH1 and CH4 who had engaged in physical violence during their present placements was 10 per cent down on the proportions who had been physically violent prior to being placed at the two Homes), whilst that of CH3 children improved by some 15 per cent. No change was recorded for CH2 children in relation to which the figure for no evidence of physical violence was 66.7 per cent both prior to and during their present placement.

Table 5.12
Proportions of foster and residential children who made court appearances as alleged offenders prior to and during their present placements

| | Prior to Placement | | During Placement | |
	%	(N)	%	(N)
Foster Children	6.9	(2)	10.3	(3)
Residential Children	32.3	(11)	20.5	(7)

Table 5.12 (above) compares the proportions of foster and residential children who made court appearances as alleged offenders prior to and during their present placements, and registers a slight, and unimportant, deterioration on the part of foster children, but an overall improvement of just over 10 per cent for residential children. The latter included an improvement of just under 20 per cent for CH1 youngsters, 16.7 per cent for children at CH3 and 9.1 per cent by CH4 children. No change was recorded for CH2 children since no children at the Home had any record of court appearances as alleged offenders.

The rates of school truancy prior to and during children's present placements reflect a general improvement for both groups with the change recorded for foster children (approximately 13 per cent fewer foster children truanting during their present placements) more impressive than that for residential youngsters (roughly 2 per cent), as Table 5.13 indicates. With respect to residential children, decreases in non-school attendance by CH1 and CH3 youngsters

Table 5.13
Proportions of foster and residential children who had truanted prior to and during their present placements

| | Prior to Placement | | During Placement | |
	%	(N)	%	(N)
Foster Children	37.0	(11)	24.1	(7)
Residential Children	35.0	(12)	32.4	(11)

(changes of some 30 per cent and 15 per cent, respectively, fewer children truanting during their present placements at CH1 and CH3) were offset by deteriorations in the performance of CH2 and CH4 younsters during their present placements (the change in both cases was just over 15 per cent).

However, the improvement in residential children's performance with respect to school behaviour problems was impressive. School behaviour problems were reported for 50 per cent of residential children prior to their present placement, but this fell to 26.5 per cent of such children during their present placements. Whilst foster children's performance in this area also appeared to have improved during their present placements, the change was not as marked as that recorded for residential youngsters. Although some 27 per cent of foster children manifested school behaviour problems prior to their present placements, this declined to 20.7 per cent of such youngsters during their present placements. CH1 children's performance improved from 90.6 per cent displaying school behaviour problems prior to their present placement to 55 per cent having such difficulties during their present placement. The improvement by CH3 children was even more dramatic. Whilst only 33.3 per cent of CH3 children were said not to have manifested behavioural problems at school prior to their placement at the Home, this was said for all such children during their stay at CH3. CH4 children also displayed progress in this area in that about 10 per cent fewer were said to have school behaviour problems during their stay at CH4 than was the case prior to their admission. However, a deterioration was recorded in relation to CH2 youngsters, with just over 15 per cent more children exhibiting school behaviour problems than was reported for such children prior to their stay at the Home.

Overall improvements were also recorded for both groups of children in relation to their educational performance. Although evidence was found suggesting that an estimated 38 per cent of foster children's educational performance fell short of satisfactory prior to their present placements, this had declined to 24.1 per cent of such children during their present placements. Prior to their present placements, the educational performance of some 44 per cent of residential children was said to be unsatisfactory. Yet during their present placements the proportion of residential children reported to be performing less than satisfactorily at school had dropped to 26.5 per cent. Before their present placements the educational performance of only 18.2 per cent of CH1 youngsters was described as satisfactory (or at least there was no evidence to the contrary). This had risen to 56.4 per cent of such children during the course of their stay at CH1. The educational performance of an estimated 16.7 per cent of CH2 children seemed to have deteriorated during their placement at the Home, whilst the performance of just over 30 per cent of CH3 youngsters had improved. Some 10 per cent of CH4 children appeared to be performing less well at school than was reported to have been the case prior to their admission.

The exercise of comparing children's performance prior to their placement at the settings where they were studied with their performance during the course of their placements appears to show a general improvement for both foster and residential children. However, it must be noted that the data are in some ways unsatisfactory, not least because the period prior to children's placements covers the whole of their lives before admission to the settings visited. The problem here is that certain children had experienced previous placements in care. Thus, improvements in performance are not necessarily attributable to the placements visited. This point particularly applies to foster children. As noted most of these youngsters were living at residential settings prior to their foster placements.

Notwithstanding these caveats, it would seem that the Children's Homes may have enjoyed some measure of success in effecting modifications in children's behaviour in relation to the important areas examined. Indeed, whilst CH1 children's performance generally compared unfavourably with that of foster children and children at the other three Authority B Homes, the improvement shown by CH1 youngsters during the course of their placements is actually quite impressive in some respects. What the data on the residential children perhaps, therefore, indicate is that the Children's Homes were reasonably successful at containing youngsters in the sense of ensuring that they attended school regularly, behaved themselves when at school, and stayed out of trouble with the law, etc. However, perhaps the foster home data at the very least also demonstrate that similar results can be achieved without the comparatively institutionally-oriented approach characteristic of care practice in the Children's Homes.

It is worth noting here that neither of the two foster placements which broke down during the course of fieldwork could really be said to have failed. Both involved youngsters over 16 years of age. One of the placements was intended to help an unmarried adolescent mother develop parenting skills *vis a vis* her young baby. The girl had left home owing to friction with her parents that was associated with the birth, etc., of her child. Her mother (who I met on a visit to the foster home during the first phase of fieldwork - see Chapter 1) seemed to hold a positive view about the placement, believing that it was more appropriate than a residential placement. However, after some months, the girl appeared to tire of taking care of her baby - which was one of the conditions stipulated in the contract agreed between the people concerned (i.e. the youngster, her social worker, the foster mother, and the fostering officer) - and she returned to live with her natural mother (who thereafter assumed responsibility for the baby's care) and father.

The second breakdown appeared temporary and (as had been the case on several previous occasions), after a short stay in a residential setting, it seemed likely that the youth concerned would return to the foster home. The lad's history had been extremely troubled, and included lengthy periods in different residential settings since birth. His manner was said to be generally aggressive and anti-social. That the foster placement had remained intact for over 2 years appeared proof of its success, since it seemed that secure accommodation was sometimes required to contain the youngster during his periodic returns to residential care. Moreover, he was reported to have made considerable overall progress during his foster placement. The fostering officers involved attributed this to the tolerance and understanding provided by his foster parents (both of whom were under 30 years of age) and the support offered by a conscientious social worker.

Notes

1. See Fuller and Stevenson(1983, p.117)

2. One activity code (either socially acceptable or deviant) for each 30-second observation/recording interval was applied when analysing data on children's behaviour with respect to each child observed interacting with target caretakers. Therefore, whilst it might be expected that the total number of activity codes applied in relation to residential children would exceed the number used for foster children, the reverse was true because, as noted in the main body of the text (see Chapter 4), interactions between foster children and their caretakers were longer in duration than those involving residential children and staff.
    The raw frequency counts for socially acceptable and deviant General Activity codes assigned in relation to children at each of the four Authority B Children's Homes were as follows:

	SAGA	DGA
CH1	215	5
CH2	176	1
CH3	257	11
CH4	238	26

3. The raw frequency counts for socially acceptable and deviant Physical Gestures recorded in relation to children at each of the four Authority B Children's Homes, were:

	SAPG	DPG
CH1	4	0
CH2	4	0
CH3	18	0
CH4	1	5

4. The following raw frequency counts of socially acceptable and deviant Bodily Expressions were recorded for children at the four Authority B Children's Homes:

	SABE	DBE
CH1	61	11
CH2	74	14
CH3	88	7
CH4	50	21

5. The raw frequency counts of socially acceptable and deviant Language codes applied with respect to children at each of the four Authority B Children's Homes were as follows:

	SAL	DL
CH1	122	9
CH2	99	16
CH3	136	10
CH4	109	12

6. Kadushin (1971) lists one of the main advantages of residential care as the opportunity it provides children for a less intense emotional relationship with parental figures. However, whilst not denying the possible value of such relationships in certain circumstances, it might argued that what the Children's Homes studied actually offered to some children was not so much less intense emotional relationships with caretakers but a virtual lack of such relationships.

156

7.   This should not be construed as implying that certain foster parents were, so to speak, "in it for the money" (i.e. that financial reward was foster parents primary motivation for initially taking on, or subsequently continuing to perform, their roles).
8.   In order to obtain an independent second opinion on this matter, I consulted my associate Roger Fuller at the National Children's Bureau (see, for example, Fuller and Stevenson, 1983) and he unreservedly concurred with the view taken by myself and by my associates at Oxford.
9.   The results produced by the computation of Mann-Witney tests for each of the five RSCS subscales were:

Strictness

	Mean rank	U	W
Foster Children	23.66		
		267.5	520.5
Residential Children	31.63		

Corrected for Ties	
Z	2-Tailed P.
-1.8386	0.0660

Child Friendliness

	Mean rank	U	W
Foster Children	35.33		
		147.0	636.0
Residential Children	21.82		

Corrected for Ties	
Z	2-Tailed P.
-3.1349	0.0017

Caretaker Support

	Mean rank	U	W
Foster Children	33.63		
		284.5	773.5
Residential Children	25.87		

Corrected for Ties	
Z	2-Tailed P.
-1.7659	0.0774

Satisfaction

	Mean rank	U	W
Foster Children	40.39		
		129.0	929.0
Residential Children	21.29		

Corrected for Ties	
Z	2-Tailed P.
-4.3764	0.0000

Behaviour

	Mean rank	U	W
Foster Children	11.42		
		34.5	205.5
Residential Children	34.49		

Corrected for Ties

Z	2-Tailed P.
-5.2853	0.0000

It should be noted that the original scoring procedure for the Behaviour subscale was problematic in that favourable responses to items (i.e. responses suggesting that subjects did not witness much by way of anti-social behaviour on the part of other children) were scored 0, whilst favourable scores for items constituting the other three subscales of the full scale (see main text) were scored 1. This difficulty was resolved by simply reversing the scoring procedure for the Behaviour scale, thus making it consistent with that of remaining subscales (a procedure adopted for each stage of RSCS data analysis).

The one-tailed Mann-Witney test might have been used given that the direction of difference could have been predicted on the basis of the findings pertaining to care practice. This would have produced statistical significance for differences between the foster and residential children in respect of all five subscales.

The Scheffe Multiple Comparison procedure demonstrated that the foster children's mean score was significantly different at the 0.05 level from CH1 children's mean score with respect to the Child Friendliness and Satisfaction subscales. The foster children's mean score also differed significantly at the 0.05 level from those of CH1, CH3 and CH4 children, but not from CH2 youngsters, with respect to the Behaviour subscale. The mean score of CH1 youngsters for the Behaviour subscale differed significantly at the 0.05 level from that of CH2 children. The mean scores of foster children were lower than those for residential children at each Children's Home with respect to the Strictness and Behaviour subscales, but higher in relation to the other three subscales. This indicates that statistical significance obtained with respect to the Mann-Witney tests performed in order to compare the mean scores of foster homes and Children's Homes cannot be attributed to the influence of extreme scores on the part of a single Children's Home.

10. The Mann-Witney test computed in order to compare the mean scores of foster and residential children with respect to the full RSCS (i.e. excluding the Strictness subscale) produced the results listed below. Only children who had completed the RSCS without omissions (see main text) were included in the analysis. This meant that the number of foster children included was reduced to 18.

	Mean rank	U	W
Foster Children	39.61		
		70.0	713.0

		Residential Children	19.56		

Corrected for Ties

Z	2-Tailed P.
-4.5479	0.0000

The Scheffe test showed that the mean score obtained by the foster children was significantly different at the 0.05 level from the mean scores of CH1, CH3 and CH4 children, but not from that of CH2 youngsters; although the foster children's mean score did exceed that of CH2 children, as can be seen below:

		Mean	Minimum	Maximum	Standard Deviation
Foster Children		26.2222	18.0000	31.0000	3.7347
CH1	"	16.8182	11.0000	23.0000	3.6556
CH2	"	22.1667	13.0000	29.0000	5.7417
CH3	"	19.0000	7.0000	24.0000	6.2929
CH4	"	19.0909	13.0000	25.0000	3.9612

11. Whilst crosstabulations and the computation of the Chi-square test were used for comparing the response of foster and residential children in relation to individual RSCS items, this approach was not followed when analysing scores for the five subscales and the full scale despite the fact that the scoring procedure adopted involved dichotomous variables. This was because to have done so would have meant that cases (i.e. children) would have made more than one contribution to the cells comprising 2 x 2 tables, which may well have effected the associated significance levels. Hence, the Mann-Witney test was regarded as reflecting a conservative approach to the analysis of the subscales and full scale.

12. The statistics resulting from the computation of the Kendall Coefficient of Concordance with respect to foster and residential children's rankings were as follows:

	W	Chi-square	D.F.	Significance
Foster Children	.3004	26.4363	4	.0000
Residential Children	.1379	18.7492	4	.0009

13. The Mann-Witney test performed comparing foster and residential children's rankings produced the results presented below. Of the 63 children on whom data was collected via the CCQ, only 60 were included in the exercise concerned. The three subjects excluded were all foster children, one of whom (a member of the sibling group comprised by three children under 10 years) did not understand the question sufficiently well

to be included, whilst the remaining two were not interviewed due to the breakdown of their placements.

A friend outside

	Mean rank	U	W
Foster Children	28.17		
		381.5	732.5
Residential Children	32.28		

Corrected for Ties

Z	2-Tailed P.
-0.9368	0.3489

Social worker

	Mean rank	U	W
Foster Children	33.60		
		361.5	837.5
Residential Children	28.13		

Corrected for Ties

Z	2-Tailed P.
-1.2385	0.2155

Staff/Foster Parent

	Mean rank	U	W
Foster Children	25.27		
		306.0	657.0
Residential Children	34.50		

Corrected for Ties

Z	2-Tailed P.
-2.1091	0.0349

A friend here

	Mean rank	U	W
Foster Children	34.07		
		251.5	749.5
Residential Children	24.90		

Corrected for Ties

Z	2-Tailed P.
-2.1400	0.0324

Member of natural family

	Mean rank	U	W
Foster Children	31.79		
		408.5	826.5
Residential Children	29.51		

Corrected for Ties
       Z   2-tailed P.
   -0.5160   0.6058

14. The number of no reports for data concerning the views of children's natural mothers were: foster children - N = 14 (48.3 per cent of foster children); residential children - N = 7 (20.6 per cent of residential children).
The percentages regarding residential children in table 5:8 are not rounded to sum to 100 exactly.

15. The number of no reports for data regarding natural fathers views about children's placements were:foster children - N = 17 (58.6 per cent of foster children); residential children - N = 11 (32.4 per cent of residential children).
The percentages for foster children in table 5:9 are not rounded to sum to 100 precisely.

16. As indicated previously, there appears to be a body of opinion which supports residential care on the grounds that it is more conducive to maintaining a child's contacts with the natural family than is fostering. If there is a descrepancy between the evidence supporting this view and the data that I collected (and which is readily acknowledged to be unsatisfactory in certain respects), it may owe something to the fact that constructive contacts between the foster children and their natural parents were encouraged by the fostering officers responsible for the Authority A special foster scheme. Moreover, it might be that the professionalised nature of the type of foster care studied meant that the foster parents concerned were more cooperative in this respect than ordinary foster parents may be. Ordinary foster parents could be more inclined than special foster parents to view natural families as a threat to their own interests *vis a vis* foster children.

17. Whilst data on children's performance prior to and during their placements were collapsed in order to resolve the problem of crosstabulations having cells with expected frquencies of <5, as pointed out earlier, this was not possible with respect to other data collected via the CCQ because of the serious distortions to the data which would have resulted (see note 1 of Chapter 2).

6 Summary and discussion

Introduction

This study has delineated and compared care practice in special foster homes and Children's Homes for older children in local authority care. Fieldwork was conducted in two local authorities over a 12 month period, and featured the application of a combination of research instruments. Quantitative techniques were used for analysing the data collected. In closing this account, the major findings reported in previous chapters will be summarised and the sorts of factors which might help to shape care practice will be explored. Finally, the possible implications of the findings for policy and practice in the substitute care field will be outlined.

1. Summary of Major Findings

Four Dimensions of Care

In Chapter 3 foster homes and Children's Homes were compared along four dimensions: the management of recurrent - mainly daily - social events, children's community contacts, the provision of physical amenities, and the controls and sanctions employed by caretakers.

The management of recurrent - mainly daily - social events

This aspect of care practice was measured by the *Index of Child-Management* (ICM). All the foster homes achieved a higher rank than the Children's Homes with respect to degree of child-orientation, and statistical significance for the overall differences observed between foster homes and Children's Homes was obtained at the 0.0001 level (two-tailed test). That statistical significance was not gained for observed differences between the Children's Homes administered by Authority A and Authority B suggests that the Authority B Homes where in-depth research was carried out were not atypical Children's Homes. An item analysis produced an *unbiased estimate of reliability* of .95, thus revealing the ICM to be a highly reliable research instrument. The ICM also proved to be a very robust measure of care practice.

The comparatively institutionally-oriented management of the daily lives of the residential children was further illustrated by documents serving as guides to the daily routines at three of the Children's Homes whose ICM scores suggested that they could be regarded as representative of the residential settings visited.

Children's community contacts

If the management of daily events was more child-oriented in the foster homes than in the Children's Homes, the community contacts of foster children also compared favourably with those of residential children. This conclusion issued from the application of the *Revised Index of Community Involvement* (RICI). Statistical significance at the 0.001 level (two-tailed test) was obtained for differences between the means of total scores assigned to the foster homes and Children's Homes. The ranks achieved by the foster homes in relation to degree of child-orientation were generally higher than those gained by the Children's Homes (CH9 did, however, succeed in entering the ranks of the foster homes). As was also found to be the case with respect to the ICM, the difference between the means of total scores awarded to the two groups of Children's Homes (i.e. Authority A and Authority B Homes) was not statistically significant. The RICI had an *unbiased estimate of reliability* of .73.

Perhaps the magnitude of the difference between the foster homes and Children's Homes on this dimension of care practice was surprising in view of the belief in some quarters that youngsters in Children's Homes receive treats and enjoy outings at a rate in excess of that afforded the average child in the community. However, it should be borne in mind that the RICI went beyond the superficial level of treats and outings. By themselves, the latter may be inadequate and misleading indices of children's involvement in community activities (for example, whilst the children at CH1 enjoyed regular outings, these usually involved trips in a mini-bus to venues outside the locality where the Home was situated, and CH1 children's contacts with the surrounding community were minimal). The term Community Homes - the official title of local authority Children's Homes - seems to denote an unfulfilled aspiration.

The physical environment

The *Revised Index of Physical Environment* (RIPE) demonstrated that the provision of physical amenities in the foster homes also generally compared favourably with that characteristically found in the Children's Homes (although one of the Children's Homes - CH7 - broke into the ranks of the foster homes with its RIPE score). Statistical significance was attained at the 0.001 level (two-tailed test) for the difference between the means of total scores for the foster homes and Children's Homes. The observed difference between the means of the total scores awarded to Authority A and Authority B Children's Homes did not produce statistical significance. The RIPE was found to have a reliability coefficient of .77 (*unbiased estimate of reliability*).

However, it was pointed out that the scoring procedure associated with the RIPE appeared to favour the Children's Homes. Moreover, the emphasis which the design of the RIPE placed on matters that could be easily and reliably measured meant that the index failed to address important issues which were less amenable to quantification. For example, the RIPE results did not reflect the institutionally-oriented exterior and interior design of some of the Children's Homes. Thus, the differences between the physical environment of the two types of setting were underestimated by the RIPE.

Controls and sanctions

Findings resulting from the application of the *Index of Controls and Sanctions* (ICS) were consistent with the trend established by the results summarised above. The scores obtained by the foster homes for the full ICS were generally more child-oriented than those gained by the Children's Homes (but the score obtained by CH9 again allowed it to enter the ranks of the foster homes). The *unbiased estimate of reliability* for the full ICS was .84. Statistical significance for the differences between the means of total scores awarded the foster homes and Children's Homes was obtained at the 0.0001 level (two-tailed test). Analysis of the full ICS also showed that Authority A Homes did not differ significantly from Authority B Homes with respect to this aspect of care practice.

What emerged from the use of the ICS was that the residential staff studied appear to have made far greater use of inappropriate/ineffective techniques of control than foster parents. It also seemed that although foster children typically participated in the rule-making process at their placements, residential children did not.

Caretaker Roles and Behaviour Towards Children

While Chapter 3 compared the foster homes and Children's Homes in terms of four aspects of child-management practice, Chapter 4 was primarily concerned with the details of behaviour manifested by the adults who are directly responsible for the daily welfare of the children studied - foster parents and residential staff.

Caretaker roles

Direct observation of the role activities of caretakers via the *Narrative Recording Schedule* (NRS) suggested that the foster parent role is characterised by social child care and, in the case of female foster parents, domestic activities. By contrast, staff roles seem to involve an emphasis on supervisory and administrative duties. This view is supported by the finding that the focal points of foster parents' activities were the living room and kitchen, whilst staff activities centred on the office of the Children's Home and locations that appear to permit the supervision and surveillance of children. These locations varied according to the interior design of the Children's Homes. Moreover, interviews with caretakers entailing the use of the ST/FPIQ (*Staff/Foster Parent Interview Questionnaire*) showed that although keeping order and general supervision of children appeared to be the major source of strain pertaining to staff roles, it is no more stressful to foster parents than their social child care activities (or indeed, the domestic tasks mainly performed by female foster parents).

However, staff seemed to underestimate the accent which their roles placed on supervisory and administrative duties. Foster parents, on the other hand, attached greater import to the control and supervision of children than the direct observations of their role activities might have led one to expect. But both groups regarded social child care as the most important aspect of their role, and would have welcomed a reduction in the emphasis which their roles placed on control and supervision.

The degree of congruence between foster parents' perceptions of their actual and ideal roles was generally greater than that found for staff; a finding which may be related to the comparatively high degree of autonomy associated with foster parents' roles. Despite the fact that foster parents were more isolated from potential sources of support than staff, most foster parents considered that the supervision they received was adequate.

Caretaker behaviour towards children

Caretakers verbal and non-verbal behaviour towards children was also studied by direct observation using the NRS.

Foster parents were discovered to use proportionately more informative speech speech (i.e. speech which offered opinion, information or explanation or asked children for opinion, information and explanation) during interactions with children than their residential counterparts. Further, a larger proportion of foster parent than staff speech was approving (the term was used to denote all informative speech which had an unambiguously positive connotation eg., praise, playful remarks, words of comfort or encouragement, or affectionate comments, etc.). Residential staff were found to employ more informative speech defined as disapproving (i.e. speech which plainly had a negative connotation e.g., criticism, censure, etc.) and more controlling speech (i.e. statements which gave orders without explanation) than did foster parents. Foster parents also used a warm tone of voice with greater frequency than staff, but a critical tone less often than staff.

Interestingly, staff were observed to manifest approving physical gestures involving bodily contact with children with greater frequency than foster parents. However almost two-thirds of such contacts recorded for staff were manifested by staff at a single Children's Home - CH3. A large proportion of staff physical contacts with children entailed male staff engaging in rough play with youngsters. Staff also used proportionately more disapproving physical gestures involving bodily contact with children (e.g., restraining children or pulling them away by the hand, as distinct from physical chastisement) than did foster parents, and foster parents were observed to show approval by way of bodily expressions such as facial expression and gesture (e.g, smiling) with proportionately greater frequency than staff. Moreover, staff engaged in disapproving bodily expressions (e.g., frowns of disapproval) more often than foster parents.

The duration of interactions between caretakers and children

The NRS observations demonstrated that interactions between staff and individual residential children tended to be fleeting encounters which were significantly shorter in duration than those typically observed between foster parents and foster children. In view of the fact that, by contrast with most of the foster parents studied, staff interact with relatively large numbers of children, it seems likely that the residential children studied generally received less adult attention than the youngsters placed in the foster homes visited. Perhaps this finding would be less significant were it not for the results regarding the nature of the staff role and the behaviour of the latter towards children previously summarised. The idea that certain residential children may receive little beyond a few terse commands or disapproving comments from their caretakers during the course of an entire day does not appear fanciful.

The initiation of interaction between caretakers and children

Foster parents and foster children were observed to initiate interaction with similar frequency. However, the data collected by way of the NRS indicated that by far the greater part of observed interaction between staff and children was initiated by staff (where interaction was initiated by residential youngsters this frequently entailed requests by the latter for information from staff, children seeking permission from staff prior to commencing some activity, and children seeking access to things kept under lock and key). This finding served further to reinforce the view that the role of staff *vis a vis* children is mainly one of control and supervision. It may also **suggest** that a degree of familiarity, reciprocity, and social closeness existed **between** foster parents and children that was absent from relations between residential staff and children.

Chapters 3 and 4 established that care practice in the foster homes was generally significantly more child-oriented than in the Children's Homes. Hence, the first general hypothesis listed in Chapter 1 - that there are characteristic variations between care practice prevailing in special foster homes and Children's Homes for older children in local authority care - was not refuted (although, of course, the direction of differences between the two forms of substitute care were not predicted in advance of statistical analysis of data collected - as evidenced by the use of two-tailed statistical tests).

Children's Perceptions and Behaviours

Chapter 5 examined the impact of care on foster and residential children.

Children's behaviour towards caretakers

Three aspects of foster and residential children's behaviour during their interactions with caretakers was compared via the NRS - general activity, affect (i.e. bodily expressions and physical gestures involving bodily contact with

166

caretakers) and language. The proportions of *socially acceptable* responses manifested by foster children exceeded those of residential children for each of the categories of behaviour listed, whilst the pattern was reversed with respect to the proportions of *deviant* responses exhibited by the two groups of children. The levels of deviant responses recorded for foster children were extremely small and would have been non-existent were it not for my exceedingly, perhaps excessively, strict adherence to the definitions of the coding categories used for analysing the data. However, the need for caution in drawing conclusions from the data on residential children was also urged in the knowledge that the deviant behaviours recorded for this group were produced by relatively large numbers of different youngsters. Thus, it appeared that at any given moment most of the residential children in the Homes visited were behaving in acceptable ways. Further, some of the behaviours labelled deviant in relation to residential children might just as readily have been interpreted as adaptive, and the nature of care practice in the Children's Homes may help to explain why research shows that older children in residential care are more likely to manifest behavioural disorders and emotional disturbance than children living in their own homes [1].

The direct observations of foster children's behaviour contrasted with the somewhat negative perceptions expressed by a number of foster parents. Such views were not, however, usually based on behaviours readily amenable to observation by an outsider, and appeared to be typically associated with the foster children's capacity for integration into the foster family and their ability to meet foster parents aspirations regarding the parent-child relationship. No such expectations pertain to residential children, with staff often apparently prepared to settle for outward conformity by children and relationships with them which have more in common with relations between inmates and staff in residential institutions or pupil-teacher relationships than they do with parent-child relations. These points perhaps indicate the importance of matching children with placements suited to their needs and characteristics. It could be argued that the expectations of some foster parents were unrealstic given the troubled backgrounds of the youngsters concerned. However, whilst certain children in care may require the opportunity for less intense emotional relationships with adults this falls a long way short of serving to justify the kind of emotional limbo which some of the youngsters in the Children's Homes visited appeared to experience.

Children's perceptions of their social environments

The application of the *Revised Social Climate Scale* (RSCS) demonstrated that foster children's perceptions of their social environments generally compared favourably with those of residential children. Foster children rated their foster parents as less strict and more supportive than residential children rated staff. These differences just failed to obtain statistical significance at the 0.05 level (two-tailed tests). Foster children rated other children whom they lived with as more friendly than did residential children; a difference that was statistically significant at the 0.001 level (two-tailed test). Moreover, foster children not only rated their satisfaction with their placements higher than residential children, but also witnessed less anti-social behaviour by their companions than their residential counterparts. Both differences were statistically significant at the 0.0001 level (two-tailed tests).

That foster children's perceptions of their placements generally compared favourably with those of residential children was confirmed by results obtained for the full scale (i.e. excluding the Strictness subscale), in respect of which the difference between the two groups was statistically significant at the 0.0001 level. An *unbiased estimate of reliability* of .86 was obtained for the full RSCS. Further, something approaching a consensus on the shortcomings of residential care was found between the views expressed by foster children with previous experience in residential settings, the residential children interviewed, and adults studied by Triseliotis and Russell (1984) who had grown up in residential care. The complaints made by the three groups focused on the sorts of factors addressed by the instruments which were used to measure care practice. However it was also noted that some of the residential children spoke very warmly of staff and were appreciative of material benefits which had been derived from their placements - for example, activities, outings, holidays, an improved diet and better clothing. Whether this deserves to be read as a genuinely positive aspect of residential children's placements or as an indictment of what was available to such children in the community (or both) is perhaps a matter for debate.

Yet irrespective of how care practice in Children's Homes compares with that provided in families, this seems an appropriate place to emphasise that standards of care, particularly physical care, in Children's Homes appear to have vastly improved since the days of the Curtis Committee (see Chapter 1). This achievement, along with the valuable role played by Children's Homes in substitute child care (see the next section of this chapter), must not be overlooked.

The centre of the foster children's lives appeared to be their foster homes. Overall foster children seemed to rate foster parents as their primary source of support. However, it was also plain that foster children's ties with their natural families remained important to them. Residential children appeared to rate their natural families as their most important source of support. Whilst it would seem that, in general, relationships between foster children and foster parents were closer than those between residential children and staff, the rating given to staff by residential children was also high. It should be noted that the findings in question appear to have been influenced by the fact that many foster children, unlike the majority of their residential counterparts, were unable to maintain contact with their natural families.

If the way children perceive their placements has any bearing on the long-term outcome of different types of substitute care, the results of the interviews with foster children may be encouraging because they appear to imply that the problems experienced by some foster parents of hard to place children are far from insurmountable.

An attempt via the *Children's Characteristics Questionnaire* (CCQ) to ascertain what children's natural parents thought about their children's placements was unavoidably less than satisfactory in certain respects. But although no firm conclusions can be drawn from the exercise reported, the data concerned may suggest that special foster children's natural parents need not be any less positive about their children's placements than the natural parents of residential children are towards placements in Children's Homes. However much may depend here on the approach adopted by those responsible for special foster schemes and the special foster parents concerned. It could be that professionalised fostering is less likely to involve strains between foster parents and natural parents than ordinary fostering because special foster parents may be more inclined to regard what they do as a vocation rather than as an attempt to fill the shoes of children's natural parents. Hence it might also be the case that the natural parents of special foster children are less likely than the natural parents of ordinary foster children to perceive foster parents as rivals. Certainly the relatively generous rates of payment made to the special foster parents studied somewhat blurred the distinction between their roles and those of residential staff.

Children's progress during their placements

Data collected by the CCQ enabled a comparison to be made between the progress of foster and residential children during the course of their placements in terms of crude but important indices. None of the observed differences between the two groups for the various areas of behaviour examined were found to be statistically significant. However the overall performance of foster children was somewhat more impressive than that of residential children in relation to the following areas: absconding, offending whilst absconding, manifestations of physical violence, court appearances as alleged offenders, offences for which children were found guilty, truancy and school behaviour problems. Interestingly, however, fewer residential than foster children were reported to be cheeky, abusive or disobedient towards their caretakers.

Both groups of children showed a general improvement when their behaviour in the placement was compared with their performance prior to placement in terms of the following: physical violence, court appearances, school truancy, behavioural problems at school and educational performance. Whilst a major shortcoming of the data is that past performance embraced the whole of the children's lives before their stay at the settings visited (which for some youngsters included other placements in local authority care) the progress made by residential children was quite impressive. Thus Children's Homes appear to enjoy some success in containing children and effecting modifications of problem behaviours.

Whilst not wishing to imply that caretakers should condone such behaviour, cheek, and so on, can be interpreted as a positive, rather than a negative, response by children. In view of the favourable findings concerning care practice in foster homes, factors such as the opportunity to establish relationships with parental figures, exhibit affection, anger, etc., might be indicated by the finding that foster children were cheekier than their residential counterparts. Surely it is not far fetched to assert that this may augur well for the development of the foster children. I am reminded here of a conversation observed between two men which followed an altercation involving one of the men and his adolescent daughter... "I would'nt let a daughter of mine speak to me like that"... said the other man, shaking his head and frowning disapprovingly... "No, ...but then a daughter of yours would'nt know how to"..., replied the first man, proudly.

However that may be, perhaps the very least suggested by the data on foster children is that similar results can be achieved with regard to ameliorating behaviour problems without the comparatively institutionally-oriented approach of the Children's Home. This view appears to be supported by the success rates for other special foster schemes reported in Chapter 1. The Kent Special Family Placement Project, for example, attempted to demonstrate that adolescents with severe problems can be placed and maintained in foster families. Yelloly's (1979) interim and independent evaluation of the scheme suggested that roughly three-quarters of the youngsters so placed improved. This seems impressive, given the troubled histories of the youngsters involved.

According to the second hypothesis formulated to provide a framework for empirical research and specified in Chapter 1, it was predicted that the responses manifested by the foster and residential children studied would vary according to the care practice they had experienced. Overall it seems that the foster children's perceptions of their placements compared favourably with those of the residential children. However, although foster children's directly observed behaviour towards foster parents also generally appeared to compare favourably with the behaviour of residential children towards staff, various factors indicate that it would be unwise to attempt to draw firm conclusions from the data concerned. Data on the progress made by foster and residential children also proved inconclusive. Yet, as already implied, it seems reasonable to suggest that the responses of the residential children were not sufficiently impressive to be regarded as offering justification for findings concerning the ways that the lives of such children differ significantly from those of children living with families.

2. Factors Which Help to Define Care Practice

It is hoped that these findings will help to make possible a more sophisticated debate on the outcome of the two major forms of substitute care than has hitherto been possible. But what sorts of factors help to shape the care practices delineated? This is a difficult question to answer, not least because the study was not designed to examine the determinants of care practice. Moreover, care practice is influenced by a multiplicity of factors which are not easy to disentangle. Accordingly, the account which follows focuses on insights that suggest ways to amend some of the major shortcomings identified.

One obvious possible explanation for the comparatively institutionally-oriented nature of care practice in the Children's Homes might be the type of children which they accommodated. King *et al* (1971) in their study of child-management practice in residential institutions for mentally retarded children tested for factors associated with the provision of child-oriented care (measured in terms of scores on their revised Child Management Scale). They found that children's handicaps were not an overriding factor in determining child-oriented care. This seems to support the view taken here. The material collected on the background characteristics of a sample of foster and residential children via the CCQ, and reported in Chapter 2, appear to suggest that the generally marked contrast between the care practices found in the foster homes and Children's Homes cannot be satisfactorily explained in terms of the differential characteristics of foster and residential children. For one thing, the foster children comprised genuinely *hard to place* youngsters who, prior to the inception of the special foster schemes, would undoubtedly have been placed in

Children's Homes of the kind studied; indeed, most were so placed prior to their placements at their foster homes. Second, although the youngsters accommodated at one of the Children's Homes - CH1 - had been delinquent with greater overall frequency than the foster children, the record of the foster children in this respect was very like that of the children placed at the other three Authority B Children's Homes. A similar point can be made in relation to behavioural problems manifested by children prior to their admission. Furthermore, despite what has been said about the youngsters placed at CH1, care practice at CH1 was no less child-oriented than at other Children's Homes. The reader can verify this by examining Table 3.1. The results tabulated show that CH1 was not found to be the most institutionally-oriented Children's Homes on any of the four dimensions of care concerned.

This is not to suggest that no differences whatsoever were found between the sample of foster and residential children. But the major differences between the two groups did not concern their behavioural characteristics. Rather it seemed that, on the whole, the foster children had perhaps suffered greater trauma with respect to their past experiences than the residential children. For example, the care histories of foster children generally exceeded those of the residential youngsters in length. Both the care careers and family histories of foster children had generally been characterised by a greater degree of disruption than those of residential children. Foster children's relationships with their natural parents and siblings were found to have been impaired or severed more often than those of residential children; and it appeared that the foster children would, unlike many of the residential children, stay in care for the remainder of their childhood. However differences between foster and residential children with respect to the duration of their present placements were not statistically significant.

A second factor that might have a major impact on care practice is the way caretakers perceive children. The ST/FPAS, reported in Chapter 4, measured caretaker attitudes towards children. The underlying dimension of the scale was termed *traditionalism* by its originators - Cawson and Perry (1977) - because it seemed to reflect the extent to which caretakers accept... "traditional values of orderly behaviour, outward expression of respect and firm discipline"... Five subscales comprised the modified version of the index used: Traditional Control, Passivity, Caretaker Status, Distance and Suppression of Problems. Except for the Caretaker Status subscale, the scores of foster parents exceeded those of staff and the observed differences between the two groups were statistically significant. The difference between staff and foster parents for the full scale was statistically significant at the 0.01 level. The *unbiased estimate of reliability* associated with the ST/FPAS was .90.

The ST/FPAS results seemed inconsistent with findings pertaining to care practice. A number of possible explanations for this discrepancy were considered. All proved inadequate. Certain junior staff implied that the way they performed their roles conflicted with their views about how they ought to work, but insufficient evidence was found to support an argument that junior staff were under pressure from their superiors to work in ways that contradicted their beliefs. Concepts such as conformity and obedience to authority appeared more promising with respect to accounting for the findings pertaining to foster parents. It seemed that foster parents may have been conditioned by fostering officers to perceive their foster children as problematic, and that this view was reinforced at monthly foster parent support group meetings. However this notion perhaps assumes an implausibly high degree of influence on the part of fostering officers. The general age difference between the two groups of caretakers might also have served to account for the ST/FPAS results, given that the scale was supposed to measure traditionalism. Yet this seemed to run the risk of confusing professed attitudes with actual behaviour. It could also be argued that if foster parents were socialised into regarding their foster children as problematic, staff had been subject to training which emphasied the unacceptabilty of authoritarian attitudes towards children. However, the problem here was that the in service training afforded staff was patchy and the values communicated to staff during the course of such training are unknown.

Given that none of these explanations are entirely satisfactory, the incongruence between the ST/FPAS results and findings associated with care practice perhaps suggests that the actual performance of foster parents and staff was heavily influenced by the contrasting realities of family and residential living. For example, whilst the attitudes of staff were clearly conducive to the provision of child-oriented care situational constraints made this difficult to achieve in practice. Therefore, just as the nature of care practice in the foster homes and Children's Homes visited cannot be satisfactorily understood in terms of the type of children accommodated, the attitudes of caretakers also appears an inadequate explanation of care practice.

In contemplating the sorts of factors which may constrain the actions of caretakers, the size of the home or institution has a common sense appeal as a determinant of care practice. King *et al* (1971) discovered that management practices were not affected by institutional size, nor was the size of living units within institutions related to child-management practice. Table 3.1 reveals that one of the most noticeable differences between the foster homes and Children's Homes was their relative size in terms of numbers of children and caretakers. CH9 broke into the ranks of the foster homes with its RICI and ICS scores and gained by far the most impressive ICM score of the 12 Children's Homes visited. CH7 also entered the ranks of foster homes with its RIPE score. What distinguishes these two Homes, and particularly CH9, from the other Children's Homes ? Their size ? Certainly, they were among the smaller of the Children's Homes studied. But so were CH8 and CH12 whose scores for the four dimensions of care tabulated in Table 3.1 were far from impressive. Moreover, although FH7 fell into the ranks of the Children's Homes with its ICS score and FH12 did the same with its RIPE score, the scores of these foster Homes on other dimensions of care practice compared favourably with those gained by Children's Homes accommodating similar numbers of children. Thus whilst size may well exercise an impact on care practice the influence of other factors is also indicated by the results reported.

King *et al* (1971) found no relationship between assigned staff ratios and scores on their Child Management Scale. However, the authors do report that child-oriented units had most staff on duty at peak periods of daily routine when they were most needed. The ambiguity in the findings reported by King *et al* (1971) is consistent with the results of this study. Whilst caretaker-child ratios in the foster homes generally compared favourably with those found in the Children's Homes, FH7, FH8 and FH12 were no more well endowed with respect to numbers of caretakers relative to numbers of children than some of the Children's Homes. Although, like size, the import of caretaker-child ratios must not be underestimated, it would appear that other factors are implicated in the process whereby care practice in Children's Homes become institutionally-oriented.

In discussing factors associated with favourable scores on their Child Management Scale, King *et al* (1971) report that child-oriented units enjoyed greater continuity of staffing than institutionally-oriented units. Heads of child-oriented units spent a significantly greater proportion of their time in activities which necessarily involved them with the children (e.g., social and physical child care), while the heads of institutionally-oriented units spent significantly more of their time in tasks which did not necessarily involve children (e.g., administrative activities). Heads in child-oriented units also managed to interact more frequently, and more warmly, and spoke more often, with children than heads of institutionally-oriented units. A similar pattern characterised the way that junior staff in child-oriented and institutionally-oriented units performed their respective roles. In institutionally-oriented units there was a more specialised division of labour, with tasks being allocated to staff on status lines, whereas child-oriented units were characterised by greater role diffusion, with both senior and junior grades of staff engaged in similar activities. Finally, King *et al* (1971) found that heads of child-oriented units were given more responsibility and were subject to less frequent inspection than the heads of institutionally-oriented units.

Two of the factors, in particular, which King *et al* (1971) found to be associated with child-oriented scores on their Child Management Scale - role diffusion among, and the exercise of autonomy by, caretakers - may suggest that in order to make Children's Homes more child-oriented the degree of bureaucratisation associated with their operation must be reduced. The features of bureaucratic organisations are listed by Smith (1979, p.24) as follows:

(1) A hierarchical authority structure based on official position rather than the individuality of the incumbent.
(2) A system of rules governing the rights and duties of these positions.
(3) A detailed system of rules and regulations for dealing with each particular case.
(4) A clear-cut and highly specialised division of labour.
(5) Impersonal social relations, with management based on written documents (the files).
(6) Recruitment of officials to a salaried career with security of tenure on the basis of technical qualifications.

It is important to remember that the characteristics adumbrated by Smith (1979) represent an ideal-type model of a bureaucratic organisation which, following Weber, can be used as a conceptual framework for analysing organisations. It may prove illuminating to compare and contrast the foster homes and Children's Homes with reference to the six characteristics listed.

Hierarchical authority structures based on official position rather than the individuality of incumbents were not observed in the foster homes. As Parsons (1964, p.133) relates: "The family is a collectivity within which the basic status-structure is ascribed in terms of biological position, that is, by generation, sex and age. There are inevitably differences of performance relative to these, and they are rewarded and punished in ways that contribute to differential character

173

formation. But these differences are not given the sanction of institutionalized social status. The school is the first socializing agency in the child's experience which institutionalizes a differentiation of status on non-biological lines"...

By contrast with the foster homes, hierarchical authority structures did exist in the Children's Homes, as Table 2.3, which compares the composition of staff groups in the twelve Children's Homes visited, shows. Care staff are separated into two groups - senior staff and junior staff. However, Table 2.3 does not reveal the further gradations observed amongst senior staff groups (e.g., Officer-in-Charge, Deputy-Officer-in-Charge, Third-Officer-in-Charge, Senior Houseparent, and so on). The differentiation within senior staff ranks in the larger Children's Homes (e.g., CH1, CH4 and CH5) was greater than that found in the smaller Children's Homes. It was also reported in Chapter 2 that domestic and ancillary staff were employed in the Children's Homes. The status of such staff was generally viewed as being inferior to that of care staff.

Adults were in authority over children at both the foster homes and the Children's Homes. Yet, whilst the staff role *vis a vis* residential children was characterised by the generalised superiority of adult status which foster parents had relative to foster children, staff were not ascriptively related to the residential children but rather performed an occupational role. To some degree, this can also be said about the foster parent who was a salaried employee of Authority A (see below); and, the financial allowance received by all the special foster parents, which contained a reward element, somewhat blurred the distinction between staff and foster parent roles. However, as already implied, it is only really in the school setting that the foster child encounters a differentiation of status on a non-ascriptive lines. By contrast the residential child experiences the latter both at school and within the Children's Home. This partly explains why it was possible in Chapter 5 to conceive of relations between staff and residential children as having more in common with staff-inmate or teacher-pupil relations than with conventional parent-child relations.

Ordinarily there are no rules governing the rights and duties of persons living in family settings, unless one counts the parental rights (which, in the case of foster children were vested in the authorities concerned and not the foster parents) discussed in Chapter 1 and the law more generally. However contracts had been drawn up in relation to each of the special foster placements that, although not legally binding (see Chapter 1, note 19), often specified expectations concerning the behaviour of foster children, foster parents and social workers - particularly the behaviour of foster children. But foster parents were not provided with written job descriptions of the kind given to residential staff, and mentioned in Chapter 4, which specified the rights and duties of staff positions. The documents concerning the daily routines in three of the Children's Homes, presented in Chapter 3, provide further evidence of the contrast between the foster homes and Children's Homes with respect to the second aspect of bureaucratic organisations distinguished in that they summarise the duties of junior staff.

Foster parents had, however, been issued with written guidelines regarding certain aspects of their foster children's care. These were required because parental rights were vested in the local authority (or the court in wardship cases - see Chapter 2). Hence, foster parents had to obtain the SSD's consent prior to, for example, taking foster children on holiday abroad, etc. Obviously this cannot be regarded as a detailed system of rules and regulations for dealing with each particular case. Procedural guides had been prepared by senior administrative staff covering various aspects of residential children's care, but these were not consulted on a daily basis by staff.

The division of labour in the foster homes was not highly specialised. Rather there appeared to be a basic division between the roles of male and female foster parents. As noted in Chapter 4, the male foster parent was usually seen as the main breadwinner, whilst the majority of female foster parents seemed to be mainly responsible for physical child care and domestic tasks. This is not to suggest that there was no overlapping of the roles performed by male and female foster parents. For example, a number of female foster parents had jobs outside the home. Moreover, it will be recalled that several lone foster parents were encountered during the course of the study, all of whom went out to work and had sole responsibility for physical child care and domestic tasks (although the youngsters concerned were more or less self-sufficient in these areas). Also, in one of the households visited the female foster parent was the main breadwinner and the male foster parent stayed at home and carried out the domestic tasks and physical child care.

By contrast with the foster homes, the division of labour in the Children's Homes was fairly specialised. As indicated in Chapters 2 and 4, care staff were employed to undertake only some of the activities associated with child care. Domestic staff carried out essential tasks such as cleaning and cooking, washing and ironing clothes, etc. In CH1, special care staff (who did not work at CH1 in the daytime) were employed to watch over children during the night. Some of the larger Homes such as CH1 and CH5 had part-time secretarial staff. Senior care staff seemed to have more administrative duties to perform than junior staff and supervised the activities of junior staff. However, as noted in Chapter 4, recent years have seen attempts to increase the participation of junior staff in areas previously the preserve of senior staff and field social workers, and the extent to which junior staff also undertook administrative type duties was reported in Chapter 4. Moreover, domestic staff at all the Children's Homes visited were observed to engage in social child care activities, care staff were observed performing domestic activities (e.g., the preparation of food, washing and ironing clothes, cleaning, etc.), senior staff shared the activities of junior staff *vis a vis* the supervision of children, and so on. Thus it should not be thought that the compartmentalisation of staff roles was absolute.

The fifth feature of bureaucratic organisations - impersonal social relations with management based on written documents (the files) - was not present in the foster homes, except in the rare cases when written directives had been received from the SSD. Files were maintained on children, and indeed, the foster parents, but these were kept at SSD offices. Communication between foster parents and agency personal (e.g., social workers and fostering officers) was typically informal and usually either involved contact by telephone or visits by fostering officers and social workers to the foster homes. Data reported in Chapter 4 show that relations between foster parents and foster children were more personalised than those which existed between staff and residential children. Files were maintained on residential children both at SSD social work offices and at the Children's Homes, and staff maintained daily records on the behaviour of children. Detailed records of daily events at the Children's Homes were made by staff and kept in the form of logbooks. Communication between different staff shifts took the form of written messages - the "changeover" or "handover" book - in addition to verbal communication. Senior staff used the changeover book to issue directives to junior staff. Punishments applied with respect to children were recorded. Diaries of forthcoming events and activities, etc., were kept. External directives from senior SSD staff were frequently received in written form. Finally, the three documents pertaining to the daily routines in three of the Children's Homes presented in Chapter 3 may also be seen as management based on written documents.

With respect to the final feature of bureaucratic organisations, all save one of the foster parents did not receive a salary. Few foster parents held qualifications in child care and their recruitment was not conditional upon holding such qualifications. However, as noted in Chapters 2 and 4, all the foster parents had undergone a preparatory course prior to receiving their foster children. By contrast with the foster parents, all care staff were salaried employees of the SSD's concerned, and contracts of employment, etc., ensured the security of their jobs. There was also a recognisable career structure within the two SSD's. As reported in Chapter 2, however, very few staff held qualifications in child care. This is not to imply that qualifications did not play a part in the recruitment of staff. On the contrary relevant qualifications were seen as a decided advantage by the two authorities.

The traces of the six elements of bureaucratic organisations observed in the foster homes appear to have been intrusions from Authority A and B, which were associated with the fact that the foster children were under the care of the two local authorities. The elements would not normally be found in family settings, and they were far more in evidence at the Children's Homes than at the foster homes. Thus Parsons' (1982, p.193) view of families ... "as 'factories' which produce human personalities"... is somewhat misleading. The production of human personalities does, indeed, appear to require a context which provides warmth, security and mutual support. Adequately functioning families appear able to offer these conditions. But families are not factories in the ordinary sense. Manifestations of the six features of bureaucratic organisations can be found in factories. Therefore, factories can be said to have much in common with residential institutions - for example, a specialised division of labour, a hierachical authority structure, and so on (indeed, Melossi and Pavarini's (1981) account of the rise of the prison which is entitled, The Prison and the Factory, attempts to examine the relationship between techniques of punishment and methods of production). However, as Goffman (1961) affirms, what distinguishes residential institutions from other social establishments such as factories is their all encompassing or total character and the fact that ... "the staff...[in]... their work, and hence their world have uniquely to do with people. This people-work is not quite like personnel work or the work of those involved in service relationships; the staff, after all, have objects and products to work upon not services, but these objects and products are people"... (Goffman, 1961, p.73).

The growth of factory production helped to strip the family of its economic functions - factory production replaced cottage based industry, and so on. The special foster homes, which involve a measure of financial reward for foster parents may, ironically, be seen as a sort of cottage industry. Special foster families are, therefore, a variant of the ideal-type conventional family (see the discussion on the family in Chapter 1). However, it seems that the Barclay committee's well meaning view of foster care as a variant of residential care encourages misconceptions about the nature of life in families, on the one hand, and residential institutions, on the other.

Notwithstanding the fact that the family is shaped by wider social, economic and political forces, by comparison with the Children's Home, the family is a naturally occurring social entity. We saw in Chapter 1 that the term family refers to any social group based on consanguinal (blood) and/or affinal relationships. The special foster home is a variation on this theme. It involves placing a child in a pre-existing family or household. By contrast, Children's Homes are specifically created for the placement of children in local authority care. Whilst the existence of the families (or households) studied was independent of the foster children, the Children's Homes were dependent for their existence on the residential children. This much is perhaps obvious, as is the identical nature of the objective of both foster and residential children's placements: the provision of care with respect to children who are unable for reasons discussed in Chapters 1 and 2 to live with their families of origin.

However, whilst substitute child care is the sole *raison d'etre* of the Children's Home, the family, according to Parsons (1982, p.193) has two basic and irreducible functions, viz., the primary socialisation of children and the stabilisation of adult personalities. In order to meet their needs in this respect, adults too require a context of warmth, security and mutual support. All the families visited were adequately functioning families in the sense that these conditions seemed to be be present (although a prime factor in the motivation of foster parents, especially those without children of their own living with them, may have been a desire to enhance these conditions). Whatever the foster child's response and whatever attitudes the foster parents may hold towards the foster child, these conditions must be preserved (or, in the case of previously solitary adults, sought). Otherwise, the family cannot provide a context for the meeting of human needs and, hence, loses its reason for existence.

Thus, the extent to which the family (or, indeed, the previously solitary adult) can adapt to difficult and disruptive behaviour on the part of the foster child is severely circumscribed. Certain foster placements will be more flexible than others in this respect. For example, placements where foster parents do not have children of their own living with them mean that the foster child's behaviour cannot endanger the welfare of other children. Families where warmth, security and mutual support are strongly in evidence are presumably better able to withstand the strains caused by the arrival of foster children than placements that are weak in these respects. The placement of special foster children is sure to expose any such weaknesses, sometimes (judging from the social work files maintained on the foster and residential children that were examined during the course of fieldwork) to the extent of precipitating the break up of families. Usually, however, when the behaviour of the foster child is such that it threatens the interests of either the other children or adults of the family - or both - or the previously solitary foster parent, breakdown of the placement occurs.

Paradoxically, therefore, it might be said that because the meeting of children's needs is only one of the functions performed by the family, and because the needs of foster children are accorded secondary import to those of the pre-existing family or household members, the foster homes were able to provide child-oriented care. Whereas the foster children had to adjust to a social environment conditioned by the fact that their caretakers were seeking to meet their own needs and those of any natural children living with them, and from which bureaucratisation was virtually absent, the residential children were obliged to adapt to the requirements of bureaucratic management. The needs of the youngsters in the Children's Homes visited were subordinate to the needs of the latter. Consequently although the Children's Homes were able to meet the basic needs of the children which they accommodated (e.g., the need for food and shelter), it is uncertain whether they satisfactorily met the higher order needs of the children concerned.

The notion that the needs of pre-existing family or household members take precedence over those of foster children may help to account for findings concerning the management of recurrent - mainly daily - social events, the controls and sanctions employed by foster parents *vis a vis* foster children, the observed role activities of foster parents, the observed behaviour of foster parents towards foster children, and the generally very positive perceptions of their social environments held by foster children (which in turn helps to account for the progress made by foster children during the course of their placements). For example, flexible daily routines, a relaxed social climate characterised by warm, informal and reciprocal relations with other household members - including the foster child - are very much in the interests of the pre-existing household member(s). Close control and supervision of the foster child by the foster parent, rigid daily routines, marked social distance between foster parent and child, a tense social climate, etc., are not. The provision of physical amenities owes a great deal to the socio-economic status of foster parents - what they can afford - and the life-style they choose; although, again, it is in the foster parent's interests to maintain a certain standard of comfort, etc.

However, it should not be thought that the needs of staff cannot to some extent be met by their employment in Children's Homes or that staff do not attempt to meet certain of their needs via such employment. But in Children's Homes the needs of children are regarded as being of paramount importance, and Children's Homes tend not to be seen as a legitimate domain for the meeting of adult needs. The proper place for the meeting of staff needs is outside the workplace by way of family life, etc. This gives rise to, and is subsequently reinforced by, the employment of multiple caretakers, which disrupts the continuity of care provided to residential children; especially since shift-systems enable staff to work fewer hours in the interests of meeting their own needs outside the Children's Homes. Thus, unlike the situation in foster homes, the needs/interests of staff and residential children to some degree appear to be in direct competition. They do not seem to converge or to dovetail in the way that adult-child interests may do in family settings. By contrast with Children's Homes, families often appear to rear children in an almost incidental fashion, which seems indicative of the degree to which the needs/interests of parents and children may be in harmony. This is not, of course, to imply that family life is invariably ideal, nor to deny that strains in parent-child relations may be occasioned by children's growth towards independence, etc.

The findings concerning foster children's community contacts may be partly explained by the level of the foster families integration into the communities where they lived, but also by other factors such as the way children in many Western countries characteristically seem to develop towards independence. Parsons (1964, p.138 - 139) offers the following useful caricature of this process: "The school age child, of course, continues to live in the parental household and to be highly dependent, emotionally as well as instrumentally on his parents. But he is now spending several hours a day away from home subject to a discipline and a reward system which are essentially independent of that administered by the parents. Moreover, the range of this independence gradually increases. As he grows older, he is permitted to range further territorially with neither parental nor school supervision, and to do an increasing range of things. He often gets an allowance for personal spending and begins to earn some money of his own. Generally, however, the emotional problem of dependence- independence continues to be a very salient one in this period, frequently with manifestations by the child of compulsive independence... Comcomitantly with this, the area for association with age-peers without detailed supervision expands. These associations are tied to the family, on the one hand, in that the home and yards of children who are neighbours and the adjacent streets serve as locations for their activities; and to the school, on the other hand, in that play periods and going to and from school provide occasions for informal association, even though organised extracurricular activities are introduced only later. Ways of bringing some of this activity under some sort of adult supervision are found in such organisations as boy scouts"...

The bureaucratisation found in the Children's Homes may, ironically, in part, reflect the role which they are required to play in foster care. Berridge (1985) argues that Children's Homes undertake what he terms a "fail safe" role *vis a vis* the substitute child care system. According to Berridge (1985), Children's Homes undertake five main tasks in the child care process: (1) reception into care (Children's Homes are used by social workers as a safety net in the absence of suitable alternatives); (2) the control of adolescents (many of whom are in care because of behavioural problems); (3) caring for groups of siblings who would otherwise be separated; (4) rehabilitation (e.g., helping to return children to their natural families); (5) dealing with placement breakdowns (notably, fostering breakdowns). The problems associated with family placement for hard to place youngsters have been highlighted during the course of this account. Rowe (1983, p.10) relates that although concern had been expressed that residential establishments in Strathclyde... "were full of fostering breakdowns"..., the research unit of Strathclyde Regional Council found that, in fact, ..."only 13 per cent of youngsters in ordinary community homes [Children's Homes] had been admitted following a family placement breakdown"... However, whilst it might be that the extent to which Children's Homes "bail out" unsuccessful family placements is sometimes exaggerated, in a sense it can be said that residential care is to community care what gold is to fiduciary or paper money.

Parenthetically, however, it seems that a similar process may occur within the residential child care sector. It was noted in Chapter 2 (see note 7) that residential placements may also breakdown and that the child in residential care who proves difficult to manage may be transferred to an alternative residential setting. This view is supported by the findings on control in the Children's Homes reported in Chapter 3. Ultimately, troublesome children may be placed in establishments with secure provision. The following passage from Millham *et al* (1981, pp.48 - 50) augments what has already been said about the possible reasons for foster placement breakdown, and perhaps provides important clues as to why Children's Home staff may resort to transferring difficult children to other residential settings; it might also help to explain the general nature of findings reported in Chapter 3 on control in the foster homes and Children's Homes. They state: "control in a community home rests, as it does in a family, in demonstrating that within its walls a child receives more physical care, more love, understanding and encouragement than he is likely to experience outside... Unless children see that they are getting something tangible out of their residential experience, control becomes increasingly difficult... The less caring the home, the more it will resort to sanctions and final transfer to solve its problems and the more the child will be conjured as intractable and difficult"... However, the discrepancy between ST/FPAS results and those associated with care practice, together with findings concerning children's perceptions of their social environments, perhaps indicates that even Children's Homes staffed by the most committed adults may find it difficult to convince some children that residential placement genuinely serves their interests, given the bureaucratic organisation of Children's Homes.

A second ideal-type concept - Goffman's (1961) concept of the total institution may help to indicate how the bureaucratisation of Children's Homes is related to their function. Whilst it is plain from what was said about the Children's Homes in Chapters 2 and 3 that none of the Homes visited were total institutions, they did manifest tendencies associated with this ideal-type construct. The key fact about total institutions is, according to Goffman (1961, p.18), that they involve the..."handling of many human needs by the bureaucratic organisation of whole blocks of people.... From this follow certain important implications.... When people are moved in blocks, they can be supervised by personnel whose chief activity is... surveillance - a seeing to it that everyone does what he has been clearly told is required of him"... Goffman (1961, p.18) is not clear which came first, the large blocks of managed people, or the small supervisory staff, but argues that the two are made for each other. In total institutions there is a basic split between a large managed group and a small supervisory staff. The staff-inmate split is one major implication of the bureaucratic management of large blocks of persons. Whilst the smaller homes did not accommodate groups of children any larger than some of the foster homes, they did have some of the other features of bureaucratic management discussed above.

The question arises as to whether or not bureaucratisation is a necessary or effective means of social organisation in the circumstances. Although the Children's Homes visited did meet some of the demands placed on them - for example, the control of disparate groups of children - it is, as noted, questionable whether they were able to adequately meet their officially purported caring role. Goffman (1961, p.73), as stated in Chapter 1, believes that ..."many institutions, most of the time, seem to function merely as storage dumps for inmates"... However, they... "usually present themselves to the public as rational organisations designed consciously, through and through, as effective machines for producing a few officially avowed and officially approved ends... This contradiction, between what the institution does and what its officials must say it does, forms the basic context of the staff's daily activity"...

The total institution is, in Goffman's (1961, p.22) view, a social hybrid - part residential community, part formal organisation. However, whilst it is useful to regard the Children's Homes studied as sharing some of the total institution's affinities with formal organisations, it is also important to recognise that a local authority Children's Home, like many total institutions, is part of a much larger formal organisation - the Social Services Department (SSD). As stated in Chapter 1, Hadley and Mcgrath (1980, p.5) assert that SSD's display the worst features of bureaucracies in that they are ..."hierarchic, rule bound and slow to respond to changes"... It might be argued that a potential strength of bureaucratisation in Children's Homes is that it permits external control of residential staff and thereby offers a safeguard to vulnerable children. Unfortunately, however, it seems that attempts to ensure accountability (e.g., via staff maintaining detailed records of daily events in the Homes, etc.) reduces the amount of time which staff are able to spend with children, thus making it more likely that staff contacts with children will be of a supervisory nature.

Ironically, attempts in recent years to improve the quality of care for children via innovations such as the key worker system (Authority A Children's Homes had a modified version of this system and termed their staff case workers; Authority B Homes also operated a similar system, but called their staff link workers), which involve staff performing duties previously regarded as the preserve of senior staff and field social workers (e.g., writing reports and attending reviews on children, participating in decisions regarding children's futures, visiting children's families, and so on), may have had the same effect [2]. Whether some staff enthusiastically undertake administrative type duties because these help to foster a professional self-conception (undermined by the fact that most residential staff, unlike their fieldwork colleagues, lack formal qualifications) is also a matter for conjecture; as is the question of whether attempts to improve the quality of care in Children's Homes have mainly benefited staff rather than children. Certainly, the key worker system has at least in part been supported by staff because, in addition to offering a means by which to improve the quality of care provided for children, it promised to enhance their status *vis a vis* field work colleagues. A fairly striking difference between the role performance of foster parents and staff was that the former spent less time discussing children but more time actually engaged in direct contact with them than did staff. To say that staff talk and foster parents do in relation to children is perhaps to overstate the case. However, it was not uncommon during fieldwork to observe a group of staff discussing children in the office whilst the children remained on the other side of the door.

Attempts to exert external control over Children's Homes reduces the degree of discretion exercised by staff. But the differential levels of autonomy afforded foster parents and staff does not merely entail more paper work, etc., for staff. It means that residential staff may have little scope for the exercise of autonomy in relation to the most practical aspects of life in the Children's Homes. For example, food is often delivered by wholesalers and retailers through arrangement with central office; decor and furnishings may be selected by administrative personnel at central office rather than by staff.

Administrative frameworks also appear to impede the extent to which youngsters in Children's Homes are able to live the sort of life experienced by the majority of the nation's children. As Fuller and Stevenson (1983, p.111) note, administrative frameworks may deny children in residential care the exercise of choice and experiences which are an essential part of growing up. The authors exemplify this point by citing the rules in some authorities governing the purchase of clothes by vouchers at certain shops (not all local authorities now follow this practice). More prosaically, if food is delivered wholesalers, etc., children do not gain from basic experiences such as regular visits to shops with caretakers.

Fuller and Stevenson (1983) also correctly report that the accounts (e.g., Docker Drysdale, 1968; Wills, 1970), referred to in Chapter 1, by those who have attempted to create specialist therapeutic miliex for the treatment of severely disturbed children, and which have had a profound impact on the progressive element in residential care, involved establishments operating in the voluntary sector. The authors argue that..." the central dilemma facing those who seek to improve the quality of residential care is how to translate the ideals and the practice of gifted individuals for the use of ordinary mortals"... More pertinently, they also question whether the charismatic leaders to whom they refer could have functioned as well as is purported (the accounts make no claims to evaluative research) in the statutory sector, and call for more research in order to understand how the insights and experience gained from... "such enlightened but idiosyncratic provision can be incorporated into the mainstream of residential care and adapted to the needs of less disturbed children"... (Fuller and Stevenson, 1983, p.113).

Of course, factors other than bureaucracy help to shape the nature of care practice in Children's Homes. Here I have in mind the findings concerning residential children's community contacts and the nature of the physical environment in the Children's Homes visited. The residential children appeared to enjoy fewer opportunities than the foster children for contact with people, places and experiences outside their placements. This probably owes more to the fact that many of the Homes were some distance from children's home areas and to the attitudes of host communities than it does to restrictions imposed by staff on children's external activities and the reception given by the former to children's visitors. That the residential children were placed with relatively large groups of age-peers may also have meant that residential youngsters tended not to seek the company of age-peers outside the Children's Homes in the way that Parsons considers youngsters in families usually do (see above). In addition to inappropriate siting, the design and size of some of the Children's Homes was clearly inimical to child-oriented care. Although buildings alone cannot ensure a reasonable quality of life, the best efforts of staff may to some extent be vitiated by the sorts of factors noted in Chapter 3.

However, bureaucracy may even help to determine the extent to which Children's Homes are integrated with host communities, and the quality of the physical environment provided for residential children, in that residential provisions appear to have an inherent tendency towards inertia and inflexibilty. Historically, the geographical distribution and size of residential provision for children may be attributed to the fact that much of it was built at a time when protection of the community and/or the removal of children from harmful family and home ties conditioned the prescriptions of policy makers. Moss (1975, pp.43 - 44) relates: "Any generation is heavily dependent on individual residential establishments, and also on the overall systems...[of]... which they form...[a].. part. These are the product of past generations and may go back for up to or even over 100 years. Individual systems and units survive, even when their original *raison d'etre*...has passed, due to the inertia caused by the high costs of replacement and the well established and influential patterns of staffing and management, with the sectional interests to which they give rise. All of these may be reinforced by an intricate network of philosophy, values and sentiment. Inflexibility comes in because old buildings, outmoded in design, scale, location and overall concept, are impossible to convert into provision in line with contemporary thinking, and are probably unsaleable or unusable as anything else but residential provision. In this way the residential scene of any period is marked by a struggle to convert, use, exploit (and finish paying for) past structures and organisations, so that they can be made to meet current needs and thinking and sustain a viable justification for their continued existence"...

Moss's (1975) comments are an appropriate place to end this account of factors which helped to shape care practice in the foster homes and children's Homes visited. They not only further indicate the extreme complexity of some of the processes involved, but also perhaps counsel against underestimating the difficulties associated with efforts to improve the quality of provision made for children in care. Moreover, enough has been said throughout this account to make it clear that even if implemented such policies are by no means certain to produce their desired effect.

3. Implications of the Study

In contemplating possible determinants of care practice, I have strayed far beyond the objectives set out in Chapter 1. This study was never intended to provide the basis for a policy blue print. However, having arrived at this point, it may be appropriate to outline how some of the major deficiencies identified might be ameliorated. Before doing this, it must be said that the special foster homes and Children's Homes of two local authorities do not constitute a representative sample of the provisions concerned. However, as noted in Chapter 2, the residential settings did comprise examples from each of Berridge's (1985) three ideal-type categories of Children's Homes. Moreover, whilst major differences in care practice were generally observed between the foster homes and Children's Homes, the differences between the means of scores obtained by Authority A and Authority B Children's Homes on the four dimensions of care examined in Chapter 3 were negligible. Thus, it would appear reasonable to suggest that the Children Homes were not atypical examples of such provision.

Given the uncertainties associated with substitute child care, measures designed to sustain and support natural families may, in various ways, be more socially and economically effective than those seeking to provide alternative modes of care. That structural factors such as poverty, homelessness, inadequate income-maintenance and day care services for lone parents, and so on, appear to be a necessary condition, if not sufficient cause, for the entry of many children into care, compels one to support the repeated calls in the literature for increased help to vulnerable families [3]. Pending the inception of policies associated with *primary* prevention, the focus in what follows will be *secondary* prevention. That is, how the experience of local authority care can be prevented from being a deprivation in itself.

Despite their shortcomings, it is clear that Children's Homes currently perform an invaluable role in relation to the substitute care system [4]. What is far from certain, however, is whether all the tasks presently undertaken by Children's Homes necessarily have to be performed in residential settings. Some of the functions carried out by Children's Homes have been mentioned already. To these may be added the following positive roles suggested for residential care (Kadushin, 1971; Prosser, 1976; Aldgate, 1978):

- it is often the choice for disturbed or older children who may not wish to identify with a new family unit
- it can provide an excellent *milieu* for the treatment of particular emotional problems
- it can be a key component in the use of part-time parenting schemes to aid those parents who are unable to cope with their children on a full-time basis
- it appears to be more conducive than fostering to maintaining children's contacts with their natural families
- it can provide opportunity for a less intense emotional relationship with parental figures.

Such are some of the positive roles claimed for residential care. However, are these roles, and the other functions of Children's Homes earlier referred to, really exclusive to residential care ? Even if it is conceded that residential care appears more conducive than foster care to maintaining children's natural family ties, data reported in Chapters 3 and 5 suggests this need not be the case. Could not the emergency and short-term placements offered by residential care be provided in family settings ? Would not preparation for long term-fostering and the rehabilitation of children with their natural families be more appropriately done in family contexts ? Similar questions can be asked about the treatment function of residential care (especially in view of special foster schemes pioneered by Kent SSD), about part-time parenting schemes, and about how breakdowns in foster placements are dealt with. Moreover, in practice, it may be that for some youngsters Children's Homes afford them not so much an opportunity for less intense emotional relationships with parental figures, but rather a sort of emotional limbo. Whilst the family appears particularly well suited to the development of very close inter-personal relationships between its members, we may also question whether placements in family settings for older children in local authority care necessarily have to entail intense emotional relationships between the caretakers and children concerned. Much seems to depend on the expectations of foster parents. These partly hinge on what sort of people are recruited, but are also conditioned by the preparation and support that foster parents receive. The need of certain children for emotional relationships with caretakers less intense than those customarily associated with parent-child relations is not beyond the comprehension of ordinary people, nor is the idea that children in care may derive positive benefit from regular contact with their natural parents. Arrangements could be made that would allow older children to be placed in family settings without the children involved experiencing a conflict of loyalties between their natural families and their surrogate families. Equally, are there really firm grounds for supposing that special foster placements could not be found for older youngsters who do not wish to identify strongly with a new family unit? *Approved lodgings* are used for children in care of working age. Why could this idea not be modified somewhat to meet the needs of youngsters below working age? Indeed, some of the foster placements visited were, in fact, operating successfully along such lines.

The view taken here is, therefore, that the flexibilty of family placement, and the range of functions which the latter could perform with respect to the substitute care of older children may be underestimated. This concurs with Rowe's (1983) conception of family placement, referred to in Chapter 1, which involves short term foster placements (serving various purposes - emergency care, assessment, respite care, etc) at one end of a fostering continuum to long-term foster placement (with or without contact between children and their natural families) and adoption at the other. However, given that many children presently in residential care continue to maintain contact with their natural families, support is also given here to Holman's (1975) view that family placement should, where possible, be informed by the inclusive model of fostering, irrespective perhaps of whether restoration of children with natural parents is the goal of social work intervention. As noted in Chapter 1, the *inclusive* model encourages contact with natural parents. It also seeks to ensure that foster children understand their situation. By contrast, the *exclusive* model discourages contact with natural parents and the foster family approximates to a natural family. In this respect, it might help if the role of the special foster parent was regarded as primarily one of service to the community and an expression of altruism and good citizenship, rather than a means by which foster parents seek to meet their parenting needs.

Expanding family placement for older children would require the recruitment of sufficient caretakers. Parker (1978) considers that increases in married women's employment, a shorter average period in a women's life of child-bearing and child-rearing, and rises in separation, divorce and remarriage, and in the numbers of lone parents are likely to adversely affect the supply of foster parents on traditional criteria. Accordingly, he argues that attention must be given to fostering by groups not previously considered suitable for this role; for example, older parents, retired people, families where both parents are working. The family settings in this study varied considerably and relatively few were conventional families; indeed some of the households visited were not families prior to the arrival of the foster child, but rather were solitary people - male as well as female [5]. Some were people whose own children were adults and living independently. It could be, therefore, that there are significant reserves of potential foster parents whose situations diverge from that of the conventional family. Similarly, there may be a substantial number of people (including large numbers of residential staff - see below) who would neither wish, or be in a position to offer, long-term care but who may be willing and able to help meet the need for special family placements of a short-term nature - including emergency receptions into care, ordinary foster placement breakdowns, part-time parenting to help natural parents who are unable to cope with their children on a full-time basis. A pool of such placements, perhaps with special foster parents paid a retainer when their service is not required, could be a valuable resource for any local authority.

Parker (1978) also affirms that rates of payment for foster parents might have to compete with wages paid in other forms of employment. The sorts of fees received by Authority A foster parents referred to in Chapter 2, which were generous by comparison with the allowances paid to ordinary foster parents, might well attract suitable people who would otherwise not be able to afford to offer their service. Interestingly, a number of the residential staff interviewed were disillusioned with what residential care had to offer children, and reported that they would prefer to foster children if the fostering fee was commensurate with their earnings. However, whilst the recruitment of sufficient numbers of foster parents may require a pragmatic acknowledgement of the factors which are likely to promote or inhibit this, once again notions such as community service, altruism and good citizenship should be the sorts of primary factors which motivate special foster parents.

Hazel (1981) claims that a professional foster placement probably costs roughly half the price of a residential placement in a CHE. Despite the fact that the cost of schooling is included in these comparisons, Fuller and Stevenson (1983) suggest that professional fostering may also be somewhat cheaper than residential care in Children's Homes of the kind studied, but that this is variable and difficult to estimate. Moreover, Walton and Elliot (1980, pp.1 - 2) rightly argue that whilst a realistic appreciation of the differential costs of services is important in balancing needs and resources, the ... "ethics of using financial arguments as anything other than secondary factors in determining policy at a general level and deciding the particular form of social work appropriate for individual clients needs to be rigorously examined. If costly forms of care - whether residential or community - are effective in helping clients, their use is fully justified"...

Clearly, the growth of family placement for older children in care would also necessitate attention being given to issues such as how best to support the foster parents concerned and monitor placements effectively without invading the privacy and usurping the authority of foster parents. It seems that one of the genuine advantages which residential care may have over family placement is that it is generally easier to monitor than the latter. This is because, unlike family settings, the bureaucratic organisation of the Children's Home is compatible with the administrative arrangements of the SSD; although we have seen that the possible strength of the Children's Home referred to is a source of major weakness also.

As previously implied, it appears likely that even if non-residential alternatives were developed to undertake many of the tasks currently performed by Children's Homes, the former would have to be complemented by a measure of non-family care. For example, it might not be possible to find a family placement for a large group of siblings; in spite of what has been said above, some youngsters may not wish to live in a family setting, some may exhaust the tolerance and patience of foster parents, and so on. Can, therefore, child-oriented care be provided in non-family settings ? The results obtained for CH9 suggests that they could. However, it would seem that there is a need to eradicate the bureaucratisation associated with the operation of the sort of Children's Homes studied.

This would appear to demand a substantial decrease in the external control exercised by the SSD's concerned and a corresponding increase in the autonomy of the staff employed in the Homes - including caretakers being given greater responsibilty for practical matters such as the buying of foodstuffs and the purchase of decor and furnishings. Increasing the autonomy of caretakers should also result in a corresponding increase in the degree of choice and normal experience afforded children in relation to matters such as clothing, diet, etc.

The caring aspect of the staff role needs to be given greater emphasis, and must not be seen as inferior to the role performed by field social workers. Increasing the amount of direct contact between children and caretakers appears to require a significant reduction in the administrative type tasks performed by staff, including a major decrease in the amount of recording and reports undertaken by staff *vis a vis* children. Record keeping is useful in the sense that it offers a means of attempting to ensure accountability. However, the special foster parents visited did not maintain detailed records on children, nor were the foster homes equipped with offices. But the foster homes appeared to be adequately monitored by the SSD's concerned, and foster parents were able to participate in decisions concerning their foster children. Liberating staff from administrative type duties would not only increase the amount of time which the latter are able to spend on social child care activities in a general, but would also increase the attention given by caretakers to specific issues such as children's educational needs; moreover, it would mean that offices could be dispensed with.

The office is not, however, merely an artefact of attempts to monitor Children's Homes. It is also a symbol and tool of the social distance between staff and children which facilitates the bureaucratic management of a larger child group by a smaller staff group. Accordingly, it seems that in order to render bureaucratic management unnecessary, the number of children accommodated in some Homes must be reduced considerably (a point which is not seen as contradicting what was said in the previous section about the impact of size on care practice). It may be that the optimum number of youngsters accommodated in each setting would not ordinarily exceed 3 or 4 (exceptions to this would be large sibling groups). This would mean that ordinary houses - council owned properties, for example - could be used. Locating these close to children's home localities might make it easier to involve natural parents in their children's care, and would increase children's participation in community activities. Reducing the numbers of children accommodated in residential settings should also make possible increased participation by children in decisions pertaining to the organisation of daily life in the units (e.g., household rules and routines, etc) and normalise daily living in general.

The community based alternative to Children's Homes that is suggested seems to follow from the findings concerning the nature of care practice in the special foster homes and Children's Homes studied, and from the arguments rehearsed regarding the factors which might help to define care practice. If the adults involved were husband and wife teams, the sort of provision advocated would be very similar to special foster placements headed by salaried, professional, foster parents. This would be entirely consistent with the arguments presented in the previous section.

It must be emphasised that the alternative model for Children's Homes proposed is not, however, an argument in favour of a return to the family group homes referred to in Chapter 1. For one thing, all the adults concerned would be salaried and, in recognition of the fact that some of the children accomodated might be very difficult to manage, where husband and wife teams were involved the husband would not have employment outside the home. Second, there would be no domestic staff employed in the homes; rather, all domestic tasks would be undertaken by caretakers and children. Third, the ratio of caretakers to children present in the homes at any given time would be about

1.2; thus,the new homes would have more adults but fewer children than the old family group homes. Fourth, the homes would operate on democratic lines; there would be no differentiation in the status of the adults; as in families, adults would have authority over children, but children would participate in decisions affecting the running of the homes and their lives more generally. Fifth, the new homes would enjoy considerably more autonomy from SSD's than the old family group homes, and it is assumed that ways would be found to ensure that the administrative frameworks of SSD's did not impede the degree to which children lived a normal life. Last, there would be no expectation on the part of the adults concerned that the children accommodated would be relatively unproblematic.

The suggested alternative to current Children's Homes represents one, inevitably flawed, necessarily roughly sketched, model only. The details must be provided by those who perform the difficult and, given the arguments rehearsed in the previous section, unenviable role of administering substitute child care provisions. Other models are, of course, possible. However, homes very similar to those proposed, involving a combination of foster home and small family group home, supported by a very high level of social work support, have been developed in the Netherlands (Social Services Committee, session 1983-84, para., 189), and some may already exist in this country also. Such initiatives are exceedingly welcome and merit applause, for imagination and experimentation on the part of those directly responsible, informed by evaluative research, are vital for the development of provisions which satisfactorily meet the needs of children in local authority care.

The latter objective ought not to be beyond reach. Work by Clarke and Clarke (1976) - referred to in Chapter 1 - and Rutter (1985), for example, appears to indicate that children are far more resilient in terms of being able to overcome adversity than is sometimes supposed. The task seems to be one of ensuring that children in local authority care are provided with compensatory experiences and opportunities likely to enhance their life chances (e.g., warmth, security and support from parent figures, continuity of care, full knowledge and understanding of their past experiences and future prospects, appropriate educational and employment opportunities, training in social skills, help in developing the practical skills of household management, etc.).

Finally, the quality of the provision which a nation or society makes for its most vulnerable members says much about the nature of that society, what it values or cherishes and chooses to disregard or to disown. The issues which have lain at the heart of this study are not esoteric. Responsibility for the welfare of the children concerned is collectively borne.

Notes

1. See, for example, reviews on the consequences of residential care by Dinnage and Pringle, 1967 and Prosser, 1976.
2. Wendelken (1983, p.54), in a handbook for social work practitioners notes that..." in large group situations, individual needs are difficult to meet. Children's homes can be encouraged to individualise their care of each child by...operating a system of 'specials' where each member of staff takes a particular responsibility for a few children. The 'special'

liaises with school and home and with the fieldworker concerned. She takes responsibility for the personal care of the child, the day-to-day decisions, his clothing and medical supervision"... The author employs the term specials to denote a role which approximates to that of key worker.

3. See the review of the literature on substitute care by Fuller and Stevenson (1983, pp.87-128).

4. There are reasonable grounds for supposing that the wholesale closure of local authority Children's Homes would stimulate a growth in private sector residential facilities. These would be difficult to monitor and an article by Laurance (1983) implies that the motives of some of those responsible for such provisions may contrast markedly with those of the founding fathers of progressive residential care who operated in the voluntary sector. Moreover, Scull's (1984) attack on the modern policy of deinstitutionalisation, whereby, for example, inmates are decanted from mental hospitals into non-existent or appauling alternatives of care, perhaps serves as a warning against well meaning attempts to abolish local authority residential provisions.

5. See Rapoport et al (ed.) (1982) for a collection of readings which show the diversity of forms taken by families in Britain. The contributors demonstrate that the strereotype, conventional, family group comprising breadwinning father, full-time housewife mother and at least two residing children is seriously misleading in Britain today. The majority of family households in contemporary Britain consist of other combinations - for example, couples (married or unmarried) without accompanying offspring, single parent households, dual worker families and varying types of reconstituted families.

Appendices

INTERNAL ORGANISATION OF SETTINGS INTERVIEW
QUESTIONNAIRE

Name of Children's Home/foster home:
Post/Role of person interviewed:
Date of interview

I would like to ask you some questions about...how your establishment is organised/your domestic arrangements...Your answers will be treated as confidential

1. First, could you give me a list of...all the people who work in this establishment, including domestic, maintenance and night staff [Note: name; post; hours per week; whether resident or non-resident. Probe: team/shift system worked by direct care staff] /the members of your family or household [Note: name; age; occupation; relationship to interviewee; where living; etc. Probe: hours worked by foster parent(s)]?

2. Could you tell me...whether any members of staff have special responsibilities in relation to the children [Note: name; post; nature of responsibility] /who has most to do with the day-to-day care of the child(ren), e.g., cooking, cleaning, washing, etc. [Probe: other areas of responsibility, e.g., attending reviews, writing reports, etc.]...?

3. Are...the children separated into groups, etc., for any activities for any part of the day [Note: activity or purpose; which children involved; which staff involved; duration... Probe: sleeping, eating, school, recreation, etc.] /there any aspects of your foster child(ren)'s daily life within the home which are kept separate from the living arrangements of the rest of the family or household [Probe: eating, recreation, meals, accommodation]?

4. Where do(es) the child(ren) go to school? [Probe: whether on site or in the community; numbers attending each (where applicable); type(s) of school attended in the community; whether (any) child(ren) is/are of working age and employed (including Government Training Schemes; where foster parents own child(ren) attend(s) school (if applicable).]

N.B.   Children's Homes only

5.   Can you tell me what the role of your establishment is within the Department's overall residential provision for children in need of substitute care?   [Probe: *official* vs. *actual* role; type of children accommodated]

6.   Could you give me the names of the children who are [N.B. Note sex]

(a) 10 - 12 years

(b) 13 - 15 years

(c) 16 years and over

THANK YOU FOR YOUR HELP

Note

Recording spaces throughout this section have been considerably shortened for the purpose of presentation.

CHILDREN'S CHARACTERISTICS QUESTIONNAIRE

Source of data collected (e.g. interview with child's social worker):

Date:

---

1. Name:
2. Date of birth:
3. Sex:
4. Legislation in force:
5. Date legislation came into force:
6. Local authority in whose care child is placed:
7. Name and type of provision where child is placed:
8. Date placed:
9. Reason for placement (i.e. brief summary):
   [Note: anticipated length of stay; purpose of placement within the overall plan of social work intervention]

10. *Previous placements in local authority care [N.B. If none, write NONE]

    Name of est./foster home   Type   Date placed   Date departed   Reasons
    for
    departure

N.B. Code reasons for departure as follows:	
Normal discargc	1
Placement for assessment/remand only	2
Emergency/temporary placement	3
For internal behaviour problems	4
Absconding	5
Offence	6
Age	7
Institution, etc. requested child's removal	8
Transferred, but reason not given	9
Other	10

11. *Has a place in an establishment, etc. for the child ever been refused?

Yes   [ ]
No   [ ]
No records   [ ]

[N.B. List number of placements refused, the type(s) of placement(s) involved, and the date(s) of the refusals]

12. *What were the reasons given for the refusal(s) by the Dept./est./admissions panel?

	1st	2nd	3rd	4th
Too old				
Too young				
Lack of places				
Has not tried other suitable places				
Would not fit in with group				
Not disturbed enough				
Too disturbed				
Too delinquent				
Too far from home				
Intelligence too high				
Intelligence too low				
Other reason [specify]				

13. *When did the child last live at home (i.e. with natural or adoptive parents, or relatives) on a full time basis with SSD consent (i.e. not as an absconder or in hiding)?

Within the last 3 months   [ ]
4 - 6 months   [ ]
7 months - 12 months   [ ]
13 months - 2 years   [ ]
3 - 4 years   [ ]
More than 4 years ago   [ ]
Has never lived at home   [ ]
No reports   [ ]

14. *When the child was living at home s/he was living with

Father and mother   [ ]
Father only   [ ]
Father and stepmother   [ ]
Father and cohabitee   [ ]
Mother only   [ ]
Mother and stepfather   [ ]
Mother and cohabitee   [ ]
Adoptive parents   [ ]
Grandparents or other relatives   [ ]
Other   [ ]
Never lived at home   [ ]
No reports   [ ]

15. *Is there any evidence of the following serious family problems affecting parents, siblings or other members of the household?

(a) Member of the family has a serious criminal record [N.B. does not include road traffic offences, minor instances of juvenile offending, etc.].
(b) Member of family has received psychiatric treatment as an inpatient, or at a day hospital (including drugs or alchoholism units).
(c) There is a substantiated record of neglect or cruelty by parents.

None of them present   [ ]
All three present   [ ]
Criminality and mental illness present   [ ]
Criminality and neglect/cruelty present   [ ]
Mental illness and neglect/cruelty present [ ]
Criminality only present   [ ]
Mental illness only present   [ ]
Neglect/cruelty only present   [ ]
Not applicable (family dead/unknown)   [ ]

16. *How many times has the child absconded from present placement?

Never   [ ]
Once   [ ]
2 - 3   [ ]
4 - 5   [ ]
6 - 9   [ ]
10 or more   [ ]
Occasionally (number unknown)   [ ]
Frequently (number unknown)   [ ]
No reports   [ ]

17. *How many previous placements have broken down due to abscondings?

0 or not applicable (no previous placements)	[ ]
1	[ ]
2	[ ]
3	[ ]
More than 3	[ ]
No information	[ ]

18. *Has the child committed offences whilst absconding from present placement?

No	[ ]
Yes (found guilty on one occasion)	[ ]
Yes (found guilty on more than one occasion)	[ ]
Evidence of offence committed, but no charge brought	[ ]
No information	[ ]

19. Did the child commit offences whilst absconding from previous placements?

No or not applicable (no previous placements)	[ ]
Yes (found guilty on one occasion)	[ ]
Yes (found guilty more than once)	[ ]
Evidence of offence committed, but no charge brought	[ ]
No information	[ ]

20. *Has the child a record of active physical violence towards people or animals?

	+Prior to Present Placement	During Present Placement
Yes, has attacked caretaker(s), other children, and members of the public	[ ]	[ ]
Yes, has attacked caretaker(s) and other children	[ ]	[ ]
Yes, has attacked caretaker(s) and members of the public	[ ]	[ ]
Yes, has attacked other children and members of the public	[ ]	[ ]
Yes, has attacked caretaker(s) only	[ ]	[ ]
Yes, has attacked children only	[ ]	[ ]
Yes, attacked members of the public only	[ ]	[ ]
Yes, attacks on pets/other animals only	[ ]	[ ]
No record of physical attacks	[ ]	[ ]
No reports	[ ]	[ ]

+ includes whilst at home

[N.B. Questions 21-25 are to be answered in relation to the child's behaviour in his/her present placement.]

196

21. *Is the child said to be otherwise generally aggressive?

Yes, towards people and property   [ ]
Yes, towards people only   [ ]
Yes, towards property only   [ ]
Yes, but no details   [ ]
No indication that s/he is aggressive   [ ]
Reports contradictory   [ ]
No reports   [ ]

22. *If violent/temper outburts are mentioned, are explanations given for the behaviour (e.g., in response to reprimand, loss of privilege or freedom, teasing by peers, etc.)?

Yes, reasons given   [ ]
No, reports specifically describe behaviour as irrational [ ]
No, behaviour unexplained   [ ]
No violent/temper outbursts mentioned   [ ]
Reports contradictory   [ ]
No information   [ ]

23. *Is the child said to lead others into trouble or to be a bad influence?

Yes, deliberately stirs up trouble/leads others into trouble, etc.   [ ]
Yes, is a bad example (others copy or admire him/her, or might do so)   [ ]
Yes, but no details given   [ ]
No indication that s/he does   [ ]
No reports   [ ]

24. *Is the child said to get on well with caretaker(s)?

Yes, well liked   [ ]
No evidence that s/he doesn't   [ ]
No caretaker(s) find(s) relationship difficult   [ ]
No, is generally unpopular   [ ]
Reports contradictory   [ ]
No reports   [ ]

25. *Is the child said to be cheeky, abusive, disobedient, to caretaker(s)?

Yes, normal mode of behaviour   [ ]
Yes, variable; at times; reports contradictory   [ ]
No evidence that s/he is   [ ]
No reports   [ ]

197

26. *Is the child said to lack guilt or concern about his/her offences and/or other anti-social acts?

Yes   [ ]
Reports contradictory   [ ]
No   [ ]
No reports   [ ]

27. *IQ level

Name of scale used:
Under 60   [ ]
60 - 69   [ ]
70 - 79   [ ]
80 - 89   [ ]
90 - 99   [ ]
100 - 109   [ ]
110 - 120   [ ]
Over 120   [ ]
No reports   [ ]

28. *Is there evidence of any of the following: brain damage at birth; other congenital deformity of the nervous system; brain damage in childhood; severe illness causing neurological deformity; epilepsy?

Yes[state]:   [ ]
No   [ ]
No reports   [ ]

29. *Is there a record of psychiatric treatment or oversight?

Has been treated in an adolescent unit or psychiatric hospital/ward   [ ]
Has been in an adolescent unit or psychiatric hospital/ward for
observation   [ ]
Has had treatment as an outpatient   [ ]
Treatment has been recommended by a psychiatrist   [ ]
Recommended for psychiatric oversight only   [ ]
No record of psychiatric treatment or oversight   [ ]
No reports   [ ]

30. *Has the child been to a child guidance clinic/accepted or recommended for a maladjusted school?

Yes[state]:   [ ]
No   [ ]
No reports   [ ]

198

31. *Is the child said to be sexually at risk or a risk to others (e.g., reports express concern because of: indecent exposure; unlawful sexual intercourse; homosexuality; incest; promiscuity; taken into care as being in moral danger; prostitution; victim of sex offence, etc.)?

Yes, both child and others at risk   [ ]
Yes, child at risk   [ ]
Yes, risk to others   [ ]
Yes, sexual problems but no details   [ ]
No   [ ]
No reports   [ ]

N.B. If at risk and/or risk to others specify:

32. *Has the child threatened or tried to commit suicide?

Has attempted suicide (made a serious attempt)   [ ]
Has inflicted injuries on him/herself (no evidence that
it was a suicide attempt)   [ ]
Has threatened to kill him/herself   [ ]
No evidence that s/he has   [ ]
No reports   [ ]

33. *Reasons for making of most recent care order (or other)?

(a) Offences against the person (e.g., assault, rape, other violent)   [ ]
(b) Breaking and entering/burglary   [ ]
(c) Larceny and other theft offences not included in (a) and (b)   [ ]
(d) Road traffic offences (including TDA)   [ ]
(e) Sex/drugs/arson offences   [ ]
(f) Breach of the peace (including threatening behaviour, etc.)   [ ]
(g) Breach of probation or supervision order   [ ]
(h) Wilful or malicious damage   [ ]
(i) Other [specify]   [ ]
(j) Not an offender (care, protection or control) [specify]   [ ]
(k) No care order, in care under CCA 1980 [specify reasons]   [ ]
(l) No care order, other [specify reasons]   [ ]
(m) No reports   [ ]

34.   *If child an offender: age on first finding of guilt (excluding charges under the Education Act or Beyond Control cases)?

8 years	[ ]
9 years	[ ]
10 years	[ ]
11 years	[ ]
12 years	[ ]
13 years	[ ]
14 years	[ ]
15 years	[ ]
16 years	[ ]
Not an offender	[ ]
No reports	[ ]

35.   *Number of court appearances as an offender (excluding Education Act or Beyond Control, but including S.1 (2) (f) CYPA 1969)?

	Prior to Present Placement	During Present Placement
None	[ ]	[ ]
1	[ ]	[ ]
2	[ ]	[ ]
3	[ ]	[ ]
4	[ ]	[ ]
5	[ ]	[ ]
6	[ ]	[ ]
More than 6	[ ]	[ ]
Numerous, exact figure unknown	[ ]	[ ]
No information	[ ]	[ ]

36.   *Total number of offences for which child has been found guilty (including any taken into consideration - t.i.c.)?

	Prior to Present Placement	During Present Placement
None	[ ]	[ ]
2 - 5	[ ]	[ ]
6 - 10	[ ]	[ ]
15 - 20	[ ]	[ ]
25 - 30	[ ]	[ ]
More than 30	[ ]	[ ]
Numerous, exact figure unknown	[ ]	[ ]
No reports	[ ]	[ ]

37. *Has the child been found guilty of the following types of offence (including t.i.c.'s)?

Assault/rape/other violent   [ ]
Taking and driving away   [ ]
Arson   [ ]
Drug offences   [ ]
No reports   [ ]

38. If the child has not been found guilty of the types of offence listed in question 37 (above), but is an offender, state the nature of offences committed.

Prior to Present Placement:

During Present Placement:

39. Is the child reported as truanting from school?

	Prior to Present Placement	During Present Placement
Very frequently	[ ]	[ ]
Occasionally	[ ]	[ ]
Never	[ ]	[ ]
No reports	[ ]	[ ]

40. Is the child's behaviour at school said to be problematic?

	Prior to Present Placement	During Present Placement
No, said to be satisfactory	[ ]	[ ]
contradictory	[ ]	[ ]
Yes	[ ]	[ ]
No reports	[ ]	[ ]

41. Is the child's educational performance said to be satisfactory?

	Prior to Present Placement	During Present Placement
Yes	[ ]	[ ]
Reports contradictory	[ ]	[ ]
No	[ ]	[ ]
No reports	[ ]	[ ]

42. Is the child handicapped?

    Yes, physically [specify]   [ ]
    Yes, mentally [specify]   [ ]
    Not handicapped   [ ]
    No reports   [ ]

43. Has the child suffered traumatic illness?

    Yes   [ ]
    No   [ ]
    No reports   [ ]

    If, YES, specify nature and date of illness and note whether illness
    occasioned separation from parents:

44. Has the child ever been separated from parents for a period of more than
    two months for reasons other than those previously noted?
    [If not, write NONE. Otherwise, state: whether from father or mother, or
    both; age of child; reasons for separation; duration of separation; other
    relevant information]

45. Has the child been rejected?

    By father   [ ]
    By mother   [ ]
    Not rejected [ ]
    No reports   [ ]

46. Composition of family (i.e. natural or adoptive)
    [State: N parents, whether living at home, ages, occupations; N siblings,
    ages, occupations (if appropriate), where living, etc]

47. **Nature of home ownership or tenancy?

    Owner-occupier   [ ]
    Standard council house or flat, etc. [ ]
    Private rented   [ ]
    Other   [ ]
    No reports   [ ]

202

48. If child of working age, is work record said to be satisfactory?
    [N.B. Includes Government training schemes]

    Yes   [ ]
    No, work record is said to be poor   [ ]
    Reports contradictory   [ ]
    Not applicable, child is unemployed and has never held a job [ ]
    Not applicable, child continuing full-time education   [ ]
    No reports   [ ]

49. Do the child's natural or adoptive parents hold a positive view of his/her
    placement?

	Father	Mother
Yes, view is said to be positive	[ ]	[ ]
View is said to be ambivalent	[ ]	[ ]
View is said to be indifferent	[ ]	[ ]
Reports contradictory	[ ]	[ ]
No, view is said to be negative	[ ]	[ ]
No reports	[ ]	[ ]

THANK YOU FOR YOUR HELP

Note

* Denotes questions based on items from a questionnaire designed by
Cawson and Martell (1979), ** denotes item based on work by Millham
et al (1975).

INDEX OF CHILD-MANAGEMENT

CH/FH: Dates of application: (a) Int: (b) Obs:
Post/Role of person interviewed:

A = Children's homes; B = foster homes; 0 = child-oriented; 2 = institutionally-oriented; 1 = mixed pattern (i.e. care practice falling somewhere between child-oriented and institutionally-oriented); X = other - to be completed when in doubt about the appropriate score at the time of data collection; I = interview item; Ob = observational item; FS = final score awarded for items where data collected via interview and observation.

Interview: I would like to talk with you about various matters concerning...the children/your foster child(ren)... What you tell me will be treated as confidential...

Rigidity of Routine

1. *
A.

    I Do children get up at the same time at weekends as they do on weekends?

    0 Different times for all on two days.
    1 Different for some or on one day only.
    2 Same time.
    X:

B.

    I Do(es) the foster child(ren) get up at the same time at weekends as s/he/they do(es) on weekdays?

    0 Different time on two days.
    1 Different for one etc., or on one day only.
    2 Same time.
    X:

2.
A.   I Do children always go to bed at the same time during the week ?

0 No, usually children would be permitted to stay up later if, say, there
was something on TV of particular interest.
1 Different for some or occasionally.
2 Yes, same time.
X:

B.
I Do(es) the foster child(ren) always go to bed at the same time during
the week?

0 No, usually s/he/they would be permitted to stay up later if, say, there
was something on TV of particular interest.
1 Different for one etc., or occasionally.
2 Yes, same time.
X:

3. *
A.   I Do the child(ren) go to bed at the same time at weekends as they do
during the week?

0 Different times for all on two days
1 Different times for some, or on one day only.
2 Same time.
X:

B.
I Do(es) the foster child(ren) go to bed at the same time as s/he/they
do(es) during the week?

0 Different time on two days.
1 Different time for one, etc., or on one day only.
2 same time.
X:

4. * +
A.
FS Ob I Do they use their bedrooms at set times?

0 0 0 No, whenever they wish to.
1 1 1 Under various conditions.
2 2 2 Yes, set times.
X:

205

B.
FS Ob I Do(es) the foster child(ren) use his/her/their bedroom(s) at set times?

0   0   0   No, whenever s/he/they wish(es) to.
1   1   1   Under various conditions.
2   2   2   Set times only.
        X:

5. * #
A.
    I   Are there set times when visitors (i.e. family, relatives and friends)
        may come to see the children?

    0   No, visitors may come any time.
    1   Any day but set times. Or, any day/time but appointment required.
    2   Certain days only.
    X:

B.
    I   Are there set times when visitors (i.e. natural family, relatives and
        friends) may come to see the foster child(ren)?

    0   No, visitors may come anytime.
    1   Any day but set times. Or any day/time but appointment required.
    2   Certain days only.

6. *
A.
    I   Is tea served at the same time each day?

    0   No, tea times are flexible, depending on children's preferences and/or
        activities.
    1   Tea times are flexible for some; or, at weekends only.
    2   Same time each day.
    X:

B.
    I   Is tea served at the same time each day?

    0   No, tea times are flexible, depending on preferences and/or activities
        of child(ren).
    1   Mixed pattern
    2   Same time each day
    X:

7. *
A.

   I Do the children have baths/showers etc. at a set time each day?

   0 No, whenever they wish to.
   1 Set times for some; or set time during the week.
   2 Set time only
   X:

B.

   I Do(es) the foster child(ren) have (a) bath(s)/shower(s) etc. at a set time each day?

   0 No, whenever s/he/they wish(es) to.
   1 Set time for one etc. or, set time during the week.
   2 Set time only.
   X:

Block Treatment

8. *
A.

   Ob Do they wait together as a group before bathing, etc?

   0 Does not apply, children take baths etc. at different times; or, none wait, all   occupied elsewhere.
   1 Some wait; or, mixed pattern.
   2 All wait.
   X:

B.

   Ob Do the children of the household wait together as a group before bathing?

   0 Does not apply.
   1 Mixed pattern.
   2 Yes, all wait.
   X:

9. *
A.

   Ob Do they wait together as a group after bathing etc?

   0 None wait, return individually; or, does not apply, children have baths at different times.
   1 Some wait; or, mixed pattern.
   2 All wait.
   X:

B.

Ob Do the children of the household wait together as a group after bathing, etc?

0 Does not apply.
1 Mixed pattern.
2 All wait.
X:

10. *
A.

Ob Tea or evening meal: do they sit waiting at tables before the meal is served?

0 Less than 2 minutes.
1 3 - 5 minutes.
2 More than 5 minutes.
X:

B.

Ob Tea or evening meal: do(es) the foster child(ren) sit waiting at the table before the meal is served?

0 Less than 2 minutes.
1 3 - 5 minutes.
2 More than 5 minutes.
X:

11. *
A.

Ob Tea or evening meal: do they sit waiting at tables after the meal is finished?

0 Less than 2 minutes.
1 3 - 5 minutes.
2 More than 5 minutes.
X:

B.

Ob Tea or evening meal: do(es) the foster child(ren) sit waiting at tables after the meal is finished?

0 Less than 2 minutes.
1 3 - 5 minutes.
2 More than 5 minutes.
X:

12. *
A.

    Ob Do children wait around doing nothing before beginning new activities after tea?

    0   None wait, all are occupied.
    1   Some wait; or, mixed pattern.
    2   All wait.
    X:

B.

    Ob Do(es) the foster child(ren) wait around doing nothing before beginning new activities after tea?

    0   No.
    1   Mixed pattern.
    2   Yes.
    X:

13.
A.
FS Ob I Must children eat everything which is set before them?

0 0 0 No, children eat only that which they wish to.
1 1 1 Some must, or mixed pattern.
2 2 2 Yes, everything.
      X:

B.
FS Ob I Must the foster child(ren) eat everything set before him/her/them?

0 0 0 No, only that which s/he/they wish to eat.
1 1 1 Mixed pattern.
2 2 2 Yes, everything.
      X:

14.
A.
FS Ob I Are there routine/group shoe cleaning sessions?

0 0 0 No, children clean their shoes on an individual basis.
1 1 1 Yes, for some; or, mixed pattern.
2 2 2 Yes, children clean their shoes as a group.
      X:

B.

FS Ob I Do the children of the household clean their shoes at a set time each
day and as a group?

0   0   0   No; or, does not apply.
1   1   1   Mixed pattern.
2   2   2   Yes.
        X:

15.

A.

FS Ob I Are there group activities for children regularly organised by staff on
weekday evenings?

0   0   0   No, children mainly find their own sources of entertainment/
            amusement.
1   1   1   For some; or, mixed pattern.
2   2   2   Yes, all evenings during the week.
        X:

B.

FS Ob I Do(es) foster parent(s) regularly organise group activities for the
children of the household on weekday evenings?

0   0   0   No, or does not apply.
1   1   1   Mixed pattern.
2   2   2   Yes.
        X:

Depersonalisation

16.

A and B.

    I   Is there a routine admissions procedure [day of admission]?

    0   No, admissions styled to needs of individual children / not applicable.
    1   Mixed pattern.
    2   Yes, all children undergo a set procedure.
    X:

17.

A.

    I   Are pre-admission visits arranged for children?

    0   Yes, all children visit at least once prior to admission (except for
        emergency admissions).
    1   Mixed pattern.
    2   No, children do not visit prior to admission.
    X:

B.

    I Did the foster child(ren) visit the foster home prior to going to live there?

    0 Yes.
    1 Mixed pattern.
    2 No.
    X:

18. #
A.

    I Do children have a say in whether they are admitted to the Home?

    0 Yes, children's views are actively sought.
    1 Some children have a say; or, mixed pattern.
    2 No, children do not participate in the decision making process.
    X:

B.

    I Did the foster child(ren) have a say in the decision to place him/her/them with the foster parent(s)?

    0 Yes, his/her/their views were actively sought.
    1 Mixed pattern.
    2 No.
    X:

19. * #
A.

    I What is done with the clothing which children arrive with on admission?

    0 Kept and used by children.
    1 Used only on visits, certain occasions; or, mixed pattern.
    2 Not used or not allowed.
    X:

B.

    I What was done with the clothing which the foster child(ren) arrived with on the day of placement?

    0 Kept and used by child(ren).
    1 Used only on visits, certain occasions; or, mixed pattern.
    2 Not used or not allowed.
    X:

20. * #
A.

    I What is done with children's other possessions (toys, books, games, watches, radios, etc.)?

    0 Kept and used by childern.
    1 Kept for a time but become communal.
    2 Not used or not allowed.
    X:

B.

    I What is done with the foster child(ren's) other possessions?

    0 Kept and used by the child(ren).
    1 Mixed pattern.
    2 Not used or not allowed.
    X:

21. * #
A.

    I How many of the children possess all of the following items of clothing: 3 shirts or blouses (or equivalent); 3 trousers or skirts (or equivalent); jacket (or equivalent - e.g., bomber jacket); 3 sweaters (or equivalent); top coat (or equivalent - e.g., anorak); dressing gown; slippers; shoes (or equivalent - e.g., trainers); sportswear? [N.B. Does not include school uniform].

    0 100%
    1 95 - 99%
    2 Less than 95%
    X:

B.

    I Do(es) the foster child(ren) possess all the items of clothing listed above in 21.A?

    0 100% of items listed.
    1 95 - 99% of items listed.
    2 Less than 95% of items listed.
    X:

22. * #
A.
FS Ob I Whereabouts do children keep their clothes?

0 0 0 In private provision (i.e. wardrobes in bedrooms).
1 1 1 In private provision - located outside bedrooms.
2 2 2 In communal provision, supplied daily; or, shared provision.
    X:

212

B.
FS Ob I Whereabouts do(es) the foster child(ren) keep his/her/their clothes?

0   0   0   In private provision (i.e. wardrobe(s) in bedroom(s)).
1   1   1   In private provision - located outside bedroom(s).
2   2   2   In communal provision, supplied daily; or, shared provision.
          X:

23. * #
A.
    I   How many of the children have possessions (e.g., toys, books, games, watches, radios, etc)?

    0   100%.
    1   95 - 99%.
    2   Less than 95%.
    X:
B.
    I   Do(es) the foster chil(ren) have possessions such as toys, books, watch(es), radio(s) etc?

    0   Yes.
    1   Mixed pattern.
    2   No.
    X:

24. * +
A.
FS Ob I Are children permitted to hang pictures, posters, photos in bedrooms?

0   0   0   Yes.
1   1   1   Mixed pattern.
2   2   2   No.
          X:

B.
FS ObI May the foster child(ren) hang pictures, posters, photos in his/her/their bedroom(s)?

0   0   0   Yes.
1   1   1   Mixed pattern.
2   2   2   No.
          X:

25. * #
A.
FS Ob I How much time do they have for free recreation?

0 0 0 At least two hours per day.
1 1 1 At least one hour per day.
2 2 2 Less than one hour per day.
    X:

B.
FS Ob I How much time do(es) the foster child(ren) have for free recreation?

0 0 0 At least two hours per day.
1 1 1 At least one hour per day.
2 2 2 Less than one hour.
    X:

26. +
A.
    Ob May children switch on the TV, radio, record player, etc., without
       first seeking permission from staff?

    0 Yes.
    1 Mixed pattern.
    2 No.
    X:

B.
    Ob May the foster child(ren) switch on the TV, radio, record player,
       etc., without first seeking permission from foster parent(s)?

    0 Yes.
    1 Mixed pattern.
    2 No.
    X:

27. #
A.
    I Are children allowed some measure of choice as to the sorts of food
      they eat (i.e. before menu is prepared and/or food cooked)?

    0 Yes, considerable choice.
    1 Mixed pattern.
    2 No.
    X:

B.

    I Is/are the foster child(ren) allowed some measure of choice as to the sorts of food s/he/they eat (i.e. before menu is prepared and/or food cooked)?

    0 Yes, considerable choice.
    1 Mixed pattern.
    2 No.
    X:

28.
A.

    Ob Do children spend long periods in their nightclothes before going to bed (i.e. over one hour prior to going to bed)?

    0   No, children change into their nightclothes shortly before, or on going to bed.
    1   Mixed pattern.
    2   Yes, all do.
    X:

B.

    Ob Do(es) the foster child(ren) spend long periods in his/her/their nightclothes before going to bed (i.e. over one hour prior to going to bed)?

    0   No, nightclothes are put on shortly before, or on going to bed.
    1   Mixed pattern.
    2   Yes.
    X:

29. *
A.

    I How are children's birthdays celebrated?

    0 Individual presents and parties.
    1 Mixed pattern.
    2 No recognition.
    X:

B.

    I How are the foster child(ren)'s birthdays celebrated?

    0 Presents and parties.
    1 Mixed pattern.
    2 No recognition.
    X:

30. #
A.

    I May children send and receive sealed correspondence?

    0 Yes, children's letters are never opened by staff.
    1 Mixed pattern.
    2 No.
    X:

B.

    I May the foster child(ren) send and receive sealed correspondence?

    0 Yes, the child(ren)'s letters are never opened by foster parent(s)
    1 Mixed pattern.
    2 No.
    X:

31. #
A.

    I May children make and receive confidential telephone calls at any time?

    0 Yes.
    1 Mixed pattern.
    2 No.
    X:

B.

    I May the foster child(ren) make and receive confidential telephone calls at any time?

    0 Yes.
    1 Mixed pattern.
    2 No.
    X:

32. * + #
A.

    I May children use whatever facilities and equipment are available for physical exercise and recreation (other than things already covered) without first obtaining permission from staff?

    0 Yes, children have unrestricted access to such facilities and equipment.
    1 Some restrictions.
    2 No.
    X:

B.

    I May the foster child(ren) use whatever facilities and equipment are available for physical exercise and recreation (other than things already covered) without first obtaining permission from foster parent(s)?

    0 Yes, child(ren) has/have unrestricted access to such facilities and equipment.
    1 Some restrictions.
    2 No.
    X:

33. #
A.
FS Ob I Do children have access to individually locked storage space for their private use?

0 0 0 Yes, all children.
1 1 1 Some children do not; or mixed pattern.
2 2 2 None do.
    X:

B.
FS Ob I Do(es) the foster child(ren) have access to locked storage space for his/her/their private use?

0 0 0 Yes.
1 1 1 Mixed pattern.
2 2 2 No.
    X:

34. #
A.
    I Where is children's pocket money kept?

    0 Children look after it themselves.
    1 Mixed pattern.
    2 In the office or in the possession of staff; or does not apply, no pocket money given.
    X:

B.
    I Where is the child(ren)'s pocket money kept?

    0 Child(ren) look(s) after it
    1 Mixed pattern.
    2 Foster parent(s) look after it; or does not apply, no pocket money given.
    X:

35. #
A.

    I Are children given the opportunity to experiment with the preparation and eating of foods?

    0 Yes, all are regularly given this opportunity.
    1 Mixed pattern.
    2 No, never.
    X:

B.

    I Is/are the foster child(ren) given opportunity to experiment with the preparation and eating of foods?

    0 Yes, regularly.
    1 Mixed pattern.
    2 No, never.
    X:

36. #
A.

    I Where appropriate do young persons have access to contraception and, if necessary, abortion services on the same basis as other young people in the community?

    0 Yes; or, not applicable.
    1 Mixed pattern.
    2 No.
    X:

B.

    I Where appropriate, do(es) the young person(s) have access to contraception and, if necessary, abortion services on the same basis as other young people?

    0 Yes; or, not applicable.
    1 Mixed pattern.
    2 No.
    X:

37.
A.

    I Are children allowed to style their hair according to their own tastes/wishes?

    0 Yes, within reason (i.e. in accordance with that which headmasters/ employers in the community typically allow).
    1 Mixed pattern.
    2 No, there are strict rules governing children's hair styles.
    X:

B.

    I Is/are the foster child(ren) allowed to style his/her/their/ hair according to his/her/their own tastes/wishes?

    0 Yes, within reason (i.e. in accord with that which headmasters/ employers typically allow).
    1 Mixed pattern.
    2 No, there are strict rules governing child(ren)'s hairstyle(s)
    X:

38.
A.

    I Do children choose own clothes when these are bought at shops?

    0 Yes.
    1 Mixed pattern.
    2 No, staff decide.
    X:

B.

    I Do(es) the foster child(ren) choose his/her/their own clothes when these are bought at shops?

    0 Yes.
    1 Mixed pattern.
    2 No foster parent(s) decide(s).
    X:

39.
A.

    I Are children's clothes purchased with cash?

    0 Yes, always.
    1 Mixed pattern.
    2 No, a voucher type scheme operates whereby children's clothes are obtained from specified shops only.
    X:

B.

    I Are foster child(ren)'s clothes purchased with cash?

    0 Yes, always.
    1 Mixed pattern.
    2 No, voucher type scheme operates, whereby clothes are obtained from specified shops only.
    X:

40.

A.

   I Is special provision made for young people (16 years and over) in order to facilitate their transition, where appropriate, to independent living?

   0 Yes, such such youngsters are accommodated in separate living provision, and look after themselves as far as possible (e.g., with respect to cooking, shopping, laundry, and money matters); or, not applicable.

   1 Mixed pattern.

   2 No provision made.

   X:

B.

   I Where applicable, is special provision made for young person(s) (16 years and over) in order to facilitate, where appropriate, his/her/their transition to independent living?

   0 Yes, youngster(s) cook(s), shop(s), clean(s), handle(s) own money, and do(es) own laundry; or, not applicable.

   1 Mixed pattern.

   2 No provision made.

   X:

41. #

A.

   I Do children have access to files and documents pertaining to themselves?

   0 Yes, all children have such access.

   1 Some children have access; or, mixed pattern.

   2 None have access.

   X:

B.

   I Do(es) the foster child(ren) have access to files and documents pertaining to him/her/them?

   0 Yes.

   1 Mixed pattern.

   2 No.

   X:

42. #
A.

    I How often is a child's placement formally reviewed?

    0 At least every 3 months.
    1 Mixed pattern.
    2 Longer.
    X:

B.

    I How often is the foster child(ren)'s placement formally reviewed?

    0 At least every 3 months.
    1 Mixed pattern.
    2 Longer.
    X:

43. #
A.

    I Are children and their parents or other representatives normally present at the review and, do they participate in decisions taken by the review body?

    0 Yes.
    1 Mixed pattern.
    2 No.
    X:

B.

    I Is/are foster child(ren), and a representative, normally present at reviews and, do they participate in decisions taken by the review body?

    0 Yes.
    1 Mixed pattern.
    2 No.
    X:

Social Distance

44. *
A.
FS Ob I Do the children have access to the kitchen?

0 0 0 Yes, all do: no restrictions.
1 1 1 Mixed pattern.
2 2 2 No.
        X:

B.

FS Ob I Do(es) foster child(ren) have access to the kitchen?

0 0 0 Yes; no restrictions.
1 1 1 Mixed pattern.
2 2 2 No.
    X:

45.

A.

    I Do the children have access to laundry facilities?

    0 Yes, no restrictions.
    1 Mixed pattern.
    2 No.
    X:

B.

    I Do(es) the foster child(ren) have access to laundry facilities?

    0 Yes, no restrictions.
    1 Mixed pattern.
    2 No.
    X:

46.

A.

    Ob How do children address staff?

    0 By first or fore names; or, auntie, uncle, etc.
    1 Mixed pattern.
    2 By terms such as Sir, Miss, etc, and/or Mr..., Mrs..., Miss..., Ms..., etc.
    X:

B.

    Ob How do(es) foster child(ren) address foster parent(s)?

    0 By first or fore name(s); or, uncle, auntie, etc.
    1 Mixed pattern.
    2 By terms such as Sir, Miss, etc., and/or Mr..., Mrs..., Miss..., Ms...., etc.
    X:

47. *
A.

Ob Do staff talk with children at mealtimes?

0   Yes.
1   Mixed pattern.
2   Supervisory remarks from staff only. Or, does not apply in some
    cases - not all staff eat with the children.
X:

B.

Ob Do(es) foster parent(s) talk with foster children at mealtimes?

0   Yes.
1   Mixed pattern.
2   Supervisory remarks only. Or, does not apply, foster parent(s)
    do(es) not have meals with child(ren).
X:

48. *
A.

Ob Do staff watch TV with children?

0   Someone usually does.
1   Someone sometimes does.
2   Sporadic involvement by staff only.
X:

B.

Ob Do(es) foster parent(s) watch TV with foster child(ren)?

0   Usually
1   Sometimes
2   Sporadic involvement only.
X:

49.
A.

I Are children and staff permitted to make drinks and snacks, etc.?

0 Yes, both groups may do so; or neither group may.
1 Some children may, along with staff.
2 Staff may do so, but children may not.
X:

B.

    I Do foster parent(s) and foster child(ren) make drinks and snacks, etc?

    0 Yes, both foster parent(s) and child(ren) do; or, both do not.
    1 Mixed pattern.
    2 Foster parent(s) may, child(ren) may not.
    X:

50.
A.

    Ob Is there a staff room on the premises?

    0   No.
    1   Yes, but children generally have access to it.
    2   Yes, and children do not generally have access to it.
    X:

B.

    Ob Do(es) foster parent(s) have a living room from which foster child(ren) is/are excluded?

    0   No.
    1   Mixed pattern.
    2   Yes.
    X:

51.
A. and B.

    Ob Is there an office on the premises?

    0   No.
    1   Yes, but child(ren) generally has/have access to it.
    2   Yes, and child(ren) do(es) not generally have access to it.
    X:

52.
A. and B.

FS Ob I Do(es) staff/foster parents have accommodation on the premises from which child(ren) is/are generally excluded?

0 0 0 No.
1 1 1 Mixed pattern.
2 2 2 Yes.
    X:

THANK YOU FOR YOUR HELP

Note

*   Denotes items based on work undertaken by King *et al* (1971) in devising their *Revised Child Management Scale*, + questions based on items included in Sinclair's (1975) *restrictiveness scale*, # items based on Taylor *et al's* (1979), *Charter of Rights for Children in Institutions*.

Appendix (d): RICI

REVISED INDEX OF COMMUNITY INVOLVEMENT

Children's Home/Foster home:

A denotes items for Children's Homes and, B, items for foster homes

---

1.
A.   How many of the children participated in some kind of organised leisure activity in the community in the last fortnight (e.g., Scouts, Guides, Disco's Youth Clubs, etc.)?

B.   Has/Have the foster child(ren) participated in some kind of organised leisure activity in the community in the last fortnight (e.g., Scouts, Guides, Disco's, Youth Clubs, etc.)?

2.*
A.   How many of the children went shopping (for clothes) in the last month?

B.   Has/have the foster child(ren) been shopping (for clothes) in the last month?

3.*
A.   How many of the children went to the cinema in the last fortnight?

B.   Has/Have the foster child(ren) been to the cinema in the last fortnight?

4.*
A.   How many of the children went to a place of public interest, such as a museum or a football match, in the last fortnight?

B.   Has/Have the foster child(ren) been to a place of public interest, such as a museum or football match, in the last fortnight?

5.*
A.   How many of the children have been on a public bus, or on a train, in the last fortnight?

B.   Has/Have the foster child(ren) been on a public bus, or on a train, in the last fortnight?

226

6.*
A. How many of the children have been to a restaurant or cafeteria in the last month?

B. Has/Have the foster child(ren) been to a restaurant or cafeteria in the last month?

7.*
A. How many of the children went to a house other than that of their parents for a visit in the last fortnight?

B. Has/Have the foster child(ren) been to a house other than that of his/her/their parents for a visit in the last fortnight?

8.*
A. How many of the children have been for a car ride in the last fortnight?

B. Has/Have the foster child(ren) been for a car ride in the last fortnight?

9.*
A. How many of those children able to do so went for overnight visits home or elsewhere in the last fortnight?

B. If able to, has/have the foster child(ren) been for an overnight visit to his/her/their natural parents home or elsewhere in the last fortnight?

10.*
A. Of the children who had their hair cut in the last 3 months, how many visited a hairdresser in the community?

B. If the foster child(ren) had his/her/their haircut in the last 3 months, did s/he/they visit a hairdresser in the community?

11.*
A. Of the children who required such services in the last 3 months, how many went to a doctor or dentist in the community (i.e. where they were fit to do so)?

B. If the foster child(ren) required such services in the last 3 months, did s/he/they go to a doctor or dentist in the community (i.e. where fit to do so)?

12.*
A. How many of the children who are able to do so went on a holiday in the last year with their families?

B. Has/Have the foster child(ren) been on a holiday with his/her/their natural family in the last year (i.e. if able to do so)?

13..*
A. How many of the children went on a holiday organised by the staff in the last year?

B. Has/Have the foster child(ren) been on a holiday with his/her/their foster parent(s) in the last year?

14.
A. How many of the children who are able to do so have received visits from their family or relatives in the last month?

B. If able to do so, has/have the foster child(ren) received a visit from his/her/their natural family or relatives in the last month?

15.
A. How many of the children have had friends stay to tea in the last month?

B. Has/Have the foster child(ren) had friends stay to tea in the last month?

16.
A. How many children have played/associated (informally) with other children in the locality in the last week?

B. Has/have the foster child(ren) played/associated (informally) with other children in the locality in the last week?

17.
A. How many of the children attend schools in the community?

B. Do(es) the foster child(ren) attend (a) local school(s)?

18.
A. How many of the children have received letters or telephone calls in the last fortnight?

B. Has/Have the foster child(ren) received (a) letter(s) or (a) telephone call(s) in the last fortnight?

19.
A. How many children have been visited by their social workers in the last month?

B. Has/Have the foster child(ren) been visited by his/her/their social worker in the last month?

Note

*   Denotes questions based on items comprising the Index of Community Involvement devised by Raynes *et al* (1979).

CHILDREN'S COMMUNITY CONTACTS QUESTIONNAIRE

Name of Children's Home/Foster home:
Date of application:
Post/Role of person interviewed:
N residential/foster children accommodated =

I would like to talk to you about the sorts of contacts the children/your foster child(ren) have/has with people and places, and so on, outside the Home/home. The information you give will be treated as confidential.

A denotes questions for Children's Homes, B, questions for foster homes

ANSWERS

1.
A.   How many children have been to a youth club or to scouts,
     or to some other activity of this sort in the last fortnight?

B.   Has/Have your foster child(ren) been to a youth club or to
     scouts or to some other activity of this sort in the last fortnight?

2.
A.   How many children went shopping for clothes in the last
     month?

B.   Has/have your foster child(ren) been shopping for clothes in
     the last month?

3.
A.   How many children went to the cinema in the last fortnight?

B.   Has/Have your foster child(ren) been to the cinema in the last
     fortnight?

4.
A.   How many children went to a place of public interest, such as
     a museum or a football match in the last fortnight?

B.   Has/have your foster child(ren) been to a place of public
     interest such as a museum or a football match in the last
     fortnight?

5.
A. How many children have been on a public bus, or on a train, in the last fortnight?

B. Has/have your foster child(ren) been on a public bus, or on a train, in the last fortnight?

6.
A. How many children have been to a restaurant or cafeteria in the last month?

B. Has/have your foster child(ren) been to a restaurant or cafeteria in the last month?

7.
A. How many children went to a house other than that of their parents for a visit in the last fortnight?

B. Has/Have your foster child(ren) been to a house other than that of his/her/their natural parents for a visit in the last fortnight?

8.
A. How many children have been for a car ride in the last fortnight?

B. Has/Have your foster child(ren) been for a car ride in the last fortnight?

9.
A. How many of the children able to do so went for overnight visits home or elsewhere in the last fortnight?

B. If your foster child(ren) has contact with his/her/their natural parents, has/have s/he/they been for an overnight visit in the last fortnight?

10.
A. Of the children who have had their hair cut in the last three months, how many went to a hairdresser off the grounds?

B. If your foster child(ren) had his/her/their haircut in the last three months, did s/he/they go to a local hairdresser?

11.
A. Of the children who required such services in the last three months, how many went to a doctor or dentist off the grounds (i.e. where they were fit to do so)?

B.   Has/have your foster child(ren) required the services of a
     doctor or dentist in the last three months? If so, and s/he/
     they was/were fit to do so, did s/he/they visit the doctor
     and/or dentist locally?

12.
A.   How many of the children able to do so went on a holiday
     in the last year with their parents?

B.   If your foster child(ren) is/are able to do so, did s/he/they go
     on holiday in the last year with his/her/their natural family?

13.
A.   How many of the children who were able to do so (i.e. they
     were living here) went on a holiday organised by the staff in
     the last year?

B.   Has/have your foster child(ren) been on a holiday with you in
     the last year (i.e. provided s/he/they have lived with you for
     a year or more)?

14.
A.   How many of the children who are able to do so received visits
     from their parents or relatives in the last month?

B.   If your foster child(ren) has/have contact with their natural
     family, has/have s/he/they received a visit from them in the last
     month?

15.
A.   How many children have had friends stay to tea in the last
     month?

B.   Has/have your foster child(ren) had friends stay to tea in the
     last month?

16.
A.   How many of the children have played/mixed informally with
     other children in the locality in the last week?

B.   Has/have your foster child(ren) played/mixed informally with
     other children in the locality in the last week?

17.
A.   How many of the children attend school off the grounds?

B.   Does your foster child(ren) attend school locally?

18.
A. How many of the children have received letters or telephone calls in the last fortnight?

B. Has/have your foster child(ren) received letters or telephone calls in the last fortnight?

19.
A. How many children have been visited by their social workers in the last month?

B. Has/Have your foster child(ren) been visited by his/her/their social worker in the last month?

THANK YOU FOR YOUR HELP

Appendix (e):   RIPE

REVISED INDEX OF PHYSICAL ENVIRONMENT

Children's Home/Foster home:
N residential/foster children =
N family members[foster homes only] =

SCORES

1.*   Ratio of bathrooms to children/family members.

2.*   Ratio of handbasins to children/family members.

3.*   Ratio of bath tubs/showers to children/family members.

4.*   Percentage of bath tubs/showers with doors that can be locked.

5.*   Ratio of mirrors to children/family members.

6.*   Percentage of bathrooms with mirrors.

7.§   Ratio of toilets to children/family members.

8.*   Percentage of toilets with paper.

9.*   Percentage of toilets with doors that can be locked.

10.*   Ratio of bedrooms to children/family members.

11.*   Percentage of children/foster children with bedside lockers.

12.*   Percentage of children/foster children with own wardrobes.

13.§   Percentage of children/foster children with different bedspreads+.

14.*   Percentage of children's/foster children's bedrooms with posters.

15.*   Percentage of children's/foster children's bedrooms with curtains.

16.*   Percentage of children's/foster children's bedrooms with mirrors.

17.*   Ratio of TVs and radios to children/family members.

18.*   Ratio of armchairs to children/family members.

19.* Ratio of occasional tables to children/family members.

20.* Percentage of bookshelves with games cupboards.

21.* Percentage of dayrooms with curtains.

22.* Percentage of dayrooms with wastebins.

23. Ratio of dayrooms to children/family members.

Notes

1. * Denotes items based on items from the Index of Physical Environment by Raynes *et al* (1979), § items based on items from the Physical Environment Inventory by Raynes *et al* (1979).

2. + i.e. number of children with bedspreads that were distinguished from those of other children by colour and/or pattern.

3. It will be noted that the RIPE did not utilise all the data collected via the Physical Environment Inventory, although some of the omitted data was used when the contrasts between foster homes and Children's Homes were discussed in Chapter 3.

PHYSICAL ENVIRONMENT INVENTORY

Children's Home/Foster Home:
Date of Application:

A. ROOMS

1. N Bedrooms =

2. N Beds =

3. N Bathrooms =

4. N Dayrooms =

5. N Dining rooms =

6. N Dining areas (between partitions) =

7. N Clothing rooms =

8. Laundry - YES [ ] NO [ ]

9. Kitchen - YES [ ] NO [ ]

10. Office - YES [ ] NO [ ]

11. Other [state]:

12. N Levels of Home/home =

13. Yard (enclosed) YES [ ] NO [ ]

14. Open areas adjacent to Home/home YES [ ] NO [ ]

B. FURNISHINGS

15. N Occasional tables =

16. N Armchairs =

17. N Couches/settees =

18. N Bookshelves =

19. N Games and toy cupboards =

20. N TVs =

21. N Record players =

22. N Radios =

23. N Day rooms with curtains =

24. N Dayrooms with wastebins =

25. N Washing machines =

26. N Dryers =

27. N = Cabinets to store dishes in kitchen

28. N Fridges =

29. N Stoves =

30. N Hotplates =

31. N Dishwashers =

32. N Drinking fountains =

C. BATHROOMS

33. N Toilets without partitions or doors with locks =

34. N Toilets with partitions only =

35. N Toilets with partitions and doors with locks =

36. Total N toilets =

37. N Showers without partitions or curtains or doors with locks =

38. N Showers with partitions only =

39. N Showers with partitions and curtains and doors with locks =

40. Total N showers =

41. N Bath tubs without partitions or doors with locks =

42. N Bath tubs with partitions only =

43. N Bath tubs with partitions and doors with locks =

44. Total N bath tubs =

45. N Urinals =

46. N Hand basins =

47. N Mirrors =

48. N Toilets with toilet paper =

D. BEDROOMS

49. N Beds per bedroom =

50. N Beds with drawers =

51. N Bedside lockers =

52. N Bedrooms with floor coverings (carpets, etc) =

53. N Bedrooms with mirrors =

54. N Bedrooms with curtains =

55. N Bedrooms with bedspreads =

56. N Children with different bedspreads

57. N Bedrooms with pictures, posters, photos, etc. =

E. DAILY CLOTHING STORAGE

58. Individual chest of drawers and/or wardrobe in bedroom - YES [ ] NO [ ]

59. Shared cupboard or chest in bedroom - YES [ ] NO [ ]

60. Labelled locker or box in clothing room - YES [ ] NO [ ]

61. All together in clothing room or laundry box or put on bed YES [ ] NO [ ]

F. YARD, GARDEN or GROUNDS

62. Benches YES [ ] NO [ ]

63. Fixed play equipment - YES [ ] NO [ ]

64. Plants and trees - YES [ ] NO [ ]

65. Grassed - YES [ ] NO [ ]

66. Fence, wall or railing YES [ ] NO [ ]

237

INDEX OF CONTROLS AND SANCTIONS

Children's Home/Foster home:

Subscale 1: Day-to-day, relatively minor infractions of rules, etc.

		USED	NEVER USED
1.	Transfer or threat of removal to another place	1	0
2.	Limitations on access to outside world	1	0
3.	Manipulation of rewards and sanctions	0	0
4.	Physical chastisement	1	0
5.	Public disapproval	1	0
6.	Praise, reward and encouragement	0	1
7.	Group punishments	1	0

Subscale 2: Serious infractions of rules, etc., such as stealing and aggression

		USED	NEVER USED
8.	Transfer or threat of removal to another place	1	0
9.	Limitations on access to outside world	1	0
10.	Voiced disappointment by adult closest to child	0	0
11.	Manipulation of rewards and sanctions	0	0
12.	Individual stricture	0	0
13.	Physical chastisement	1	0
14.	Public disapproval	1	0
15.	Group punishments	1	0

Subscale 3: Moral, social, sexual matters, etc.

		USED	NEVER USED
16.	Transfer or threat of removal to another place	1	0
17.	Limitations on access to outside world	1	0
18.	Personal example	0	1
19.	Physical chastisement	1	0
20.	Public disapproval	1	0
21.	Group punishments	1	0
22.	Counselling (i.e. sensitive, tolerant and good humoured)	0	1

CONTROL INTERVIEW QUESTIONNAIRE

Children's Home/Foster home:
Post/Role of Person interviewed:
Date of interview:

I would like to talk with you about the ways that... you and your colleagues/you and your husband/wife / you ...keep control over ...the children / your foster child(ren). What you tell me will be treated as strictly confidential.

1. In front of me, I have a list of some of the methods which are used to control children in care. As I read each method out, can you tell me whether...you and your colleagues / you and your husband/wife / you... either (a) use it or (b) never use it?

    [N.B. Explain the meaning of the terms used, giving practical examples. Record answers by placing a tick in the appropriate spaces].

CONTROLS	USED	NEVER USED
Transfer or threat of removal to another place	[ ]	[ ]
Limitations on access to the outside world (e.g., stopping home leave at weekends or visits to friends)	[ ]	[ ]
Use of drugs	[ ]	[ ]
Voiced disappointment by adult closest to child	[ ]	[ ]
Personal example	[ ]	[ ]
Manipulation of rewards and sanctions (e.g., pocket money, access to treats and outings such as visits to the cinema, late TV, or staying up late; sanctions might include household chores such as mowing the lawn, washing the van, etc.).	[ ]	[ ]
Use of secure room	[ ]	[ ]
Individual stricture	[ ]	[ ]
Corporal punishment	[ ]	[ ]
Public disapproval	[ ]	[ ]

Praise, reward and encouragement	[ ]	[ ]
Group punishments	[ ]	[ ]
Counselling (i.e. of a sensitive, tolerant, and good humoured nature)	[ ]	[ ]

2. Are there any other methods which...you and your colleagues / you and your husband/wife / you... use and which we have not talked about?

    [N.B. If YES, record in space provided below. If NO, go straight to question 3]

3. Now could you tell me which methods... you and your colleagues / you and your husband/wife / you... use for controlling the child(ren) on a day-to-day basis (i.e. for relatively minor infractions of rules, expectations, and so on)?

    [N.B. Explain the meaning of the question, where necessary, giving practical examples. If required, read out the methods said to be used by interviewee. Record answers by placing ticks in the appropriate spaces. If none of the methods listed below are used by caretaker(s) for dealing with relatively minor infractions of rules, etc., ascertain what methods are employed and record in space provided below]

CONTROLS	USED	NEVER USED
Transfer or threat of removal to another place	[ ]	[ ]
Limitations on access to the outside world	[ ]	[ ]
Use of drugs	[ ]	[ ]
Voiced disappointment by adult closest to child	* * *	* * *
Personal example * * * * * * *	* * *	* *
Manipulation of rewards and sanctions	[ ]	[ ]
Use of secure room	[ ]	[ ]
Individual stricture * * * * * * *	* * *	* *
Corporal punishment	[ ]	[ ]

241

Public disapproval	[ ]	[ ]
Praise, reward and encouragement	[ ]	[ ]
Group punishments	[ ]	[ ]
Counselling	* * * * * * * *	* * * *

OTHER CONTROLS

4.   Can you say which methods...you and your colleagues / you and your husband/wife / you... use for dealing with serious matters such as stealing, aggression, and so on (i.e. serious violations of rules, etc.)?

[N.B. Follow, as appropriate, procedure adopted for question 3]

CONTROLS	USED	NEVER USED
Transfer or threat of removal to another place	[ ]	[ ]
Limitations on access to the outside world	[ ]	[ ]
Use of drugs	[ ]	[ ]
Voiced disappointment by adult closest to child	[ ]	[ ]
Personal example * * * * * *	* * * * *	
Manipulation of rewards and sanctions	[ ]	[ ]
Use of secure room	[ ]	[ ]
Individual stricture	[ ]	[ ]
Corporal punishment	[ ]	[ ]
Public disapproval	[ ]	[ ]
Praise, reward and encouragement * *	* * * * *	
Group punishments	[ ]	[ ]
Counselling * * * * * *	* * * * *	

OTHER CONTROLS

242

5.   What methods do...you and your colleagues / you and your husband/wife
      / you ... use for dealing with moral, social and sexual matters ?

      [N.B. Follow, as appropriate, procedure adopted for questions 3 and 4]

CONTROLS	USED	NEVER USED
Transfer or threat of removal to another place	[ ]	[ ]
Limitations on access to the outside world	[ ]	[ ]
Use of drugs	[ ]	[ ]
Voiced disappointment by adult closest to child * * * * * *		
Personal example	[ ]	[ ]
Manipulation of rewards and sanctions * * * * * * * *		
Use of secure room	[ ]	[ ]
Individual stricture * * * * * * * * * * * *		
Corporal punishment	[ ]	[ ]
Public disapproval	[ ]	[ ]
Praise, reward and encouragement * * * * * * * * *		
Group punishments	[ ]	[ ]
Counselling	[ ]	[ ]

OTHER CONTROLS

6.   Do you have a tariff or scale of sanctions (e.g,. the more serious the
      misdemeanour, the more severe the punishment)?

      [N.B. Where necessary, explain the meaning of the question giving
      practical examples. Record answer by placing a tick in the appropriate
      space below]

      YES   [ ]
      NO   [ ]

243

[If YES, ascertain the sanctions involved and the behaviours to which they are applied. Record answer in space provided below. If NO, pass on to question 7]

7. Are sanctions or punishments fixed by rule or do...you and your colleagues / you and your husband/wife / you... vary them at your discretion?

    [N.B. Where necessary, explain the meaning of the question giving practical examples. Record answer by placing a tick in the appropriate space below]

    FIXED BY RULE   [ ]
    VARIED AT CARETAKER DISCRETION   [ ]

    [N.B. If some sanctions are fixed by rule whilst others are varied at caretaker discretion, ascertain the nature of the behaviours to which fixed sanctions are applied and those which are subject to the exercise of discretion. Record answer in space provided below. Otherwise, move on to question 8].

8. Are the rules of the...Home/household...clear and understood by the child(ren)?
    [Record answer by placing a tick in the appropriate space below]

    YES   [ ]
    NO   [ ]

    [Probe: means by which child(ren) is/are made aware of the rules and record in space provided below. Then, go to question 9. If there are no rules, etc., terminate the interview]

9. Are the rules open to discussion with the child(ren), and can they be changed as a result of such discussion?

    YES (i.e. on both counts)   [ ]
    No (i.e. on one or both counts)   [ ]

    [Probe: extent to which child(ren) participate(s) in rule making process. Request examples of such participation. If no participation by child(ren), probe reasons. Record answer in space provided below]

THANK YOU FOR YOUR HELP

STAFF/FOSTER PARENT INTERVIEW QUESTIONNAIRE

Children's Home/Foster home:
Date of interview:

I would like to talk with you about your background and job/role. What you
tell me will be treated as strictly confidential. There are no right or wrong
answers, only those which apply to you.

1.   Name:

2.   Post/role:

3.   Sex:

     Male   [ ]
     Female   [ ]

4.#   Marital status:

     Married   [ ]
     Single   [ ]
     Widowed   [ ]
     Divorced   [ ]
     Separated   [ ]

5.#   Age:

     Under 20   [ ]
     21 - 30   [ ]
     31 - 40   [ ]
     41 - 50   [ ]
     51 and over   [ ]

6.#   Number of own children:

     Under 16 years   [ ]
     16 years and over [ ]
     None   [ ]

7.# Do you hold any formal qualifications relating to working with children?

YES   [ ] - specify:
NO   [ ]

8.# When did you begin work in this establishment / contract fostering
/ special fostering?

Date:

9.# What previous experience do you have of work with children in local
authority care or other peoples children?

[N.B. If none, write NONE. Otherwise, list previous experience under
the headings provided below]

Type of setting	Duration of work		Post/Role
	from	to	

10. What other employment experience do you have?

[N.B. IF none, write NONE. Otherwise, list last three jobs (including
present job) only, under the headings provided below]

Job/Post	Duration of employment	
	from	to

11.* Could you tell me what your...role in this establishment / role as a
contract / special foster parent...involves (i.e. what you do)?

[Record answer in space provided below]

12.* Is your job or role, on the whole, as you feel it should be?

[Probe areas of satisfaction and/or dissatisfaction. Record answer in
space provided below]

13.* How was your job or role described to you?

[Probe respondents prior knowledge about what job or role would involve; and, whether job or role conforms to or differs from initial expectations. Record answer in space provided below]

14.* How much of a free hand do you have in the way that you carry out your work / role?
[Probe which decisions respondent can make alone, which decisions have to be referred and to whom. Record answer in space provided below]

15.* Here are ten aspects of the role which those who look after children in care can be asked to do. Could you put them in the order of importance which they have for your role as it is? [N.B. If senior member of staff, order of priority which individual thinks establishment gives to them]?

DOMESTIC (e.g., ordering supplies; replacement of clothing and equipment; laundry; caring for child(ren)'s diet, health and appearance; supervising laundry changing, cleaning, etc.).

ADMINISTRATION (e.g., arranging timetables, work rotas, leave, pocket money, privileges, etc.).

EDUCATION (e.g., remedial and other classroom teaching; educational outings and visits; teaching constructive use of leisure through sports and activities; helping child(ren) with homework, etc.).

WORK TRAINING (e.g., teaching trade skills, good work habits and a responsible attitude to work, etc.).

KEEPING ORDER AND GENERAL SUPERVISION (e.g., maintaining a reasonable standard of behaviour in the Home/home; supervising showers, meals, getting up and going to bed, and similar parts of the routine; enforcing the rules of the Home/home, etc.).

PROTECTING SOCIETY (e.g., taking precautions against child(ren) committing thefts locally, or getting involved with fights or vandalism outside, etc.).

CARE PLANNING (e.g., attending case conferences and reviews; writing progress reports on child(ren); talking to psychologists and others concerned with the children, etc.).

247

CONTACT WITH CHILD(REN)'S NATURAL FAMILY/FAMILIES (e.g., visiting natural parent(s), contacting child(ren)'s social worker(s); taking child(ren) to visit his/her/their natural parent(s); talking to natural parent(s) when s/he/they visit child(ren), etc.).

SHOWING CONCERN FOR CHILD(REN) (e.g., discussing his/her/their behaviour and problems; taking an interest in his/her/their everyday affairs and activities, etc.).

SOCIAL TRAINING (e.g., teaching politeness, table manners, cleanliness and essentials of social behaviour).

1.
2.
3.
4.
5.
6.
7.
8.
9.
10.

16.* Now could you put the same ten in the order of importance which you think they should have?

1.
2.
3.
4.
5.
6.
7.
8.
9.
10.

17.* Of the ten, which do you feel are the hardest (i.e. the biggest strain on staff/foster parents)?

[N.B. Record answer in space provided below]

18.* What do you think is the cause of the strain for the two you have chosen?

[N.B. Record answer in space provided below]

248

19.* What do you think could be done to ease or remove this strain?

[N.B. Record answer in space provided below]

[N.B.Omit questions 20 - 25 for senior staff]

20.§ How often do you talk about the child(ren)'s problems and/or progress with each of the following?

RESIDENTIAL STAFF ONLY

[N.B. Record answers by placing ticks in the appropriate spaces]

	Most days	About once a week	About once a month	Less often/ never
Other care staff at your establishment	[ ]	[ ]	[ ]	[ ]
Senior care staff at your establishment	[ ]	[ ]	[ ]	[ ]
Social workers	[ ]	[ ]	[ ]	[ ]
Professionals other than social workers (e.g., doctors, teachers, psychologists)	[ ]	[ ]	[ ]	[ ]
Parents or relatives of children	[ ]	[ ]	[ ]	[ ]

FOSTER PARENTS ONLY

	Most days	About once a week	About once a month	Less often/ never
Your husband or wife (if married, etc.)	[ ]	[ ]	[ ]	[ ]
Other foster parents	[ ]	[ ]	[ ]	[ ]
Fostering officer(s)	[ ]	[ ]	[ ]	[ ]
Social worker	[ ]	[ ]	[ ]	[ ]
Professionals other than social workers (e.g., doctors, teachers, psychologists)	[ ]	[ ]	[ ]	[ ]
Natural parents or relatives of children	[ ]	[ ]	[ ]	[ ]

249

21.§ Do you go to ...staff meetings/meetings with other foster parents..?

[N.B. Record answer by placing a tick in the appropriate space]

Yes, about once a week or more often   [ ]
Yes, about once a month   [ ]
Yes, but only occasionally   [ ]
No, never   [ ]

[Probe reasons for occasional attendance or non-attendance and record answer in space provided below]

22.§ Do you have a written job/role description?

YES   [ ]
NO   [ ]

23.§ Have you been given any written rules about your work/role?

YES   [ ]
NO   [ ]

24.§ Have you received any in-service training since you...started work here/began contract/special fostering...?

YES   [ ]
NO   [ ]

[If YES, ascertain the nature of the training and its duration, etc. Record answer in space provided below. If NO, go straight to question 25]

25.§ How much do you find that each of the following help you in your work/role?

RESIDENTIAL STAFF ONLY

[N.B. Record answers by placing ticks in the appropriate spaces]

	Very helpful	Helpful	Average	Unhelpful	Very unhelpful
Other care staff here	[ ]	[ ]	[ ]	[ ]	[ ]
Senior care staff here	[ ]	[ ]	[ ]	[ ]	[ ]
Social Workers	[ ]	[ ]	[ ]	[ ]	[ ]
Other professionals	[ ]	[ ]	[ ]	[ ]	[ ]
Children's parents, etc.	[ ]	[ ]	[ ]	[ ]	[ ]

FOSTER PARENTS ONLY

	Very helpful	Helpful	Average	Unhelpful	Very unhelpful
Your husband/wife (if married)	[ ]	[ ]	[ ]	[ ]	[ ]
Other foster parents	[ ]	[ ]	[ ]	[ ]	[ ]
Fostering officer(s)	[ ]	[ ]	[ ]	[ ]	[ ]
Social Worker	[ ]	[ ]	[ ]	[ ]	[ ]
Other professionals	[ ]	[ ]	[ ]	[ ]	[ ]
Natural parent(s), etc.	[ ]	[ ]	[ ]	[ ]	[ ]

26.§ Do you have regular supervision sessions with your immediate superior (or other) which enable you to discuss matters concerning your work/role - e.g., your progress, problems, etc?

YES   [ ]
NO   [ ]

27.§ Do you feel that you receive adequate support/supervision from your superiors/local authority?

YES   [ ]
NO   [ ]

[If NO, ascertain reason(s) and record in space provided below]

28.* What are your future plans as far as...this establishment/contract/special fostering...is concerned?

[Probe whether... staying at establishment (and for how long) or leaving (when, why and where going to), etc./will continue to foster child(ren) - and for how long - or not (and why not); whether plans to foster other child(ren). Record answer in space provided below.]

THANK YOU FOR YOUR HELP

251

Notes

1. # Denotes items based on work by King *et al* (1971), * questions based on work by Cawson (1978), and § items based on work by Raynes *et al* (1979).

2. The constraints of time did not permit the analysis of all data collected by the ST/FPIQ.

3. Recording spaces have been shortened considerably for the purpose of presentation.

Appendix (h): ST/FPAS

STAFF/FOSTER PARENT ATTITUDE SCALE

Name of staff/foster parent:
Date:
Children's Home/foster home:

Traditional Control

| | Strongly Disagree | | | | | Strongly Agree |

1. Staff/foster parents should maintain order at all times, otherwise the sort of child you deal with would tend to get out of control.   1 2 3 4 5 6

2. It's no good having rules if you don't apply them strictly.   1 2 3 4 5 6

3. Modern practice in substitute child care is tending to become too permissive.   1 2 3 4 5 6

4. If the sort of child you deal with is left to his/her own devices in recreation time, he/she is likely to get into mischief.   1 2 3 4 5 6

5. In general, the sort of child you deal with needs fairly close supervision to keep him/her from getting into trouble.   1 2 3 4 5 6

6. Children should receive pocket money only as a reward for good work or behaviour.   1 2 3 4 5 6

7. The sort of child you deal with is too immature to be allowed much say in how the Home/home is run.   1 2 3 4 5 6

253

8. In a Home/home like this it is
   not possible to give the
   child(ren) any say in things like
   mealtimes and bedtimes.   1   2   3   4   5   6

9. Practical experience is more
   important for staff/foster parents
   than theoretical knowledge.   1   2   3   4   5   6

10. Home(natural parents) leave
    (where possible), as a rule,
    should be given only to
    children who earn it through
    good behaviour.   1   2   3   4   5   6

Passivity

11. Places such as this, where
    children in care live, should be
    organised so that children feel
    as much as possible as if they
    were living at home (i.e. with
    their natural parents).   1   2   3   4   5   6

12. Children in care who cause least
    trouble are the ones most likely
    to get on well after discharge.   1   2   3   4   5   6

13. A child should be protected from
    tasks which are too hard or tiring
    for him/her.   1   2   3   4   5   6

14. If a child loses his temper with
    a member of staff/foster parent,
    it's always best to leave him/her
    to cool down rather than to make
    an issue out of it.   1   2   3   4   5   6

15. With an immature child of the
    sort you look after, it's
    important not to make demands
    or put pressure on him/her.   1   2   3   4   5   6

16. One of the main aims of a
    Home/foster home like this is
    to keep the emotional
    temperature down.   1   2   3   4   5   6

17. Children should be kept away
from tasks which might be
discouraging to them.　　　　　1　　2　　3　　4　　5　　6

18. It's better to try to trick a child
into doing something rather
than to make an issue of it.　　1　　2　　3　　4　　5　　6

19. As far as posible children in
care should be placed in a group
where most others are like them
in age and temperament.　　　1　　2　　3　　4　　5　　6

20. The sort of child you deal with
is ruled by his/her emotions,
ordinary people by their reason.　1　　2　　3　　4　　5　　6

Caretaker Status

21. A child who is cheeky to staff/
foster parents should not be
allowed to get away with it.　　1　　2　　3　　4　　5　　6

22. Children who are allowed to get
away with misbehaviour will
never learn to get on with
bosses or supervisors at work.　1　　2　　3　　4　　5　　6

23. One of the main aims of a
placement like this is to teach a
child respect for authority.　　1　　2　　3　　4　　5　　6

24. The sort of child you look
after needs to learn that staff/
foster parents know what is
good for him/her.　　　　　　1　　2　　3　　4　　5　　6

25. Staff/foster parents who insist
on an outward show of respect
from children are often more
concerned with their own status
than with the child's needs.　　1　　2　　3　　4　　5　　6

26. Children who are allowed to use
staff/foster parents first names or
nicknames will usually have
little respect for them.　　　　1　　2　　3　　4　　5　　6

255

27. Staff/foster parents should not
normally refer to each other by
their first names in front of
children.   1   2   3   4   5   6

28. Staff/foster parents being too
friendly with children makes for
poor discipline.   1   2   3   4   5   6

Distance

29. There is something about the sort
of child you deal with that makes
it easy to tell him or her from an
ordinary child   1   2   3   4   5   6

30. Although the sort of children
which you deal with seem just
like other children, it is
dangerous to forget for a
moment that they are delinquent/
disturbed.   1   2   3   4   5   6

31. The sort of child you look
after can't be friends with his
peers, let alone adults.   1   2   3   4   5   6

32. The trouble with giving too
much attention to the kind of
children you look after is that
they usually want to take
advantage of you.   1   2   3   4   5   6

33. The kind of children you have to
deal with have lost the ability to
make warm relationships.   1   2   3   4   5   6

34. The sort of child you are paid to
look after lacks the ability to tell
right from wrong.   1   2   3   4   5   6

35. Although this type of child
seems friendly, it is usually
only skin deep.   1   2   3   4   5   6

36. If this type of child is friendly
to you, s/he is probably
trying to get his/her own way
about something.   1   2   3   4   5   6

37. It's a mistake to expect the sort
of child you deal with to behave
as if s/he were normal. 1   2   3   4   5   6

Suppression of Problems

38. One of the main advantages of
sending a child to a place like
this is that s/he can forget
about past troubles. 1   2   3   4   5   6

39. It's best for children with a
problem or worry not to think
about it, but to keep busy with
more pleasant things. 1   2   3   4   5   6

40. You should think twice before
prompting a child to talk about
his/her problems or anxieties,
as it may stir up emotions the
child can't deal with. 1   2   3   4   5   6

41. If a child is encouraged to keep
on talking about his/her worries,
it will reinforce his/her anxieties. 1   2   3   4   5   6

42. If a child seems to want to keep
his/her troubles to him/herself,
it is best to leave him/her and
not try to get him/her talking. 1   2   3   4   5   6

43. It's risky for inexperienced
staff/foster parents to delve too
deeply into a child's problems. 1   2   3   4   5   6

44. When children in care are
worried about their [natural]
family it's best to try to keep
their minds off it. 1   2   3   4   5   6

THANK YOU FOR YOUR HELP

Appendix (i): NRS

NARRATIVE RECORDING SHEET

Children's Home/Foster home:
Date of observation:
Time observation commenced:

T	L	TA	ICH	ICR	TOV	NARRATIVE RECORD OF STAFF/ FOSTER PARENT ACTIVITIES AND INTERACTIONS WITH CHILD(REN)

Notes

1.   NRS recording sheet: T = target caretaker; L = location of observation; TA = activity of target caretaker; ICH = interaction initiated by child; ICR = interaction initiated by caretaker; TOV = tone of voice used by caretaker.

2.   Design and Application of Structured Observational Technique

In devising the method of observation employed, I experimented with various techniques, ranging from highly structured (i.e. extremely precise with respect to what would be observed), pre-coded, observation and recording schedules, to relatively unstructured schedules. Following the procedure adopted by King *et al* (1971), very impressive observer reliabilities were obtained for two highly structured observational instruments based on work by Bartak and Rutter (1975). However, despite the fact that a good deal of time, effort and money (which included the costs of a second observer) had been invested in the development of these instruments, it seemed that their coding categories excluded important aspects of caretaker-child interaction (this appeared to be attributable to the fact that Bartak and Rutter (1975) had devised the codes for assessing teacher-pupil interaction); that is, the codes did not appear to adequately embrace a sufficient range of possible caretaker behaviours. Subsequent trials served to confirm this suspicion.

Accordingly, the less structured narrative record technique was developed. The major strengths of this method seemed to be: first, alternative codes could be derived from the narrative data should pre-existing codes prove an inadequate means by which to analyse caretaker role activities and interactions with children; second, the narrative record approach meant that it was possible to combine two previously separate observational instruments and, hence, save time during data collection; third, the narrative record method did not abstract behaviour from its social context to the extent that the highly structured observational techniques did. But much experimentation was required in order to produce a technique suitable for application in the substitute care settings concerned. This necessitated a number of return visits to CH1, between the first and second major phases of data collection, in order to carry out further trials. Unfortunately, finances did not permit the employment of a second observer for this undertaking, which meant that observer reliability could not be obtained.

However, the coding categories used in analysing NRS data were based on those employed in several previous researches in related fields; namely, studies by Bartak and Rutter (1975), Cawson (1978), King *et al* (1971) and Raynes *et al* (1979) - see below. Thus, many of the coding categories used had been shown to be reliable. That is, codes derived from Bartak and Rutter (1975), King *et al* (1971) and Raynes *et al* (1979). The coding categories taken from Cawson (1978) were not formulated for use in structured observation. As noted in Chapter 4, these codes were used for collecting data on caretaker activities. The King *et al* (1971) coding categories were also used for this purpose, and Chapter 4 shows that the results produced by the two sets of categories were consistent. That the findings obtained via the application of the NRS are valid seems to be corroborated by the fact that the results produced were not only entirely consistent with the impressions gained during the course of fieldwork, but also by the check that the narrative data facilitated on the appropriateness of the codes used in analysis. Moreover, the multi-method approach adopted enabled NRS results to be verified by findings associated with other research instruments used. NRS findings pertaining to caretaker role activities and behaviour towards children can be compared with the results presented in Chapter 3. Whilst the same cannot be said about NRS data relating to children's responses, the codes used for analysing the latter were taken directly from the work of Bartak and Rutter(1975), and their reliability has already been commented on.

Observations had to be focused on caretakers rather than children. This became clear during visits to Authority A foster homes and Authority B Children's Homes during the period when access to research venues was being negotiated. These visits revealed the extreme, and - given the exceedingly limited resources, in terms of both time and money available - insurmountable, difficulties that an attempt to observe, systematically, the behaviour of older children in substitute care settings would have entailed, in view of (a) the considerable freedom of movement allowed some such children and (b) the fact that the children were obviously, for the most part, healthy, active, youngsters. It was evident, therefore, that observations of children could not be undertaken independently of their interactions with caretakers; equally, that the observations of caretaker-child interaction would have to be targeted on caretakers. This meant, for example, that initial plans to observe children's interactions with their peers had to be discarded; as did the idea of observing children's activities, independent of their interactions with caretakers.

One potential shortcoming of structured observation is that the patently visible observer can engender changes in behaviour that may diminish the validity of comparisons. In order to overcome this problem considerable time was allocated to the task of establishing relations of trust with foster parents, residential staff and children during the first phase of fieldwork, and also during the second period of fieldwork when the structured observations were carried out. In each of the research settings concerned, structured observations were not conducted until all other aspects of data collection had been successfully completed. This meant that all the foster parents and residential staff involved had previously participated in lengthy and searching interviews concerning various aspects of their work and all the foster children and many of the residential children had been afforded the opportunity of expressing their perceptions about their social environments (or placements). Hence, by the time observations were carried out, subjects were relaxed in the observers presence.

Prior to observing, attempts were made to accustom subjects to the equipment - stopwatch and clipboard, etc. - that was used for the task, and to the idea of being directly observed. For example, I would sometimes simply carry the clipboard and stopwatch about with me in a given Children's Home a day or so prior to conducting observations, or undertake trial runs of observations, or merely have the equipment visible to subjects several hours before commencing observations in foster homes (this aspect of the work was, so to speak, "played off the cuff", and my approach was conditioned by an assessment of how amenable to being observed subjects appeared; to have adopted a standard approach would have squandered a good deal of time because other techniques described in this and the preceding paragraph meant that subjects at most of the research settings were adequately primed or prepared for observation). The presence of younger children was also helpful here because in taking an interest in, and often playing with, the stopwatch they appeared to succeed in somehow removing any disturbing connotations which the equipment might have held for other subjects. The clipboard selected was bright red in colour and the spotwatch used was a very distinctive shade of green. The two were fixed together, giving the appearance of a toy, rather than an accessory of inspection. It was explained to foster parents and staff that the observations were not a time and motion study of their activities; a point which seemed to reassure residential staff, in particular, and one that had to be made in view of the fact that the observations were focused on caretakers rather than children. Foster parents and staff were also reassured that the observations were not intended to assess the role performance of individual caretakers, and also that participants would not be identified when the data collected were reported.

In addition to general resource constraints, a major limitation on the number of hours observation possible was the relatively unstructured nature of the NRS. Highly specific observation schedules are comparatively easy to complete and require little effort on the part of the observer. By contrast, because the NRS involved a narrative record of what was observed, completing the schedule was an arduous task, requiring physical stamina and considerable concentration. However, the snap shot view of life in foster homes and Children's Homes produced by the NRS observations was highly revealing and made the effort involved worthwhile.

3. Categories Used for Analysing NRS Data

Caretaker role activities

Categories derived from Cawson (1978)

D = DOMESTIC (e.g., ordering supplies; replacement of clothing and equipment; laundry; caring for child(ren)'s diet, health and appearance; supervising laundry changing, cleaning, etc.).

A = ADMINISTRATION (e.g., arranging timetables, work rotas, leave, pocket money, privileges, etc.).

E = EDUCATION (e.g., remedial and other classroom teaching; educational outings and visits; teaching constructive use of leisure through sports and activities; helping child(ren) with homework, etc.).

WT = WORK TRAINING (e.g., teaching trade skills, good work habits and a responsible attitude to work, etc.).

KOGS = KEEPING ORDER AND GENERAL SUPERVISION (e.g., maintaining a reasonable standard of behaviour in the Home/home; supervising showers, meals, getting up and going to bed, and similar parts of the routine; enforcing the rules of the Home/home, etc.).

PS = PROTECTING SOCIETY (e.g., taking precautions against child(ren) committing thefts locally, or getting involved with fights or vandalism outside, etc.).

CP = CARE PLANNING (e.g., attending case conferences and reviews; writing progress reports on child(ren); talking to psychologists and others concerned with the children, etc.).

CCNF = CONTACT WITH CHILD(REN)'S NATURAL FAMILY/FAMILIES (e.g., visiting natural parent(s), contacting child(ren)'s social worker(s); taking child(ren) to visit his/her/their natural parent(s); talking to natural parent(s) when s/he/they visit child(ren), etc.).

SCC = SHOWING CONCERN FOR CHILD(REN) (e.g., discussing his/her/their behaviour and problems; taking an interest in his/her/their everyday affairs and activities, etc.).

ST = SOCIAL TRAINING (e.g., teaching politeness, table manners, cleanliness and essentials of social behaviour).

M = MISCELLANEOUS (e.g., any activity which cannot be coded in terms of the categories set out above).

Categories derived from King et al (1971)

D = DOMESTIC (e.g, cleaning; polishing; washing clothes; making beds; dusting; ironing; mending or darning; washing up; drying up; laying tables; clearing tables; cooking food; locking doors; etc.).

CF = FUNCTIONAL CHILD CARE (e.g., getting child(ren)up; putting child(ren) to bed and tucking him/her/them in; combing child(ren)'s hair; cutting up food for child(ren); pouring drinks; serving out food; serving food onto plates; tying laces; giving out medicines; giving nursing attention of any kind; asking child if s/he wants more of something; saying hello and goodbye to child(ren), saying grace at table, etc.).

CS = SOCIAL CHILD CARE (e.g., playing any kind of formal or informal game with child(ren) or amusing him/her/them; reading stories; singing with or to child(ren); educational activities and games; reading letter to child; going off on a trip; watching TV with child(ren) and sitting down with him/her/them; showing child(ren) how to do something, etc.).

A = ADMINISTRATIVE (e.g., paper work of any kind - registers, medical records, record books, charts, time-tables, reports, etc.; answering telephone; dealing with visitors of any kind - social workers, doctors, natural parents, milkmen, etc.; talking to people about administrative matters; giving instructions to junior staff or directing staff activities; junior staff asking senior staff for instructions or receiving them; putting child(ren)'s pocket money away; checking stocks of various kinds, etc.).

S = SUPERVISORY (e.g., supervising movement of child(ren) from one room to another; supervising toileting; bathing, washing etc.; watching caretaker(s) or child(ren) carrying out activities; giving instructions to child(ren) - "don't do that"; telling child(ren) off - however mildly; telling child(ren) to get things; calling child(ren) back from somewhere etc.; switching TV on and off; standing watching TV with child(ren); attending assemblies; restraining child(ren) from going off somewhere or fighting etc.; interfering in a situation to prevent child(ren) from harming self/selves or other(s); sitting at table apart from table at which child(ren) sit(s); walking around in garden with child(ren) but not playing with him/her/them; handing plates to child(ren) to lay table; standing waiting for child(ren), etc.).

M = MISCELLANEOUS (e.g., chit-chat between caretakers when they are not doing anything else; caretaker talk to observer; caretaker in toilet or washing hands etc.).

Caretaker Behaviour

Verbal behaviour (i.e. defined by verbal content of behaviour)

INFORMATIVE SPEECH (i.e. speech which offers opinion, information or explanation and asks child(ren) for opinion, information or explanation).

ISA = INFORMATIVE SPEECH APPROVING (i.e. all informative speech which is unambiguously **approving** or favourable or positive in nature; including, verbal praise - e.g., telling child that s/he is good; telling child that s/he can have some reward; playful remarks - e.g., teasing child in an unambiguously friendly manner or sharing a joke or light moment with child; offering words of comfort, consolation, commiseration, sympathy, encouragement, etc.; affectionate and admiring comments; etc.).

ISD = INFORMATIVE SPEECH DISAPPROVING (i.e. all informative speech which is unambiguously disapproving or unfavourable or negative; including, verbal disapproval or criticism, censure or condemnation - e.g., telling child s/he is bad; withdrawing or threatening to withdraw some benefit from child; threatening child in some other way; sarcasm; etc.).

ISVN = INFORMATIVE SPEECH VALUE NEUTRAL (i.e. any informative speech which is neither approving or disapproving but instead falls somewhere between the two; that is, informative speech which has a neutral value content).

CS = CONTROLLING SPEECH (i.e. statements which give orders without explanation - e.g., "do this", "do that", etc.)

PC = PERFUNCTORY COMMENT (e.g., "hello", "goodbye", etc.)

OT = OTHER TALK (i.e. all caretaker speech which cannot be classified in terms of any of the categories set out above).

TOV = TONE OF VOICE USED BY CARETAKER: W = warm; N = neutral; C = critical.

Non-verbal behaviour

APPROVING NON-VERBAL BEHAVIOURS (i.e. all non-verbal behaviours which are unambiguously approving or affectionate in nature).

APG = APPROVING PHYSICAL GESTURES INVOLVING BODILY CONTACT (e.g., cuddling, patting, kissing, playful wrestling, etc.).

ABE = APPROVING BODILY EXPRESSIONS SUCH AS FACIAL EXPRESSION AND GESTURE (e.g., smiling, blowing kisses, winking, etc.).

DISAPPROVING NON-VERBAL BEHAVIOURS (e.g., all non-verbal behaviours which are unambiguously disapproving or rejecting or negative in nature).

DPG = DISAPPROVING PHYSICAL GESTURES INVOLVING BODILY CONTACT (e.g., striking, poking, pushing, pulling, dragging child, pulling child's hair, etc.).

DBE = DISAPPROVING BODILY EXPRESSIONS SUCH AS FACIAL EXPRESSION AND GESTURE (e.g., frowning at child in a disapproving manner, wagging finger at child, lifting hand as if to threaten child with physical chastisement, etc.).

VALUE NEUTRAL NON-VERBAL BEHAVIOURS (i.e. all non-verbal behaviour with a neutral value content).

VNPG = VALUE NEUTRAL PHYSICAL GESTURES INVOLVING BODILY CONTACT (e.g., steadying child lest s/he fall, etc.).

VNBE = VALUE NEUTRAL BODILY EXPRESSIONS SUCH AS FACIAL EXPRESSION AND GESTURE (e.g., shrugging shoulders and using facial expression to convey, or help convey, the message "search me" or "I don't know", etc.).

AT = ATTENTION (i.e. where caretaker makes no response other than turning to the child, walking over to him/her, or looking at him/her so as to meet his/her gaze with no particular gesture, facial expression or use of voice).

IGN = IGNORES (i.e. where caretakers fail to acknowledge child in any of the ways previously set out, whilst appearing aware of the child's presence and/or behaviour).

IGNT = IGNORES-TOLERATES (i.e. where caretakers ignore testing behaviours manifested by children).

IGNR = IGNORES-REJECTS (i.e. where caretakers ignore a child who is behaving in a socially acceptable manner and who is seeking attention).

Children's Behaviour

General Activity

SAGA = SOCIALLY ACCEPTABLE GENERAL ACTIVITY (i.e. where child engages in an activity which is permitted and appropriate to time and place or an activity which is intended for him/her).

DGA = DEVIANT GENERAL ACTIVITY (i.e., where child engages in an activity which is prohibited or inappropriate to time and place or an activity which is not intended for him/her).

Affect

Physical gestures involving bodily contact

SAPG = SOCIALLY ACCEPTABLE PHYSICAL GESTURES INVOLVING BODILY CONTACT (e.g., hugging, etc., appropriate to situation).

DPG = DEVIANT PHYSICAL GESTURES INVOLVING BODILY CONTACT (e.g., striking caretaker, etc.)

Bodily expressions such as facial expression and gesture

SABE = SOCIALLY ACCEPTABLE BODILY EXPRESSIONS SUCH AS FACIAL EXPRESSION AND GESTURE (e.g., smiling, etc., appropriate to situation).

DBE = DEVIANT BODILY EXPRESSIONS (e.g., scowling, sulking, etc.)

Language

SAL = SOCIALLY ACCEPTABLE LANGUAGE (i.e. acceptable forms of communicative speech, appropriate to situation).

DL = DEVIANT LANGUAGE (i.e. unacceptable forms of speech such as verbal abuse, etc.).

CBM = CHILDREN'S BEHAVIOUR MISCELLANEOUS (i.e. behaviours that cannot be coded in terms of any of the categories set out above).

4. Times of Observation and Who Observed

Foster homes	Time of observation	
	From	to
FH1		
Mr.	6.15 p.m.	7.20 p.m.

265

FH2
| Mrs. | 4.00 p.m. | 4.30 p.m. |
| Mr. | 4.35 p.m. | 5.05 p.m. |

FH3
Mrs.	4.55 p.m.	5.10 p.m.
	6.38 p.m.	6.42 p.m.
Mr.	7.23 p.m.	8.10 p.m.

FH4
| Mrs. | 4.30 p.m. | 4.58 p.m. |
| | 5.44 p.m. | 6.25 p.m. |

FH5
Mrs.	4.05 p.m.	4.16 p.m.
	5.05 p.m.	5.30 p.m.
Mr.	5.35 p.m.	6.05 p.m.

FH6
| Mrs. | 4.17 p.m. | 5.17 p.m. |

FH7
| Mrs. | 4.12 p.m. | 5.12 p.m. |

FH8
| Mrs. | 5.00 p.m. | 5.30 p.m. |
| Mr. | 5.32 p.m. | 6.02 p.m. |

FH9
| Mrs. | 4.03 p.m. | 4.35 p.m. |
| Mr. | 4.38 p.m. | 5.08 p.m. |

FH10   No observations carried out (see Chapter 4)

FH11
| Mrs. | 4.32 p.m. | 5.02 p.m. |
| Mr. | 5.05 p.m. | 5.35 p.m. |

FH12   No observations carried out (see Chapter 4)

Children's Homes	Time of observation		Grade	Sex
	from	to		
CH1				
Staff A	1.55 p.m.	2.05 p.m.	Houseparent	Male
Staff B	3.30 p.m.	4.00 p.m.	Team Leader	Male
Staff C	4.15 p.m.	5.15 p.m.	Houseparent	Male
Staff D	8.00 p.m.	8.30 p.m.	Deputy O-I-C	Male
Staff E	8.40 p.m.	9.00 p.m.	Houseparent	Male

CH2				
Staff A	3.30 p.m.	4.00 p.m.	Deputy O-I-C	Female
Staff B	4.10 p.m.	4.40 p.m.	Houseparent	Male
Staff A	4.45 p.m.	5.15 p.m.	Deputy O-I-C	Female
Staff B	5.15 p.m.	5.45 p.m.	Houseparent	Male
Staff A	6.10 p.m.	6.40 p.m.	Deputy O-I-C	Female

CH3				
Staff A	10.50 a.m.	11.20 a.m.	Houseparent	Male
Staff B	11.40 a.m.	12.10 p.m.	O-I-C	Female
Staff B	2.00 p.m.	2.30 p.m.	O-I-C	Female
Staff C	3.40 p.m.	4.10 p.m.	Houseparent	Male
Staff C	4.33 p.m.	5.03 p.m.	Houseparent	Male

CH4				
Staff A	3.30 p.m.	4.00 p.m.	Deputy O-I-C	Male
Staff B	4.10 p.m.	4.40 p.m.	Houseparent	Male
Staff C	4.55 p.m.	5.25 p.m.	Houseparent	Female
Staff A	5.50 p.m.	6.20 p.m.	Deputy O-I-C	Male
Staff B	6.45 p.m.	7.15 p.m.	Houseparent	Male

REVISED SOCIAL CLIMATE SCALE

Name of child:
Date:
Children's Home/Foster home:

N.B. YES = TRUE; NO = FALSE

Strictness

1. If you argue with the staff/foster parents here, you get into trouble.   YES   NO

2. The staff/foster parents here discourage criticism.   YES   NO

3. You can criticise the staff/foster parents here to their faces.   YES   NO

4. You get into serious trouble if you don't obey the rules here.   YES   NO

5. The staff/foster parents here are strict.   YES   NO

6. If you swear in front of the staff/foster parents here, you get into trouble.   YES   NO

7. The staff/foster parents here hardly ever order you around.   YES   NO

8. The staff/foster parents here allow you to be cheeky.   YES   NO

9. The staff/foster parents here take fighting by the kids seriously.   YES   NO

Child Friendliness

10. The kids here laugh if you talk about your feelings.   YES   NO

11. If a kid is upset the others try to help.   YES   NO

12. Kids rarely help each other.   YES   NO

13. It takes a long time to get to know the other kids.	YES	NO
14. The other kids help newcomers.	YES	NO
15. When a kid is upset s/he tries to hide it from the others.	YES	NO
16. This is a friendly place.	YES	NO

Caretaker Support

17. The staff/foster parents here go out of their way to help you.	YES	NO
18. The staff/foster parents here know what kids want.	YES	NO
19. The staff/foster parents here have very little time to encourage you.	YES	NO
20. The staff/foster parents here hardly ever chat informally with you.	YES	NO
21. You usually talk to the staff/foster parents if you have a personal problem.	YES	NO
22. The staff/foster parents here rarely go out of their way to help you.	YES	NO
23. The staff/foster parents here spend very little time talking with you.	YES	NO
24. The staff/foster parents here get fed up if you get upset easily.	YES	NO
25. The staff/foster parents here try to do something if you've got a complaint.	YES	NO
26. The staff/foster parents here encourage you to talk about your feelings.	YES	NO

Satisfaction

27. Being here is better than you expected.	YES	NO
28. You're ashamed of this Home/home.	YES	NO
29. You're proud of this Home/home.	YES	NO
30. You'd worry if this Home/home got a bad name.	YES	NO

31. You'd be ashamed to tell your mates outside that you're here.	YES	NO
32. The first you hear about things here is when they happen to you.	YES	NO
33. It's a waste of time being in a Home/home like this.	YES	NO

Behaviour

34. Kids here get away with a lot without getting caught.	YES	NO
35. There's a fight here almost every day.	YES	NO
36. Kids here often boast about breaking the law.	YES	NO
37. There's hardly ever a serious fight here.	YES	NO
38. Weak kids are sometimes forced to give things to stronger kids.	YES	NO
39. Kids here often lose their tempers with one another.	YES	NO
40. If you leave things lying around here they will get stolen.	YES	NO
41. There's very little swearing here.	YES	NO

Additional Questions

1. If you had a personal problem on your mind, who would you discuss it with?
Can you rank the following in order of preference?

> A friend outside
> Your social worker
> One of the staff/foster parents here
> A friend here
> A member of your natural family

Order of preference
1.
2.
3.
4.
5.

270

2. If another boy/girl like you came to live here, what would s/he enjoy?

    [Probe areas of satisfaction, etc. and record in space provided below]

3. Is there anything which a newcomer might not like about being in a place like this?

    [Probe areas of dissatisfaction and record in space provided below]

THANK YOU FOR YOUR HELP

Bibliography

Ainsworth, F. and Fulcher, L.C. (1981), *Group Care for Children*, Tavistock.

Ainsworth, M.D. (1962), *Deprivation of Maternal Care: A Reassessment of its Effects*, World Health Organisation.

Aldgate, J. (1976), 'The Child in Care and his Parents', *Adoption and Fostering*, 84, 2.

Aldgate, J. (1978), 'Advantages of Residential Care', *Adoption and Fostering* , 92, 2.

Aldgate, J. (1982), 'Foster and Adoptive Families' in Rapoport, R.N., Fogarty, M.P. and Rapoport, R., (1982) (eds), *Families in Britain*, Routledge and Kegan Paul.

Anderson, M. (1982) (ed), *Sociology of the Family*, Penquin.

Anderson, R. (1978), *Representation in the Juvenile Court*, Routledge and Kegan Paul.

Ansley, F. (1976), quoted in Bernard, J. (1976), *The Future of Marriage*, Penquin.

Arensberg, C.M. and Kimball, S.T. (1968), *Family and Community in Ireland*, Harvard University Press.

Aries, P. (1960), *Centuries of Childhood*, Penquin.

Arnold, D.O. (1970), 'Dimensional Sampling: An Approach for Studying a Small Number of Cases', *The American Sociologist*, May 1970.

Asch, J.E. (1951), 'Effects of Group Pressure upon the Modification and Distortion of Judgement in Guetzkow, H. (ed), *Groups, Leadership and Men*, Carenegie Press.

Association of Social Workers (1967), *New Thinking About Institutional Care*, Association of Social Workers.

Balbernie, R. (1966), *Residential Work with Children*, Pergamon.

Barclay, P. (1982), *Social Workers: Their Roles and Tasks*, Report of the Barclay Committee, Bedford Square Press.

Bartak, L. and Rutter, M. (1975), 'The Measurement of Staff-Child Interaction in Three Units for Autistic Children' in Tizard, J., Sinclair, I. and Clarke, R.V.G., (1975) (eds), *Varieties of Residential Experience*, Routledge and Kegan Paul.

Barton, R. (1959), *Institutional Neurosis*, Wright.

Beedell, C. (1970), *Residential Life with Children*, Routledge and Kegan Paul.

Behen, B. (1958), *Borstal Boy*, Hutchinson.

Benston, M. (1972), 'The Political Economy of Women's Liberation' in Glazer-Malbin, N. and Waehrer, H.Y., (1972), *Women in a Man-Made World*, Rand McNally.

Berridge, D. (1985), *Children's Homes*, Blackwell.

Berry, J. (1975), *Daily Experience in Residential Life*, Routledge and Kegan Paul.

Blalock, H.M. (1972), *Social Statistics*, McGraw-Hill.

Blau, P.M. (1963), *The Dynamics of Bureaucracy*, University of Chigago Press.

Blau, P.M. and Scott, W. (1963), *Formal Organisations: A Comparative Approach*, Routledge and Kegan Paul.

Blom-Cooper, L. (Chairman) (1985), *A Child in Trust: The Report of the Panel of Inquiry into the Circumstances Surrounding the Death of Jasmine Beckford*. London Borough of Brent.

Bott, E. (1957), *Family and Social Network*, Tavistock.

Bottoms, A.E. and McWilliams, W. (1979), 'A Non-Treatment Paradigm for Probation Practice', *British Journal of Social Work*, 9, 2.

Bottoms, A.E. and Preston, R. (1980) (eds), *The Coming Penal Crisis*, Scottish Academic Press.

Bowlby, J. (1946), *Forty-Four Juvenile Thieves*, Tindall and Cox.

Bowlby, J. (1951), *Maternal Care and Mental Health*, World Health Organisation.

Bowlby, J. (1953), *Child Care and the Growth of Love*, Penquin.

Bowlby, J. (1969), *Attachment and Loss (Vol.1): Attachment,* Hogarth.

Bowlby, J. (1973), *Attachment and Loss (Vol.2): Separation: Anxiety and Anger*, Hogarth.

Bowlby, J. (1976), *The Making and Breaking of Affectional Bonds*, Tavistock.

Bowlby, J. (1980), *Attachment and Loss (Vol.3): Sadness and Depression*, Hogarth.

Burn, M. (1956), *Mr. Lyward's Answer,* Hamish Hamilton.

Butterworth, E. and Holman, R. (1975) (eds), *Social Welfare in Modern Britain*, Collins

Bynner, J. and Stribley, K.M. (1979) (eds), *Social Research: Principles and Procedures*, Open University Press.

Campbell, D.T. and Stanley, J.C. (1963), *Experimental and Quasi-Experimental Designs for Research*, Rand-McNally.

Carlebach, J., (1970), *Caring for Children in Trouble*, Routledge and Kegan Paul.

Cartwright, A. (1964), *Human Relations and Hospital Care*, Routledge and Kegan Paul.

Cawson, P. (1978), *Community Homes: A Study of Residential Staff*, HMSO.

Cawson, P. and Martell, M. (1979), *Children Referred to Closed Units*, HMSO.

Cawson, P. and Perry, J. (1977), 'Environmental Correlates of Attitude Among Residential Staff', *British Journal of Criminology*, 17, 2.

Cicourel, A.V. (1968), *The Social Organisation of Juvenile Justice,* John Wiley.

Clarke, A.M. and Clarke, A.D.M. (1976), *Early Experience: Myth and Evidence,* Open Books.

Clarke, R.V.G. and Cornish, D.B. (1972), *The Controlled Trial in Institutional Research - Paradigm or Pitfall for Penal Evaluators?,* HMSO.

Clarke, R.V.G. and Martin, D.N. (1975), 'A *Study of Absconding and its Implications for the Residential Treatment of Delinquents* ' in Tizard, J. *et al* (1975) (eds), *op. cit.*

Close, P. (1985), 'Family Form and Economic Production' in Close, P. and Collins, R., (eds), *Family and Economy in Modern Society,* Macmillan.

Cloward, R.A. and Ohlin, L.E. (1961), *Delinquency and Opportunity,* John Wiley.

Cohen, A. (1955), *Delinquent Boys: The Culture of the Gang,* Free Press.

Cohen, S. (1974), 'Human Warehouses: The Future of Our Prisons', *New Society,* 14 November, 1974.

Cohen, S. (1979a), 'Crime and Punishment 1: Can We Balance Justice, Guilt and Intolerance?', *New Society,* 1 March, 1979.

Cohen, S. (1979b), 'Crime and Punishment 2: Community Control - A New Utopia', *New Society,* 15 March, 1979

Conger, J.J. (1973), *Adolescence and Youth: Psychological Development in a Changing World,* Harper and Row.

Conway, E.S. (1957), *The Institutional Care of Children: A Case History,* Ph.D. thesis, University of London; cited in Triseliotis, J. and Russell, J. (1984), *op. cit.* (see below).

Cooper, D. (1972), *The Death of the Family,* Penquin.

Cooper, J. (1978), *Patterns of Family Placement,* National Children's Bureau.

Cornish, D.B. and Clarke, R.V.G. (1975), *Residential Treatment and its Effects on Delinquency,* Home Office Research Studies No.32, HMSO.

Crompton, M. (1982), *Adolescents and Social Workers,* Heinemann.

Cronbach, L.J. (1951), cited by Smith, H.W., (1975), *Strategies of Social Research: The Methodological Imagination,* Prentice-Hall.

Davis, A. (1981), *The Residential Solution: State Alternatives to Family Care* , Tavistock.

Department of Health and Social Security (1974a), *Report of the Committee of Inquiry into the Care and Supervision Provided in Relation to Maria Coldwell*, HMSO.

Department of Health and Social Security (1974b), *The Family in Society: Dimensions of Parenthood*, HMSO.

Department of Health and Social Security (1974c), *The Family in Society: Preparation for Parenthood*, HMSO.

Department of Health and Social Security (1977), *Social Services Statistics*, HMSO.

Department of Health and Social Security (1980), *Research into Services for Children and Adolescents*, HMSO.

Department of Health and Social Security (1981), *Observation and Assessment, Report of a Working Party*, HMSO.

Department of Health and Social Security (1982a), *A Study of the Boarding Out of Children*, HMSO.

Department of Health and Social Security (1982b), *The Provision of Child Care: A Study of 8 Local authorities in England and Wales*, HMSO.

Department of Health and Social Security, Social Work Service, London, Region (1982), *Residential Care for Children in London*, DHSS.

Department of Health and Social Security (1985), Social Services Inspectorate of the DHSS, *Inspection of Community Homes*, 1985, DHSS.

Dinnage, R. and Pringle, M.L. Kellmer (1967), *Residential Child Care - Facts and Fallacies*, Longman.

Ditchfield, J.A. (1976), *Police Cautioning in England and Wales*, HMSO.

Docker Drysdale, B. (1968), *Therapy in Child Care*, Longman.

Donzelot, J. (1979), *The Policing of Families: Welfare Versus the State*, Hutchinson.

Douglas, J.W.B. (1964), *The Home and the School*, MacGibbon and Kee.

Duncan Mitchell, G. (1979), *A New Dictionary of Sociology*, Routledge and Kegan Paul.

Eichorn, D. (1968), 'Adolescence', *International Encyclopedia of the Social Sciences*, Macmillan.

Elliot, D. (1981), 'Juvenile Justice' in Jones, H., (1981) (ed)*Society Against Crime: Penal Theory Now*, Penguin.

Engels, F. (1972), *The Origin of the Family, Private Property and the State*, Lawrence and Wishart.

Erikson, E. (1968), 'Life Cycle', *International Encyclopedia of the Social Sciences*, Macmillan.

Erikson, E. (1975), *Childhood and Society*, Penquin.

Etzioni, A. (1964a), *Modern Organisations*, Prentice-Hall.

Etzioni, A. (1964b) (ed), *A Sociological Reader on Complex Organisations*, Holt, Rinehart and Winston.

Eversley, D. and Bonnerjea, L., (1982), 'Social Change and Indicators of Diversity' in Rapoport, R.N., *et al* (1982) (eds), *op. cit.* (see below).

Eysenck, H.J. (1964), *Crime and Personality*, Routledge and Kegan Paul.

Fagan, L. and Little, M. (1984), *The Forsaken Families: The Effects of Unemployment on Family Life*, Penquin.

Feeley, D. (1972), 'The Family' in Jenness, L. (1972) (ed), *Feminism and Socialism*, Pathfinder Press.

Fink, H. (1981), *Social Philosophy*, Methuen.

Fletcher, R. (1966), *The Family and Marriage in Britain*, Penquin.

Fogarty, M. and Rodgers, B. (1982), 'Family Policy: International Perspectives' in Rapoport, R.N. *et al*, (1982) (eds), *op. cit.* (see below).

Fogelman, K. (1983) (ed), *Growing up in Great Britain: Papers from the National Child Development Study*, Macmillan.

Foucault, M. (1977), *Discipline and Punish: The Birth of the Prison*, Penquin.

Fox, R.G. (1971), 'The XYZ Offender: A Modern Myth', *Journal of Criminal Law, Criminology and Police Science*, 62, 1.

Fraser, D. (1973), *The Evolution of the British Welfare State: A History of Social Policy Since the Industrial Revolution*, Macmillan.

Freeman, M.D.A. (1981), *The Child Care and Foster Children Acts*, 1980, Sweet and Maxwell.

Fromm, E. (1974), *The Anatomy of Human Destructiveness*, Jonathan Cape.

Fuller, R. and Stevenson, O. (1983), *Policies Programmes and Disadvantage: A Review of the Literature*, Heinemann.

George, V. (1970), *Foster Care Theory and Practice*, Routledge and Kegan Paul.

Gerth, H.H. and Mills, C.W. (1948) (eds), *From Max Weber: Essays in Sociology,* Routledge and Kegan Paul.

Goffman, E. (1961), *Asylums: Essays on the Social Situation of Mental Patients and Other Inmates*, Penquin.

Goffman, E. (1976), *The Presentation of Self in Everyday Life*, Penquin.

Goldberg, E.M. and Hatch, S. (1981), *A New Look at the Personal Social Services*, Policy Studies Institute.

Goldfarb, W. (1943), 'The Effects of Early Institutional Care on Adolescent Personality', *Journal of Experimental Education*, 12.

Goode, W.J. (1963), *World Revolution and Family Patterns*, The Free Press.

Gough, I. (1979), *The Political Economy of the Welfare State*, Macmillan.

Hadley, R. and Mcgrath, M. (1980) (eds), *Going Local: Neighbourhood Social Services*, Bedford Square Press.

Hall, P. (1976), *Reforming the Welfare: The Politics of Change in the Personal Social Services*, Heinemann.

Hall, P., Land H., Parker, R. and Webb, A. (1975), *Change, Choice and Conflict in Social Policy*, Heinemann Educational Books.

Hallett, C. (1982), *The Personal Social Services in Local Government*, Allen and Unwin.

Hallet, C. and Stevenson, O. (1980), *Child Abuse: Aspects of Interprofessional Co-operation*, Allen and Unwin.

Halsey, A.H. (1977) (ed), *Heredity and Environment*, Menthuen.

Halsey, A.H. (1986) (3rd edn), *Change in British Society*, Oxford University Press.

Haralambos, M. (1980), *Sociology: Themes and Perspectives*, University Tutorial Press.

Hargreaves, D.H. (1967), *Social Relations in a Secondary School*, Routledge and Kegan Paul.

Harris, C.C. (1983), *The Family and Industrial Society*, Allen and Unwin.

Hazel, N. (1981), *A Bridge to Independence*, Blackwell.

Hazel, N. and Cox, R. (1976), *First Report of the Special Family Placement Project*, Kent County Council Social Services Department.

Hazel, N., Cox, R. and Ashley-Mudie, P. (1977), *Second Report of the Family Placement Project*, Kent County Council Social Services Department.

Hazel, N., Cox, R., Ashley-Mudie, P. and Roberts, J. (1978), *Family Placement Project Third Annual Report 1976-77*, Kent County Council Social Services Department.

Heal, K., Sinclair, I. and Troop, J. (1973), 'Development of a Social Climate Questionnaire for use in Approved Schools and Community Homes', *British Journal of Sociology*, 24.

Heywood, J.S. (1959), *Children in Care: The Development of the Service for the Deprived Child*, Routledge and Kegan Paul.

Hoggett, B. (1981), *Parents and Children*, Sweet and Maxwell.

Holman, R. (1973), *Trading in Children: A Study of Private Fostering*, Routledge and Kegan Paul.

Holman, R. (1975), 'The Place of Fostering in Social Work', *British Journal of Social Work*, 5, 1.

Holman, R. (1976), *Inequality in Child Care*, Child Poverty Action Group.

Holman, R. (1978), *Poverty: Explanations of Social Deprivation*, Martin Robertson.

Home Office (1965), *The Child, the Family and the Young Offender* (Government White Paper), HMSO.

Home Office (1968), *Children in Trouble* (Government White Paper), HMSO.

Home Office Advisory Council on Child Care (1968), *Begone Dull Care*, HMSO.

Home Office Advisory Council on Child Care (1970), *Care and Treatment in a Planned Environment*, HMSO.

Hood, R. and Sparks, R. (1970), *Key Issues in Criminology*, Weidenfield and Nicolson.

Huff, A.J. and Huff, C. (1973), *Early Human Development*, Oxford University Press.

Ignatiev, M. (1978), *A Just Measure of Pain*, Panthean Books.

Jenkins, S. and Norman, E. (1972), *Filial Deprivation and Foster Care*, Columbia University Press. Also cited in Fuller, R. and Stevenson, O., (1983), *op. cit.*

Johnson, J.M. (1978), *Doing Field Research*, The Free Press.

Jones, H. (1979), *The Residential Community: A Setting for Social Work*, Routledge and Kegan Paul.

Jones, K. (1967), 'The Development of Institutional Care' in *New Thinking About Institutional Care* Association of Social Workers (1967), *op. cit.*

Jones, K. and Fowles, A.J. (1984), *Ideas on Institutions: Analysing the Literature on Long-term Care and Custody*, Routledge and Kegan Paul.

Jordan, B. (1982), 'Families and the Personal Social Services' in Rapoport, R.N. *et al*, (1982) (eds), *op. cit.* (see below).

Justice of the Peace (1982) [An article which discusses provisions contained in the Criminal Justice Act, 1982].

Kadushin, A. (1971), 'Child Welfare' in Maas, H.S. (ed), *Research in the Social Services*, National Association of Social Workers, USA.

Kahan, B. (1979), *Growing up in Care*, Blackwell.

Kahn, J. and Elinor Wright, S. (1980), *Human Growth and the Development of Personality*, Pergamon.

Kerlinger, F.N. (1973), *Foundations of Behavioural Research* , Holt, Rinehart and Winston.

King, M. (1981), *Childhood, Welfare and Justice: A Critical Examination of Children in the Legal and Child Care Systems*, Batsford Educational Limited.

King, R.D., Raynes, N.V. and Tizard, J. (1971), *Patterns of Residential Care: Sociological Studies in Institutions for Handicapped Children*, Routledge and Kegan Paul.

Kristof, W. (1963) cited by Smith, H.W., (1975), *op. cit.* (see below).

Laing, R.D. (1971), *Self and Others*, Penquin.

Laing, R.D. (1976), *The Politics of the Family*, Penquin.

Laing, R.D. and Esterson, A. (1970), *Sanity, Madness and the Family*, Penquin.

Laslett, P., (1982), Forward to Rapoport, R.N. *et al*, (1982) (eds), *op. cit.*

Lasson, I. (1980),*Where's My Mum: A Study of the Forgotten Children in Long-Term Care*, Pepar Publications.

Laurance, J. (1983), 'Is Big Business Moving into Caring?', *New Society*, February, 1983).

Leach, E.R. (1967), *A Runaway World*, BBC Publications.

Leighton, N., Stalley, R. and Watson, D. (1982), *Rights and Responsibilities: Discussion of Moral Dimensions in Social Work*, Heinemann.

Lemert, E. (1951), *Social Pathology*, McGraw Hill.

Lowe, G.R. (1974), *The Growth of Personality: From Infancy to Old Age*, Penquin.

Maier, H.W. (1969), *Three Theories of Child Development*, Harper and Rowe.

Maluccio, A.N. and Sinanoglu, P.A. (1981), *Parents of Children in Foster Care: An Annotated Bibliography*, Connecticut Practitioners Press.

Mandell, B.R. (1973), *Where Are the Children? A Class Analysis of Foster Care and Adoption*, Lexington Books.

Matthews, R. (1979), 'Decarceration and the Fiscal Crisis' in *Capitalism and the Rule of Law*, National Deviancy Conference.

Matza, D. (1964), *Delinquency and Drift*, John Whiley.

Maxwell, A.E. (1961), *Analysing Qualitative Data*, Menthuen.

McLellan, D. (1977) (ed), *Karl Marx: Selected Writings*, Oxford University Press.

Melossi, D. and Pavarini, M. (1981), *The Prison and the Factory*, Macmillan.

Merton, R.K. (1938), 'Social Structure and Anomie', *American Sociological Review*, 13.

Milgram, S. (1974), *Obedience to Authority: An Experimental View*, Tavistock.

Millham, S., Bullock, R. and Cherret, P. (1972), 'Social Control in Organisations', *British Journal of Sociology*, 23, 4.

Millham, S., Bullock, R. and Cherret, P. (1975), 'A Conceptual Scheme for the Comparative Analysis of Residential Institutions' in Tizard, J., *et al*, (eds), (1975), *op. cit.* (see below).

Millham, S., Bullock, R. and Hosie, K. (1978), *Locking Up Children: Secure Provision Within the Child Care System*, Saxon House.

Millham, S., Bullock, R., Hosie, K. and Heak, M. (1981), *Issues of Control in Residential Child Care*, HMSO.

Millham, S., Bullock, R. and Cherret, P., (1975), *After Grace - Teeth*, Human Context Books.

Mischel, W. (1973), 'Toward a Cognitive Social Learning Reconceptualisation of Personality', *Psychological Review*, 80.

Mishra, R. (1981), *Society and Social Policy: Theories and Practice of Welfare*, Macmillan.

Mishra, R. (1984), *The Welfare State in Crisis: Social Thought and Social Change*, Wheatsheaf.

Mitchell, J.J. (1971), *Women's Estate*, Penquin.

Moos, R.H. (1968), 'The Assessment of Social Climates of Correctional Institutions', *Journal of Research in Crime and Delinquency*, 5.

Morris, A., Giller, H., Szwed, E. and Geach, H. (1980), *Justice for Children* , Macmillan.

Morris, P. (1969), *Put Away*, Routledge and Kegan Paul.

Morris, T. and Morris, P. (1963), *Pentonville*, Routledge and Kegan Paul.

Moser, C.A. and Kalton, G. (1971), *Survey Methods in Social Investigation*, Heinemann.

Moss, P. (1975) in Tizard, J. *et al*, (eds) (1975), *op. cit.* (see below).

Napier, H. (1972), 'Success and Failure in Foster Care', *British Journal of Social Work*, 2, 2.

Nissel, M. (1982), 'Families and Social Change Since the Second World War' in Rapoport, R.N. *et al*, (1982) (eds), *op. cit.* (see below).

Norusis, M.J. (1983), *SPSSX - Introductory Statistics Guide*, McGraw Hill Book Company.

Nunnally, J. (1967), *Psychometric Theory*, McGraw Hill.

Oakley, A. (1982a), *Subject Women*, Fontana.

Oakley, A. (1982b), 'Conventional Families' in Rapoport, R.N. *et al*, (1982) (eds), *op. cit.* (see below).

Office of Population, Censuses and Survey's (1980) *Classification of Occupations and Coding Index*, HMSO.

Packman, J. (1968), *Child Care: Needs and Numbers*, Allen and Unwin.

Packman, J. (1975), *The Child's Generation: Child Care Policy from Curtis to Houghton*, Blackwell.

Page, R. and Clarke, G. (1977) (eds), *Who cares? Young People in Care Speak Out*, National Children's Bureau.

Pappenfort, D.M. and Kilpatrick, D.M. (1969), 'Child-Caring Institutions, 1966: Selected Findings from the First National Survey of Children's Residential Institutions', *Social Service Review*, 43, 4.

Parker, R.A. (1966), *Decision in Child Care*, Allen and Unwin.

Parker, R.A. (1978), 'Foster Care in Context', *Adoption and Fostering*, 93, 3.

Parker, R.A. (ed), (1980), *Caring for Separated Children: Plans Procedures and Priorities*, Macmillan.

Parsloe, P. (1978), *Juvenile Justice in Britain and the United States: The Balance Between Needs and Rights*, Routledge and Kegan Paul.

Parsons, T. (1937), *The Structure of Social Action*, McGraw Hill.

Parsons, T. (1951), *The Social System*, The Free Press.

Parsons, T. (1960), *Structure and Process in Modern Societies*, The Free Press.

Parsons, T. (1964a), *Essays in Sociological Theory*, The Free Press.

Parsons, T. (1964b), *Social Structure and Personality*, The Free Press.

Parsons, T. (1969), *Politics and Social Structure*, The Free Press.

Parsons, T. and Bales, R.F. (1955), *Family, Socialisation and Interaction Process*, The Free Press.

Parsons, T. (1982), 'The Isolated Conjugal Family', in Anderson, M. (1982) (ed), *op. cit.*

Pearl, D. and Gray, K. (1981), *Social Welfare Law*, Croom Helm.

Perrow, C. (1970), *Organisational Analysis: A Sociological View*, Tavistock.

Perrow, C. (1979), *Complex Organisations*, Scott, Foresman.

Pikunas, J. (1968), *Human Development: An Emergent Science*, McGraw-Hill.

Plowman, G. (1967), 'The structure and Dynamics of Institutions' in *Association of Social Workers*, (1967), *op. cit.*

Priestley, P., Fears, D. and Fuller, R. (1977), *Justice for Juveniles: The 1969 Children and Young Persons Act - A Case for Reform?* Routledge and Kegan Paul.

Pringle, M.L. Kellmer (1967), *Adoption - Fact and Fallacies*, Longman.

Pringle, M.L. Kellmer and Bossio, V. (1960), 'Early Prolonged Separations and Emotional Adjustment', *Journal of Child Psychology and Psychiatry*, 1.

Prosser, H. (1976), *Perspectives on Residential Care* , National Foundation for Educational Research.

Prosser, H. (1978), *Perspectives on Foster Care*, National Foundation for Educational Research.

Rapoport, R.N., Fogarty, M.P. and Rapoport, R. (1982), (eds). *Families in Britain*, Routledge and Kegan Paul.

Rapoport, R.N. and Rapoport, R. (1982), 'British Families in Transition' in Rapoport, R.N. *et al*, (1980) (eds), *op. cit.*

Raynes, N.V., Pratt, M.W. and Roses, S. (1979), *Organisational Structure and the Care of the Mentally Retarded*, Croom Helm.

Report of the Care of Children Committee (1946, reprinted, 1969), HMSO.

Report of the Committee on Local Authority and Allied Personal Social Services (1968), HMSO.

Roberts, G. (1978), *Essential Law for Social Workers*, Oyez.

Rosen, A.C. (1971), 'The Social and Emotional Development of Children in Long-Term Residential Care', *Therapeutic Education*, Spring.

Rothman, D.J. (1971), *The Discovery of the Asylum: Social Order and Disorder in the New Republic*, Little, Brown.

Rowe, J. (1983), *Fostering in the Eighties*, British Agencies for Adoption and Fostering.

Rowe, J. and Lambert, L. (1973), *Children Who Wait - A Study of Children Needing Substitute Families*, Association of British Adoption Agencies.

Rutter, M. (1980), *Helping Troubled Children*, Penquin.

Rutter, M. (1983), *Maternal Deprivation Reassessed*, Penquin.

Rutter, M. (1985), 'Resilience in the Face of Adversity: Protective Factors and Resistence to Psychiatric Disorder', *British Journal of Psychiatry*, 147.

Scull, A. (1975), *Madness and Segregative Control: The Rise of the Insane Asylum*, American Sociological Association.

Schur, E.M. (1973), *Radical Non-Intervention: Rethinking the Delinquency Problem*, Prentice-Hall.

Scull, A. (1977 and 1984) (1st and 2nd edns), *Decarceration: Community Treatment and the Deviant - A Radical View*, Polity Press.

Shaw, M. and Hipgrave ,T. (1982), 'Specialist Fostering', *Adoption and Fostering*, 6, 4.

Shaw, M. and Hipgrave, T. (1983), *Specialist Fostering*, Batsford/BAAF.

Shaw, M. and Lebens, K. (1976), *What Shall We Do With the Children*, Association of British Adoption and Fostering Agencies, Leaflet No.2, ABAFA.

Silverman, D. (1970), *The Theory of Organisations: A Sociological Framework*, Heinemann.

Sinclair, I. (1975), 'The Influence of Wardens and Matrons on Probation Hostels' in Tizard, J. *et al*, (eds) (1975), *op. cit.* (see below).

Sinclair, I. and Heal, K. (1976), Diversity Within the Total Institution: Some Evidence from Boy's Perceptions of Community Homes, *Policy and Politics*, 4.

Sinonglu, P.A. and Maluccio, A.N. (1981), *Parents of Children in Placements: Perspectives and Programs*, Child Welfare League of America.

Smelser, N. (1982), 'The Victorian Family' in Rapoport, R.N. *et al*, (1982) (eds), *op. cit.*

Smith, G. (1979), *Social Work and the Sociology of Organisations* , Routledge and Kegan Paul.

Smith, H.W. (1975), *Strategies of Social Research: The Methodological Imagination*, Prentice Hall.

Social Services Committee, (Session 1982-1983), *Children in Care*, House of Commons Paper 26, i-ii, HMSO.

Social Services Committee (Session 1983-84), *Children in Care*, Volume 1, House of Commons Paper, 360-1, HMSO.

Spitz, R.A. (1949), 'The Role of Ecological Factors in Emotional Development in Infancy', *Child Development*, 20, 3.

SPSS Inc. (1983), *SPSSX User's Guide*, McGraw-Hill.

SSRIU (1976), *First Year at Fairfield Lodge*, Social Services Research and Intelligence Unit, Portsmouth Polytechnic/Hampshire Social Services Department.

SSRIU (1977), *Children on the Rates*, Social Services Research and Intelligence Unit, Portsmouth Polytechnic/Hampshire Social Services Department.

Startup, R. and Whittaker, E.T. (1982), *Introducing Social Statistics*, Allen and Unwin.

Stevenson, O. (1972), *Strength and Weakness in Residential Care*, Alden Press.

Street, D., Vinter, R.D. and Perrow, C. (1966), *Organisation for Treatment: A Comparative Study of Institutions for Delinquents*, Free Press.

Sylva, K., Roy, C. and Painter, M. (1980), *Childwatching at Playgroup and Nursery School*, Grant McIntrye.

Taylor, L., Lacey, R. and Bracken, D. (1979), *In Whose Best Interests: The Unjust Treatment of Children in Courts and Institutions*, Cobden Trust/MIND.

Thomas, N. (1973), 'The Seebohm Committee on the Personal Social Services' in Chapman, R., (ed), *The Role of Commissions in Policy Making*, Allen and Unwin.

Tizard, B. (1975), 'Varieties of Residential Nursery Experience' in Tizard, J. *et al*, (eds) (1975), *op. cit.*

Tizard, B. (1977), *Adoption: A Second Chance*, Open University Press.

Tizard, B., Carmichael, H., Hughes, M. and Pinkerton, G. (1980), 'Four Year Olds Talking to Mothers and Teachers' in Hersor, L.A. *et al*, (eds), *Language and Language Disorders in Childhood*, a book supplement to the Journal of Child Psychology and Psychiatry, No.2, Pergamon Press.

Tizard, B., Cooperman, O., Joseph, A. and Tizard, J. (1972), 'Environmental Effects on Language Development: A Study of Young Children in Long-Stay Nurseries', *Child Development*, 43.

Tizard, B. and Hodges, J. (1978), 'The Effect of Early Institutional Rearing on the Development of Eight-Year-Old Children', *Journal of Child Psychology and Psychiatry*, 19.

Tizard, B. and Joseph, A. (1970), 'The Cognitive Development of Young Children in Residential Care', *Journal of Child Psychology and Psychiatry*, 11, 3.

Tizard, J. (1975), 'Quality of Residential Care for Retarded Children' in Tizard, J. *et al*, (1975) (eds), *op. cit.*

Tizard, J., Sinclair, I. and Clarke, R.V.G. (eds.) (1975), *Varieties of Residential Experience*, Routledge and Kegan Paul.

Tizard, J. and Tizard, B. (1971), 'The Social Development of Two Year Old Children in Residential Nurseries' in Schaffer, H.R. (1971) (ed), *The Origins of Human Social Relations*, Academic Press.

Tod, R.N.J. (1976a), *Children in Care, Papers on Residential Work*, Vol.1, Longman.

Tod, R.N.J. (1976b), *Disturbed Children, Papers on Residential Work*, Vol.2, Longman.

Townsend, P. (1962), *The Last Refuge: A Survey of Residential Institutions and Homes for the Aged in England and Wales*, Routledge and Kegan Paul.

Townsend, P. (1970), *The Fifth Social Service: A Critical Analysis of the Seebohm Proposals*, Fabian Society.

Townsend, P. (1979), *Poverty in the United Kingdom: A Survey of Household Resources and Standards of Living*, Penquin.

Townsend, P. (1981), *Sociology and Social Policy*, Penquin.

Trasler, G. (1955), 'The Effects of Institutional Care Upon Emotional Development', *Case Conference*, 4, 2.

Triseliotis, J. (1983), 'Issues of Identity and Security in Adoption and Long-Term Fostering', *Adoption and Fostering*, 7, 1.

Triseliotis, J. and Russell, J. (1984), *Hard to Place: The Outcome of Adoption and Residential Care*, Heinemann.

Tutt, N. (1982), 'Justice or Welfare'? *Social Work Today*, 14, 7.

Veitch, A. (1986), 'How You Have Been Hearing Only One Side of the Stories', *The Guardian*, August 13, 1986.

Walter, J.A. (1977), 'A Critique of Sociological Studies of Approved Schools', *British Journal of Criminology*, 17, 4.

Walter, J.A. (1978), *Sent Away: A Study of Young Offenders in Care* , Saxon House.

Walton, R.G. and Elliot, D. (1980), *Residential Care: A Reader in Current Theory and Practice*, Pergamon.

Warham, J. (1977), *An Open Case: The Organisational Context of Social Work*, Routledge and Kegan Paul.

Webb, E.J., Campbell, D.T., Schwartz, D. and Sechrest, L. (1966), *Unobtrusive Measures: Non-Reactive Research in the Social Sciences* , Rand McNally.

Wendelken, C. (1983), *Children In and Out of Care*, Heinemann.

Wessex Children's Regional Planning Committee (1976), *A Study of Placement Recommendations*, Wessex Children's Regional Planning Committee.

West, D.J. and Farrington, D.P. (1977), *The Delinquent Way of Life*, Heinemann.

Willmott, P. and Young, M. (1960), *Family and Class in a London Suburb*, Routledge and Kegan Paul.

Wills, D. (1970), *A Place Like Home*, Allen and Unwin.

Wills, W.D. (1973), *Spare the Child: A Study of an Experimental Approved School*, Penquin.

Wing, J.K. and Brown, G.W. (1970), *Institutionalism and Schizophrenia: A Comparative Study of Three Mental Hospitals 1960 - 1968*, Cambridge University Press.

Wolff, S. (1976), *Children Under Stress*, Penquin.

Wolfgang, M.E., Savitz, I. and Johnson, N. (1962), *The Sociology of Crime and Delinquency*, John Wiley.

Wolkind, S.N. (1974), 'Sex Differences in the Aetiology of Anti-Social Disorders in Children in Long-Term Residential Care', *British Journal of Psychiatry*, 125.

Wollkind, S.N. and Rutter, M. (1973), 'Children Who have Been in Care: An Epidemiological Study', *Journal of Child Psychology & Psychiatry*, 14, 2.

Wootton, B. (1959), *Social Services and Social Pathology,* Allen and Unwin.

Yelloly, M. (1979), *Independent Evaluation of 25 Placements*, Kent County Council Social Services Department.

Young, M. and Willmott, P. (1962), *Family and Kinship in East London*, Penquin.

Young, M. and Willmott, P. (1975), *The Symmetrical Family*, Penquin.

Younghuspand, E. (1978), *Social Work in Britain: 1950-1975*, [2 Vols.], Allen and Unwin.

Yule, W. and Raynes, N.V. (1972), 'Behaviour Characteristics of Children in Residential Care in Relation to Indices of Separation', *Journal of Child Psychology and Psychiatry*, 13.